汉英翻译

理解古代江西 上

付添爵 陈夜雨 黄秋菊 ◎ 主编

江西人民出版社
Jiangxi People's Publishing House
全国百佳出版社

图书在版编目（CIP）数据

理解古代江西：汉英翻译.上/付添爵，陈夜雨，
黄秋菊主编. -- 南昌：江西人民出版社，2023.12
 ISBN 978-7-210-15233-0

Ⅰ.①理… Ⅱ.①付… ②陈… ③黄… Ⅲ.①翻译—
文化研究—江西 Ⅳ.① H059

中国国家版本馆 CIP 数据核字（2024）第 030705 号

理解古代江西——汉英翻译（上）
LIJIE GUDAI JIANGXI——HAN-YING FANYI（SHANG）

付添爵 陈夜雨 黄秋菊 主编

责 任 编 辑：饶　芬
装 帧 设 计：马范如

江西人民出版社 出版发行
Jiangxi People's Publishing House
全国百佳出版社

地　　　　址：	江西省南昌市三经路 47 号附 1 号（邮编：330006）
网　　　　址：	www.jxpph.com
电 子 信 箱：	jxpph@tom.com
编辑部电话：	0791-86898683
发行部电话：	0791-86898815
承　印　厂：	北京虎彩文化传播有限公司
经　　　销：	各地新华书店

开　　本：	787 毫米 × 1092 毫米　1/16
印　　张：	15.5
字　　数：	210 千字
版　　次：	2023 年 12 月第 1 版
印　　次：	2023 年 12 月第 1 次印刷
书　　号：	ISBN 978-7-210-15233-0
定　　价：	68.00 元

赣版权登字 -01-2023-660

版权所有　侵权必究

赣人版图书凡属印刷、装订错误，请随时与江西人民出版社联系调换。
服务电话：0791-86898820

前　言

一、教材定位

自古翰林多吉水,从来朝士半江西。2022年8月,"理解当代中国"系列教材力主推出汉译外(十个语种)翻译教程,践行了"翻译传播,国之大者"。应时所需,"理解江西文化,翻译文化江西"成为本教材建设及课堂研究的地方性知识建构与话语塑造,正所谓"翻译传播,省之要务"。由此,本教材编写秉持"文化传播与话语塑造"之宗旨,以"传统中国译论研究"为内核、文化记忆为引擎、汉英翻译为主线,力争贴近省情,更好地服务于本省文化翻译教育格局。

详述之,本教材选取古代江西代表性"人(思想)、物(器物、遗产)"的相关翻译文本,旨在对古代江西文化进行翻译叙事与教育建构。编著的方法与路径可概括为：以古代江西名人为线索,运用文本比较分析法,即通过对每个人物的经典作品与经典译文进行对比分析,揭示翻译传播的相关问题,同时辅以相关翻译理论的解读,使读者对既存的翻译样态作出思考,进而反思如何"翻译江西文化之声,传播文化江西形象"。

简言之,本教材立足于"理解江西文化",以知识翻译与话语传播为纲目,致力于汉译英系列教材建设及其课堂应用研究,梳理文脉、钩沉记忆、彰显经典,兼具翻译教育与课程思政的现实功能与效用,力主"翻译文化江西",打造富有地方性知识与话语的翻译教程与课堂实践,更好地服务于地方性文化翻译教育事业,实践独具特色的"新文科"理念。

二、教材价值

本教材的预期效益主要体现为理论阐释与实践应用两个方面，具体表现为：

（1）填补传播地方性知识的翻译教材空白；

（2）响应课程思政理念下的翻译教学改革；

（3）践行江西文化走出去的翻译教育使命；

（4）推行讲好赣鄱故事与文化的教育方略；

（5）落实新文科理念下的翻译研究与教学。

相应地，本教材的特色、创新点如下：

（1）特色。

本教材的特色主要在于将"理解当代中国"系列教材进行地方性知识与话语转化，确立"理解江西文化，翻译文化江西"的学术定位，明晰了教材建设及其课堂应用的具体实现方式与路径。

（2）创新点。

本教材的创新点在于以知识翻译与话语传播为纲目，"教（课堂实践）""研（教材建设）"并举，发挥翻译教育与课程思政的现实功能与效用，实践独具地方性知识与话语的"新文科"理念。

三、使用说明

本教材以"中国传统翻译思想纵览"开篇，选取十位古代江西名人作为教学主题，共设十一个单元。每个单元所循体例为"译事·译研""鉴赏·评析""译论·比较""实践·译笔""阅读·延展"。其中，"译事·译研"包括某位古代江西名人的生平简介，其相关作品译介、传播与评价等；"鉴赏·评析"主要是基于文本翻译的解读与论述，兼及相关翻译理论的介绍、品评与反思；"译论·比较"是相关翻译思想发微，并结合具体译本，启发学习者作出能动性比较与探讨;"实践·译笔"属于翻译练习,鼓励学习者将理论融入实践,进而通过实践反哺理论;"阅读·延展"是翻译理论与翻译思想的品格提升,通过阅读名家名论,加深学生对文化翻译的理解,透析翻译传播的本质,深思地方性知识的对外形象建构。

整体而言,本教材在选材方面恪守经典原则,英译文本皆出自翻译名家(含赣籍译者),同时秉持版权自觉意识,对相关引用明确标注出处。除去文本引用,本教材每一个单元都花大量笔墨进行了原创性解读与论述,不当之处,还望方家批评指正!

四、特别致谢

以研促教,教研相长。本教材是2021年江西省高校人文社会科学项目"晚清民国译家翻译教育思想之记忆深描与书写"(YY21214)以及江西省教育科学"十四五"规划2021年度项目"文化记忆下近现代赣籍译家翻译教育思想研究"(21YB057)的相关研究成果。本教材能够顺利出版离不开江西人民出版社饶芬编辑的倾心相助,谨致以最诚挚的谢意。

目 录

第一单元	中国传统翻译思想纵览	001
第二单元	田园隐士·东晋陶渊明	020
第三单元	豫章一阁·初唐王勃	040
第四单元	词人宰相·北宋晏殊	063
第五单元	万世文章·北宋欧阳修	082
第六单元	宰相诗人·北宋王安石	104
第七单元	理学至尊·南宋朱熹	127
第八单元	浩然气节·南宋文天祥	144
第九单元	格致泰斗·明代王阳明	161
第十单元	戏剧鼻祖·明代汤显祖	182
第十一单元	科技先锋·明代宋应星	200

主要参考文献 ······ 219
参考答案（实践·译笔）······ 225

第一单元

中国传统翻译思想纵览

一、"翻译思想"还是"翻译理论"

回顾 20 世纪中国思想史的撰写历程，以思想史命名的著作没有以哲学史命名的著作多。从谢无量六卷一册的《中国哲学史》，到自称"中国治哲学史开山之人"胡适的《中国哲学史大纲》，再到冯友兰版、任继愈版的《中国哲学史》，无一不是以"哲学"之名来述"思想"之事。毫无疑问，哲学史的撰述，不仅有相当多的经验可供借鉴，而且从一开始就有一个来自西方和日本的、现成而明确的样式可以使用甚至套用（葛兆光，2013），即"哲学本一西洋名词，今欲讲中国哲学史，其主要工作之一，即就中国历史上各种学问中，将其可以西洋所谓哲学名之者，选出而叙述之"（冯友兰，2014）。

然而，古代中国没有"哲学"之名，也没有切合这一名称意义的知识、思想与学术体系。相反，中国接受和使用"思想史"的概念相当早，介绍"思想史"的班兹（Barnes）的《社会科学史纲》虽然是 1940 年才由向达翻译并由商务印书馆出版，但是在 1935 年，容肇祖就已经编出了《中国思想史参考资料》，1936 年陈钟凡和蔡尚思讨论编撰《中国思想史》，并明确了"序述各时代思想的体系，派别，及其演进的进程，是为思想史（History of Thought）"。正如唐君毅所说："哲学之名，本中土所未有，如昔所谓道术、理学、心学、玄学之名,与西方所谓哲学意义皆不相同"。而在西方学术话语笼罩的时代,"哲学"之名开始统摄古代中国的思想与学术,这实在很成问题。持同样理念的人还有章太炎、梁启超、金岳霖、冯友兰、陈启云、傅斯年、蔡元培、胡适等[①]。

"思想"与"理论"应当有所分野。二者的一个最大分歧就在于各自依赖不同的"思想史"与"哲学史"的研究方法。中国学术惯以"思想"冠名,注重"用格言、警句、比喻、事例等形式表述思想",而西方以概念工具、研究思路和叙述框架为挈领的哲学研究则偏爱"理论"综述。因而,或可主张既避免使用"理论"一词来强行归纳中国翻译研究脉络,也少用"思想"一语来鉴别梳理西方翻译体系,而是各按其脉,各归所属。

欲究其本,必梳其史。翻译是人类社会普遍存在的语言活动与交流方式,是思想史的一个重要组成部分。可以说,自部落之间出现往来、战争、融合开始,翻译就已经发挥其历史作用了。若按雅各布逊的翻译三分法,超越语言翻译层面,即将符号翻译也纳入其范畴,翻译的历史源头并不晚于语言本身的出现与形成,其历史至少同步于语言的历史。正如谭载喜(1991)指出的:"无论在中国还是在西方,翻译都是一项极其古老的活动。事实上,在整个人类历史上,语言的翻译几乎同语言本身一样古老。两个原始部落

---

① 章太炎在讲《国学概论》时说道,"今姑且用'哲学'二字罢",可见他的一丝无奈。梁启超在《中国历史研究法补编》中不太想用"哲学"之名,而想代之以中国式的"道术"。金岳霖在冯友兰《中国哲学史》的审查报告中说,"如果一种思想的实质与形式都异于普通哲学,那种思想是否是一种哲学,颇是一问题"。陈启云在《两汉思想文化史的宏观意义》中认为,就连冯著《中国哲学史》也实际上"名为哲学史,其实只是由一位哲学家本其哲学素养而写成的思想史"。傅斯年在《与顾颉刚论古史书》第三《在周汉方术家的世界中几个趋向》中说:"我不赞成(胡)适之先生把记载老子、孔子、墨子等之书呼作哲学史,中国本没有所谓哲学,多谢上帝,给我们民族这么一个健康的习惯……大凡用新名词称旧事物,物质的东西是可以的,因为相同,人文上的事物是每每不可以的,因为多是似同而异。"(见《傅斯年选集》第三册,文星书店1967年版,第424页)。胡适在批判性地整理国故时的两大目标,一是文学史,一是中国哲学史,"后来我总欢喜把'中国哲学史'改称为'中国思想史'"(见《胡适文集》第一册,北京大学出版社1998年版,第415页)。

间的关系，从势不两立到相互友善，无不有赖于语言和思想的交流，有赖于相互理解，有赖于翻译。"

据史料，早在夏代，我国黄河流域的先民就已同外贝加尔湖和米努辛斯克地区的居民有了交往。据《册府元龟·外臣部·朝贡》记载："夏后即位七年，于夷来宾"，"少康即位三年，方夷来宾"。异域来宾朝贺，语言交流先行，翻译必担当重要使命。《周礼·秋官》中关于翻译官象胥[①]（负责接待远方来朝使节）的记载也充分说明我国翻译活动之历史悠久。除了周朝的象胥，还有秦朝的典客、唐朝的鸿胪寺、元朝的会同馆、明朝的四夷馆、清初的四译馆和鸦片战争后的京师同文馆等，历朝历代都设置了配有译员的外事机构。在西方，翻译实践活动也同样源远流长。据法国翻译理论家米歇尔·巴拉尔研究，口译活动最早见于公元前两千多年上埃及埃利潘蒂尼岛古王国王子的石碑铭文。广义上，西方最早的译作是公元前三世纪前后七十二名犹太学者在埃及亚历山大城翻译的《圣经·旧约》，即《七十子希腊文本》；严格意义上来说，西方的第一部译作是大约公元前三世纪中叶安德罗尼柯在罗马用拉丁语翻译的希腊荷马史诗《奥德赛》。

二、中国传统翻译思想简史

学者罗新璋（1984）简略地将中国传统翻译思想归结为"案本—求信—神似—化境"。马祖毅指出，从周到清这一漫长的历史阶段，我国出现了三次翻译高潮，即从东汉到宋的佛经翻译，明末清初和从鸦片战争到清末的两次西学翻译。另外，从"象胥""舌人"这类翻译个体户，到"翻译公所""翻译书院"等政府性翻译机构，再到如今遍布各大高校的"翻译学院""翻译系"等经院研究所，都构成翻译思想的研究对象。本单元按照陈福康（2015）的译史划分，将中国传统翻译思想大致分为五个历史时期：古代译史之东

[①] "象胥，掌蛮夷闽貉戎狄之国使，掌传王之言而谕说焉，以和亲之。若以时入宾，则协其礼与其言辞传之。"见马祖毅. 中国翻译简史："五四"以前 [M]. 北京：中国对外出版公司，1998：2.

汉到唐宋的佛经翻译、古代译史之明清科技翻译、近代译史之清末民初西学翻译、近现代译史之"五四"到1949年前的社科文学类翻译、现当代译史之新中国成立后的翻译。

1. 古代译史之东汉到唐宋的佛经翻译

佛经翻译源于何时尚无定论。据史料记载，东汉桓帝建和二年（148）时，安世高已开始较大规模地从事译经活动了。自此，"千年译经活动"从东汉末年安世高开始，到魏晋南北朝进一步发展，再到唐代达到鼎盛，在北宋开始式微，在元代已接近尾声。而现存最早记录佛经翻译思想的文章当推译经名家支谦所作的《法句经序》[①]。源于中国古典文论的"文""质"思想被用于古代佛经翻译，从"尚质"与"尚文"之争，到"厥中"之调和，这一时期的翻译思想试图从"内部（本体）研究"层面揭示翻译的本真面目。

（1）初级阶段

东汉末至西晋是佛经翻译的草创时期即初级阶段，这一时期共译经书约五百七十部，安清、支谶、支谦、竺法护是其中的杰出译家代表。

安清，字世高，西域安息人，原是安息王国的王子。据梁慧皎《高僧传》记载，安世高志业聪敏，自幼喜好佛教，通晓外国典籍及七曜五行医方异术和鸟兽之声。父王死后，安世高让国于叔，出家修道，学习禅经，颇通小乘经典。后来成为游方僧，游遍诸国，并于东汉桓帝建和二年抵达关中洛阳。至汉灵帝建宁中年，安世高于洛阳译经已有20余年，译籍共有35部41卷，现存22部26卷。其中有《大安般守意经》《人本欲生经》《阴持入经》《地道经》等，开创了后世禅学之源。安清译经的主要内容是传播小乘佛教的基本教义和修行方法。由于通晓汉语，安世高翻译的经文能较准确地传达出原文的本来含义，其译笔高于同期译者。《高僧传》对他译文的评论是："义理明析，文字允正，辩而不华，质而不野。"即指安世高的译文说理清晰、

[①] 该序原未署名，收入梁僧祐所编《出三藏记集》卷七时，注为"未详作者"。后经考证，该序作者实乃吴国居士、译经名家支谦无疑。

用词恰当，语言不铺张、不粗俗，恰到好处。其译文讲求"贵而不饰"，即注重译经内容，不注重文字修饰。

支谶，又名支娄迦谶，西域月支国人。支谶通晓汉语，他至关中弘法稍晚于安世高，译有《道行般若经》《般舟三昧经》《首楞严三昧经》等，又有《阿闍世王》《宝积》等十余部经。据僧祐《出三藏记集》记载，支谶译出的佛经是 14 部 27 卷，其中《般若道行经》10 卷，《般舟三昧经》1 卷，《首楞严三昧经》2 卷。支谶一派属于月支国系，其派所传乃大乘佛法，支谶所译《般舟三昧经》《首楞严三昧经》皆是大乘佛典的代表之作，其译文比较流畅，但为了保留原文的面目，往往多用音译。

安世高和支谶开了中国翻译史上"直译派"的先河，也可称二人为"直译派"的宗师，故"译界开创二杰"非安世高和支谶莫属。他们为了遵从原文形式，免不了重复词句、颠倒结构，对于某些术语的翻译有时也有偏颇。

支谦，名越，字恭明，祖上为月支人，生于中国。其受业于同族支亮，支亮则受业于支谶，三人有"天下博知，不出三支"之称。支谦认为在不同语言中"名物不同，传实不易"。而在"译胡为汉"时，难在"审得其体"，至少"虽不能密"，也应"粗得大趣"。起先他认为"质直"不雅，但之后也认为译经只要做到"易晓"和"勿失厥义"，强调"实宜径达"，"因循本质，不加文饰"。支谦所作的《法句经序》中蕴含了三层翻译思想：其一，提出译事之难；其二，反映"质派"观点；其三，映衬翻译思想根植于中国传统文化。

从东汉末至西晋这一时期的佛经翻译具有以下四个特点：

第一，翻译佛经的主要力量为外国僧人，汉人知识分子是其辅助力量。此时的翻译尚未得到政府的支持，全是"私译"而无官译，是在民间信徒的资助下分散进行的。

第二，古代佛经无原写本，仅仅依靠师徒口耳相传。印度佛经写本出现极晚，故而早期佛经翻译全凭口授，即通过外僧背诵经文，一人口译成汉语，这个过程叫"传言"，再由另外的人"笔授"，也就是录成汉字。译经属于私人活动,又多凭口授,所以不能有选择地对佛典加以介绍;译经时依靠口授,没有校对的原本,再加上传言者的水平良莠不齐,译经的可靠度就不能充分保证。

第三,从翻译方法的角度来说,东汉末到西晋处于草创时期,译经师多抱着虔诚和敬重的态度来翻译佛典,译经时难免心存顾忌,担心违背经旨。同时译经师经验有限,而且语言知识匮乏,多采用直译法。

第四,中国的统治阶级对佛教弘扬的神学观点加以利用,一方面接受佛教,另一方面根据自身所需来改造佛教。

(2)发展阶段

东晋至隋末是佛经翻译的发展时期,这一时期主要的翻译家有释道安、鸠摩罗什、真谛、彦琮等。

释道安,俗姓卫,常山扶柳(今河北冀州)人。他出身书香门第,12岁出家受戒,从佛图澄受业,后成为其大弟子。在襄阳期间,道安整理了新旧佛经经典译本,编出目录,遂成《综理众经目录》。此目录是汉、魏和两晋时期中原佛典的目录总纂,亦是名副其实的第一部经录,开中国佛典目录学之先河。公元383—385年,苻坚开始组织翻译佛经,道安在长安"译场"中发挥了极其重要的作用,主持译出佛经14部180卷,约百万字。

对于佛经翻译,道安主张"矜慎",实际上就是坚持直译原则。结合长安译经的实践经验,在《摩诃钵罗若波罗蜜经抄序》中,道安提出了著名的"五失本""三不易"的翻译理论。"五失本"即译经有五种不可避免的原因导致梵文经本丧失其本真,"三不易"则指译经三大难处。

译胡为秦,有五失本也:一者,胡语尽倒,而使从秦,一失本也。二者,胡经尚质,秦人好文,传可众心,非文不合,斯二失本也。三者,胡经委悉,至于叹咏,叮咛反覆,或三或四,不嫌其烦,而今裁斥,三失本也。四者,胡有义说,正似乱辞,寻说向语,文无以异,或千五百,刈而不存,四失本也。五者,事已全成，将更傍及，反腾前辞，已乃后说，而悉除此，五失本也。

然《般若经》，三达之心，覆面所演，圣必因时，时俗有易；而删雅古，以适今时，一不易也。愚智天隔，圣人巨阶；乃欲以千岁之上微言，传使合百王之下末俗，二不易也。阿难出经，去佛未久，尊者大迦叶令五百六通，迭察迭书；今离千年，而以近意量裁，彼阿罗汉乃兢兢若此，此生死人而平平若此，岂将不知法者勇乎？斯三不易也。

"五失本"乃是道安佛经翻译的底线，说明"译胡为秦"之后佛典信息必有所丧失，但这也是"译胡为秦"必须付出的代价。"三不易"则强调翻译者想要忠实原文乃大不易，这需要译者如履薄冰、用笔谨慎，丝毫不能放纵。道安"五失本、三不易"的理论凸显出直译的原则，而这一原则在长安译经时期处于主导地位。故梁启超说："后世谈译学者，咸征引焉。要之翻译文学程式，成为学界一问题，自安公始也。"

道安对佛经翻译的贡献，主要是"译场"的创建和组织管理。在道安之前，佛经翻译并没有"译场"，而是由西域胡僧和汉人弟子自由组合的私译。汉桓帝时安世高在洛阳译经，是由其口授而汉人严佛调记录；支谶亦是由其口授，汉人孟福记录；西域僧人竺法护在中土译经时，则是由聂承远、聂道真父子承担记录工作并润色文字。这些佛经翻译组合在民间没有规模可言，处于自生自灭的状态，可称之为私译。"长安译场"的创建开中国"官译"的先河，使得佛经翻译由"私译"改为"官译"，这对于中国翻译思想史来说意义重大。佛经翻译从此开始获得国家财力的支持，由于资金来源方面没有后顾之忧，佛经翻译自道安长安译经之后繁荣兴盛。

鸠摩罗什，天竺人氏，世家相国。罗什9岁随母至罽宾（今克什米尔地区），拜师学法，学习小乘。12岁时，又随母回龟兹。在龟兹期间，他因学究大小乘，兼通五明之学，辩才卓越而声誉日盛。鸠摩罗什组织过两个译场，先后为逍遥园和大寺。他译经的显著风格是文丽其辞，但并不刻意追求绮文俪句。"文丽"

是指具有音乐审美意义，既浅显易懂又朗朗上口，即富有音律感，便于吟诵。

罗什译经倾向于意译，即在"不失本旨"的前提下，去繁就简，删减一再重复以及纯属凑数的文辞，令译本更加简洁、流畅，意思更加清晰，译文更有文采，唱诵时更切合梵文音律。这一点可谓翻译方法的一大进步，也是"意译派"比"直译派"高明之处。这说明中土译经正在逐步走向成熟，正努力朝着形式与内容相得益彰的方向发展。针对前人译经概不署名的情况，鸠摩罗什也提倡译者署名，以此来表示对译文负责。此外，据《鸠摩罗什传》记载："改梵为秦，失其藻味，虽得大意，有似嚼饭与人，非徒失味，乃令呕秽也。"这一妙喻是其翻译思想的重要体现，也最早从文学欣赏角度论及了翻译文体与风格的问题。

从东晋至隋朝这一时期的佛经翻译具有以下三个特点：

第一，翻译活动由"私译"转为官译，由个人翻译转入了集体翻译。

第二，从原来以单一的胡本为依据变为多种梵本，译者有更多的余地选择翻译经文的种类，译经的系统性和译文的正确性得以增强。

第三，在翻译理论和技巧上有所突破。

(3) 全盛阶段

唐朝是我国佛教发展的全盛时期，因此佛经翻译也在唐朝达到了顶峰。根据马祖毅的划分，唐代的译经情况，以玄奘为中心，可分为三个时期：公元645年前的译经情况、玄奘19年的译经情况和公元664年以后的译经情况。

公元645年前的译经情况。唐初来到长安的外籍僧侣，较著名的是波罗颇迦罗蜜多罗，简称波颇。波颇先在大兴善寺译出《宝星陀罗尼经》10卷，后又于胜光寺译出《般若灯论释》15卷、《大乘庄严经论》13卷。自贞观三年至贞观七年这4年间，波颇主持翻译了3部经籍。唐代译经始于波颇，他是唐代译经的开工之臣。

玄奘19年的译经情况。玄奘，俗称"三藏法师"，姓陈，名祎，洛州缑氏人。13岁出家，习大乘经论，继而游学相州、赵州等地，遍访名师。后西行求法，行程5万里，历时17年。唐贞观三年，玄奘从长安出发前往西域，经过长途跋涉抵达北天竺那烂陀寺，从戒贤法师学习《瑜珈》等论。因造《会宗论》调和中观、瑜珈两派争论，又作《破恶见论》驳斥小乘僧人所写的七百颂，玄奘受到大小乘僧的推崇，从此便"名震五天"了。贞观十九年，玄奘载誉返回中土，所带梵文经籍共657部。

玄奘译文精美，译风严谨，远超前人。他精通梵文，深晓佛理，汉文程度高深，翻译时出口成章，只需记录下来即可。玄奘的翻译主张为"既须求真，又须求俗"。他主张直译和意译的完美结合，既不赞同道安等人的直译，又不赞成鸠摩罗什等人的意译。他的译文弃骈取散，既忠实于原文，又注重文体风格，以朴素的文体真实地传达出佛经的内容，不仅使译文达到了"和谐"的理想境界，而且大大影响了唐代文体的改革。他还制定了五不翻原则：一、秘密故；二、含多义故；三、此无故；四、顺古故；五、生善故。"五不翻"是玄奘多年译经的心得，何者可意译，何者不可，何者可翻，何者"不翻"，他都分门别类、清清楚楚地罗列出来。"五不翻"指出意译的五个禁区，也就是用音译法解决了自古以来困扰佛经翻译的"名实不谨"的问题。除了"五不翻"之外，玄奘还有很多创新的翻译技法，如补充法、省略法、变位法、分合法、译名假借法和代词还原法共6种翻译技巧。由此可见玄奘的译文质量之高，翻译技巧运用之纯熟，达到了形式与内容高度统一的地步。正如柏乐天所说，"他是把原文读熟了，嚼烂了，然后用适当的汉文表达出来"（马祖毅，1980）。

玄奘通过长途跋涉西行求法，丰富了自己的佛学造诣，才能够"妙善梵语、精通佛理"。他回到长安后潜心译经，不断完善唐朝的译场制度，译出经文数量之多、质量之高，令人望尘莫及。在译经时，他不仅首创"五不翻"原则，而且在译文中巧妙运用了翻译技巧，融"文""质"二者于一体，直译意译，驾轻就熟。由此，"有史以来翻译家中的第一人"便诞生了。

公元664年以后的译经情况。玄奘19年的译经工作为之后的翻译活动打下了坚实的基础，他所完善的译场制度，经实叉难陀和义净承袭并有所发展。这时著名的翻译家，有实叉难陀、义净、菩提流志、不空、般若等人。武则天称帝后，将佛教的地位提升于道教之上。她当国之世，亦是唐代佛教最盛之时。

唐朝时期的佛经翻译具有以下四个特点：

第一，主译者以本国僧人为主，他们都兼通梵汉，深晓佛理。

第二，译经的计划性更强，节译选译的少，翻译全集的多。

第三，译场制度方面进一步发展和完善。

第四，所译的佛经在忠实原著方面，大大超越了前代。

（4）式微阶段

佛经翻译到北宋时基本结束。宋朝的译经总数和唐代差不多，但论典极少，质量上不如唐代，影响不大。宋代译经多为密教的小部经典，统治者发现密教与传统佛教相违逆，禁止翻译此类经典，使宋代译经受到极大挫折。此后，由于政局等原因，除个别少数民族地区的个别时期有过一些有组织的翻译活动，国内大的文字、学术翻译活动基本停顿了近600年之久。其间，翻译思想处于停滞与空白状态。

2. 古代译史之明清科技翻译

14—16世纪欧洲爆发的文艺复兴运动波及西方社会各个角落，形成了一场民族民主运动和科学主义运动。16世纪，欧洲的一部分国家已进入资本主义原始积累时期，殖民主义开始向东方扩张。但当时日趋衰落的明王朝仍保有不可小觑的实力，西方殖民者无法单纯依靠坚船利炮打开中国大门，教会方面也无法"武力清道"。西方传教士把基督教文化传播到中国的同时，也将西方的科学技术著作译介到了中国，从而掀起了唐宋佛经翻译之后的第二次翻译高潮，中国人也得以首次全面了解西方科学技术和文化。

16世纪以后，很多西方传教士来到中国。根据马祖毅（1998）的研究，"明末清初来华的传教士中，知名的总计在70名以上，一般都有译著，成书300余种，除宣扬宗教迷信的书籍外，其中有关科学的占120种左右。"这一时期的代表人物有意大利人利玛窦（Matteo Ricci）、罗雅谷

(Jacques Rho)、德国人汤若望（Adam von Bell）、比利时人南怀仁（Ferdinand Verbiest），中国方面有被誉为"科技译祖"的徐光启以及有"中华之才"之称的李之藻。

其中最负盛名的当属利玛窦。利玛窦，字西泰，意大利传教士，是将欧洲科技传入中国的先驱。他与徐光启合译了《几何原本》《测量法义》《测量异同》等，与李之藻合译了《同文算指》《浑盖通宪图说》《圜容较义》等，其中《同文算指》介绍了西方的笔算方法，包括笔算的计数法、四则运算、开平方、开立方等。除此之外，他也将中国的经典（如四书）介绍给西方世界，开了中国典籍外译之先河。

被耶稣教会人士称为"中国圣教三柱石"之一的徐光启（另外两人为李之藻和杨廷筠），是明末清初著名的大翻译家，也是最早将翻译的范围从宗教以及文学等领域扩大到自然科学技术领域的翘楚。"欲求超胜，必须会通；会通之前，先须翻译"，这便是徐光启光彩耀目的翻译思想。具体而言，这一思想有两大特点：一是求知、求真理，"裨益当世"；二是抓重点，抓"急需"，并能够从哲学方法论角度着眼。

明末清初科技翻译之所以盛行一时，有其独特的历史文化背景因素。

第一，明清之际的中国皇帝，除雍正皇帝外，对欧洲传教士的态度一般比较宽容友好，这是传教士得以在中国立足并做出成绩的必要条件。

第二，明末清初，西方在科技领域取得了很大的进步，而此时的中国由于一直处于封建社会，长期闭关锁国，科技不发达。先进的西方科技思想和新颖精密的科学仪器经过传教士传入中国，很多都是中国人闻所未闻的，这引起了中国人极大的兴趣。

第三，中国士大夫帮助西方传教士学习汉语，并对传教士的著译稿进行笔录、润色、作序介绍、刻印流传。

明末清初的科技翻译高潮提高了中国的科学水平，为我国科技翻译事业的发展作出了杰出贡献。

3. 近代译史之清末民初西学翻译

1840年爆发的鸦片战争，结束了清王朝的闭关自守。从此，中国逐步沦为半殖民地半封建社会。随着欧美列强的军事和经济入侵，西方的各种思想文化也开始涌入中国。泱泱中华在昔日的"蛮夷"面前节节败退并割地赔款，这使中国知识分子陷入了深深的忧患之思。但同时，他们开始积极探索从西方引进和借鉴救国强国之道，从而掀起了中国历史上第三次翻译高潮——西学翻译。这次翻译高潮一直持续到1919年的五四运动。这一时期的翻译主体主要包括以奕䜣、曾国藩、张之洞、左宗棠为代表的洋务派，西方各国在华教会机构，以及以康有为、梁启超为代表的维新派。

鸦片战争后，以奕䜣为代表的洋务派兴起了一场"自强、求富"的洋务运动，指导思想是"中学为体，西学为用"。洋务派设立的翻译机构主要有京师同文馆和江南制造局翻译馆（简称翻译馆）。

1862年，清政府在奕䜣等的奏请下设立了京师同文馆。后又在1868年增设了翻译馆，专事翻译西方著作。京师同文馆翻译的主要作品有《万国公法》《格物入门》《法国律例》等。比较而言，翻译馆译出的作品质量要比同文馆的质量高出很多，译作内容包括声学、光学、学务、天学、政治、商学等多个方面。

甲午中日战争后，中国面临亡国灭种之危。一大批知识分子联合起来，希望通过变法自强挽救中国，资产阶级维新派登上历史舞台。在维新派推动下，译书之风大盛，各报馆翻译东西方报纸及书籍者30余家。当时主要的报刊有《时务报》《实学报》《格致新闻》《中外纪文》等。维新派人士中最著名的翻译家是严复，其次是梁启超，而在外国文学翻译方面成就较高的当数林纾。

严复，福建侯官人，字几道。1867年进入船政学堂学习，除了学习传统典籍和英文外，他还攻读数学、物理、化学、天文等课程。严复19岁毕业，24岁赴英留学，接触了西方资产阶级的政治文化思想。1879年回国，任北洋水师学堂总教习。他基于爱国热情，通过译书、办报纸等宣传变法维新思想，抨击封建专制，提倡民主科学。他的译著都是西方资本主义的哲学、政治著作，宣扬天赋人权和自由、平等、博爱，对当时的社会产生了很大的影响。严复主要译作有《天演论》（T. Henry Huxley, *Evolution and Ethnics and Other Essays*）、《群己权界论》（John Stuart Mill, *On Liberty*）、《穆勒名学》（John Stuart Mill, *System of Logic*）等。

严复的翻译使用的都是古代文言，用他自己的话说就是"用汉以前的字法句法"。他这样做是因为他认识到，"这些书对于那些仍在中古的梦乡里酣睡的人来说是多么难以下咽的苦药，因此他在上面涂了糖衣，这糖衣就是士大夫们所心折的汉以前的古雅文体。雅，乃是严复的招徕术"（王佐良，1989）。在翻译《天演论》时，严复提出了中国近代最有名的"信、达、雅"翻译思想：

> 译事三难：信、达、雅。求其信，已大难矣。顾信矣不达，虽译犹不译也，则达尚焉。海通以来，象寄之才，随地多有；而任取一书，责其能与于斯二者，则已寡矣。其故在浅尝，一也；偏至，二也；辨之者少，三也。

这三字思想言简意赅，影响深远，后人多将其奉为翻译之圭臬。

梁启超，字卓如，号任公，别署"饮冰室主人"，广东新会人，与其师康有为一起倡导维新变法。他翻译的东西不多，但在翻译评论和翻译史方面作出了巨大的贡献。他编有《西学书目表》，并写有《西学书目表序》；在翻译史方面，他对佛经翻译及明清之际的科技翻译的研究卓有成效，写过《佛教之初输入》《翻译文学与佛典》等著名文章。梁启超创造了一种半白半文、通俗易懂的新文体。他的译述态度严肃，力求忠实，比之王韬、严复所译外国诗更加通俗、顺口流畅。

梁启超的译学思想尤其反映在他的万言《论译书》中，他提出："今日而言译书，当首立三义：一曰，择当译之本；二曰，定公译之例；三曰，养能译之才。"即从翻译内容、译名统一、译才培养等方面阐述当时翻译工作中最重要的理论问题。

晚清时期，文学翻译之风大盛。在文学翻译的译家中，最有名的是林纾，他是中国文学翻译事业的先行者和奠基人。

林纾，福建闽县人，原名群玉，字琴南。林纾与严复相似，也是使用文言文翻译，但他翻译的主要是西方文学作品，如《茶花女》《块肉余生述》《鲁滨逊漂流记》《黑奴吁天录》等。由于林纾本人不懂外文，他的翻译都是通过别人口述、自己笔录完成的。林纾在译述时主要使用了以下方法：意译的增饰；意译删削与撮译；夹注的使用。

林纾的翻译虽然不如严复的翻译那样影响强烈，但使思想闭塞的中国知识分子接触到了不少一流的外国作家，在思想上接受了外国文学先进思想的洗礼，相当程度上促进了中国文学的发展，对中国政治界和思想界也有一定程度的影响。他认为只有翻译才能开民智，才能抵御列强，否则类似于"不习水而斗游者"。他还强调在翻译时译者应该投入自己的主观感情，译者必须与原作者或作品中人物的心灵相沟通，正如其为所译《鹰梯小豪杰》写的序言中的翻译所感：

或喜或愕，一时颜色无定，似书中之人，即吾亲切之戚畹。
遭难为悲，得志为喜，则吾身直一傀儡，而著书者为我牵丝矣。

4. 近现代译史之"五四"到1949年前的社科文学类翻译

五四运动是中国历史上划时代的大事。从这时起，一大批知名的学者和翻译家广纳博取，翻译了大量外国文学、社会科学、哲学等作品，在中国历史上掀起了又一次翻译高潮。这一时期的主要代表人物为胡适、鲁迅、郭沫若、茅盾、林语堂等。

鲁迅，原名周树人，浙江绍兴人，中国现代文学的奠基者，中国翻译文学的开拓者。他翻译的主要是俄国及苏联的作品，如契诃夫的《坏孩子和别的奇闻》、果戈理的《死魂灵》等。此外，他还翻译了日本和东欧国家的一些作品。孙郁曾在《收获》杂志上提到：鲁迅首先是翻译家，其次是作家。尤其在早年，他的文学活动"注重的倒是在绍介，在翻译"。据统计，他总共翻译过14个国家近百位作家的200多种作品，超过300万字，比著作的文字还要多（仝灵，1980）。

"硬译"已成为鲁迅翻译思想中的关键词。他对"硬译"的看法有这样几层意思（陈福康，2015）：

（1）"硬译"与"死译"有区别，并不是故意的"曲译"；

（2）"硬译"自有需要它的读者对象，它在他们之间生存；

（3）"我的译作，本不在博读者的'爽快'，却往往给以不舒服"，因为思想对立的人觉得"气闷，憎恶，愤恨"，是当然的，至于那些对理论知之不多的"批评家"，本是应该有"不贪'爽快'，耐苦来研究这些理论的义务的"；

（4）"硬译"不仅为了"不失原来的精悍的语气"，同时也可以"逐渐添加了新句法"，经过一段时间，可能"同化"而"成为己有"；

（5）"自然，世间总会有较好的翻译者，能够译成既不曲，也不'硬'或'死'的文章的，那时我的译本当然就被淘汰，我就只要来填这从'无有'到'较好'的空间罢了。"

可见，鲁迅之所以采取"硬译"，更多的是怀着改造国民语言、重塑国民文学、启发国民心智的初衷。他"站在中国语言改革的角度，怀着改造中国语言的博大思想"，即"'硬译'有助于在中国建构新语言和新文学，从而树立新文化、培养新民智"（罗选民，2016）。虽然"硬译"是鲁迅一直未变的翻译方法，或者说，他的"硬译"主张从来就没有改变过，但在一篇翻译的后记里，鲁迅承认自己的翻译晦涩难解，自己的"硬译"手法并不是理想的翻译方法：凡是翻译，必须兼顾这两面，一当然力求其易解，一则保存着原作的丰姿。

郭沫若，四川乐山人。中国著名的作家、诗人、戏剧家、文学家，同时也是杰出的翻译家。他的译作颇丰，如托马斯·葛雷的《墓畔哀歌》、雪莱的《雪莱诗选》、歌德的《少年维特之烦恼》、托尔斯泰的《战争与和平》、泰戈尔的《泰戈尔诗选》等；政治经济学经典著作，如马克思的《政治经济学批判》、马克思与恩格斯合著的《德意志意识形态》；美学考古学著作，如《西洋美术史提要》《美术考古学发现史》等；科学文艺著作，如《生命之科学》《人类展望》等。

郭氏翻译思想侧重于理论建设。他指出，在译者方面，应该唤醒译书家的责任心，望真有学殖者出而为完整的翻译；在读者方面，应该从教育着手，劝知识未定的青年先从事基础知识的储积，注重语学的研究，多养成直读外籍的人才，望国内大书场多采办海外的名著。他还创造性地提出了"风韵译"，为翻译美学作出了贡献。

> 诗的生命，全在它那种不可把捉之风韵，所以我想译诗的手腕于直译意译之外，当得有种"风韵译"。……字面、意义、风韵，三者均能兼顾，自是上乘。即使字义有失而风韵能传，尚不失为佳品。若是纯粹的直译死译，那只好屏诸艺坛之外了。

林语堂，福建龙溪人，我国著名的文学翻译家、博学型的作家和卓越的语言学家。"两脚踏东西文化，一心评宇宙文章"，这是林语堂一生思想、文学创作和文学翻译道路的写照。他用英语创作了一系列轰动欧美文坛、影响深远的作品，并将《论语》《老子》《庄子》《浮生六记》等中国优秀作品介绍给西方读者，对传播中国优秀文化作出了杰出的贡献。

林语堂将翻译视为一门艺术，且认为翻译艺术倚赖三条：

> 第一是译者对于原文文字上及内容上透彻的了解；
> 第二是译者有相当的国文程度，能写清顺畅达的中文；
> 第三是译事上的训练，译者对于翻译标准及手术的问题有正当的见解。

"手术"即"手段、技术、方法"。他还提出翻译的三条标准：忠实、通顺、美。这三重标准与严复的"信、达、雅"大体上是正相比符的，且这也是译者的三种责任体现，即译者对原著者的责任、译者对中国读者的责任、译者对艺术的责任。三责具备，可谓具有真正译家的资格。

关于翻译的"忠实"，他从语言学角度提出四义，即非字译、须传神、非绝对、须通顺。关于翻译的"通顺"，他又从心理学角度提出须以句为本位，须完全根据中文心理。关于翻译的"美"，他认为："翻译语用之外，还有美一方面须兼顾的，理想的翻译家应当将其工作做一种艺术。以爱艺术之心爱它，以对艺术谨慎不苟之心对它，使翻译成为美术之一种。"

民国是我国译学思想取得较大进步的时代。这一时期的杰出译者都是文学和翻译的双料大家，翻译思想熠熠生辉。

第一，翻译主张的倾向与趋归，基本与形成的文学社团、文学流派相一致。如文学研究会中的郑振铎、茅盾、朱自清等对译学思想的贡献；与文学研究会相对峙的创造社的代表人物郭沫若、成仿吾等在译学上的重要建树；左翼作家联盟的鲁迅、瞿秋白等更是为无产阶级革命文学翻译奠定了基础。

第二，这一时期围绕翻译思想的批评、讨论和争辩尤为热闹，促进了译学思想的发展。如新文学运动者批评严复、林纾，尤为著名的是鲁迅与瞿秋白的讨论、鲁迅与梁实秋的论争，前者属于左翼文坛内部交流，后者则带有浓烈的政治思想斗争色彩。但诸多争论都对端正翻译事业的方向起到了重要作用。

5. 现当代译史之新中国成立后的翻译

新中国成立后，百废待兴，翻译建设也被提上议程，数量和质量上都有了质的飞跃，呈现出新的面貌。这一时期的代表人物有茅盾、傅雷、钱锺书等。

茅盾在1954年第一届全国文学翻译工作会议上作了题为"为发展文学翻译事业和提高翻译质量而奋斗"的报告。报告指出：

>在过去，极大多数的文学翻译工作，是在分散的、自流的状态中进行的。……我们的国家已进入社会主义建设和社会主义改造时期，一切经济、文化事业已逐渐纳入组织化计划化的轨道，文学翻译工作的这种混乱状态，决不能允许其继续存在。文学翻译必须在党和政府的领导下由主管机关和各有关方面，统一拟订计划，组织力量，有方法、有步骤的来进行。

茅盾站在历史的新高度，强调介绍世界各国的文学是一个光荣而艰巨的任务，指出文学翻译工作必须有组织有计划地进行，进而提高到艺术创造的水平。茅盾再次强调加强文学翻译工作中的批评与自我批评和集体互助精神，培养新生力量。茅盾还认为集体翻译不是很适当的方法，因为翻译是一种个体劳动，尤其是文学翻译，如果把一个作品由几个人分译，要想求得译文风格的一致是很有困难的。他还认为校订工作是集体互助精神的又一方面的表现，是翻译事业中的重要一环，而最后一环则是刊物或出版社的编辑工作。总之，茅盾的这个报告非常全面，高瞻远瞩，具有深刻的指导意义，影响深远。

傅雷，字怒安，上海南汇人。从20世纪20年代末开始他就致力于法国文学的翻译介绍工作。傅雷的翻译思想体现在以下几个方面：

首先，强调翻译工作者必须认真了解对方（指原作和原作者等）和了解自己，必须加强自身的学识修养。其次，指出中西思维方式、美学情趣方面的异同，认为翻译决不可按字面硬搬，而必须保存原作的精神和美感特征，做到"传神"是很不容易的。最后，他继承了中国近代自鲁迅、茅盾、郭沫若、闻一多以至林语堂、朱生豪等人关于艺术作品翻译须"传神"的观点，又结合自己对于艺术的精湛修养，反复强调了"重神似不重形似"的翻译思想。

>以效果而论，翻译应当象临画一样，所求的不在形似而在神似。

以实际工作论，翻译比临画更难。临画与原画，素材相同（颜色，画布，或纸或绢），法则相同（色彩学，解剖学，透视学）。译本与原作，文字既不侔，规则又大异。

新中国成立后的翻译思想主要有以下特点：

第一，对翻译的原则、标准和方法等基本问题作进一步的讨论。

第二，新时期翻译研究注意从新角度出发，与新学科相结合，吸取其他相关学科的新成果。

第三，新时期的翻译研究对各种具体的、专门的翻译工作进行了较深入的探讨。

第四，这一时期更加注重介绍和引进国外翻译研究的各种成果，也更注重我国各个阶段翻译经验的总结。

第五，我国译学界正式提出建立翻译学。

翻译史是"记叙人类社会翻译活动和人们对翻译的认识的历史"（方梦之，2011），"不从历史视角加以考察，译学研究必然不完整"（Bassnett，1980）。某种意义上，学科建设与发展的广度与深度受限于基础性理论研究以及学科史的思想书写。如果说前者提供了一种原力觉醒，那么后者则展现了学术底蕴。因此，鲁迅所谓的"治学要先治史"极具洞见。因为"一门学科要有开拓和突破，既需要拓展自身的研究空间，亦需要深入了解学科自身的发展史"（邹振环，2019）。翻译史之于翻译学学科具有重要的框架引领与规导意义是不言而喻的。对于中国的翻译学习者而言，了解本土传统翻译思想颇有"认祖归宗"的道统建构与仪式内涵。在当今中国文化"走出去"的大背景下，把握中国翻译思想的脉络，从传统译思中汲取本土性力量，不仅能够更好地解释本土的翻译实践问题，也能够将本土的思想资源作为"他山之石"供予参鉴。

第二单元

田园隐士·东晋陶渊明

一、译事·译研

有着"隐逸诗人之宗""田园诗文之祖"之称的陶渊明是中国文化史上的"隐逸田园"第一人。梁启超（2010）曾明确称赞"我们国里头四川和江西两省，向来是产生大文学家的所在。陶渊明便是代表江西文学第一个人"。陶渊明的隐逸实践和飘然文风互为彰显，在人与自然的关系上开启了超越其所属时代的生命体验与探索（傅修延，2019），远早于18世纪倡导"回归自然"的卢梭、19世纪发出"自然歌者"的华兹华斯以及主张"寄居超验"的梭罗。时至今日，陶渊明所塑造的"桃花源"形象及其思想主张不仅穿越时空规导着现代中华文化，也跨越疆界影响着异域文明。

陶渊明及其诗文的对外译介可溯及19世纪末，而系统翻译则迟至20世纪50年代。英国汉学家艾克尔（William Acker）在1952年所译的 *T'ao the Hermit：Sixty Poems by T'ao Ch'ien*，365—427 为英语世界中的第一本译陶作品。其后，张葆湖和辛特莱尔于1953年合译陶诗全集 *The Poem of T'ao Ch'ien*。1970年，海陶玮（James Robert Hightower）所译的 *The Poetry of T'ao Ch'ien* 囊括了陶渊明所有的诗和赋。1983年，戴维斯（Albert Richard Davis）在剑桥出版社出版其译作 *T'ao Yuanming*（AD 365—427）：*His Works and Their Meaning*。20世纪90年代，美国诗人兼翻译家亨顿（David

Hinton）翻译 *The Selected Poems of T'ao Ch'ien*。国内方面，自 20 世纪 80 年代始，方重（《陶渊明诗文选译》，1984）、谭时霖（《陶渊明诗文英译》，1992）、杨宪益和戴乃迭（《陶渊明诗选：汉英对照》，1999）、汪榕培（《英译陶诗》，2000）、许渊冲等先生与翻译家对陶渊明诗文进行了英译。可以说，对陶渊明及其作品的译介体现了其人其文走出中国文化疆界、面向多元世界，并逐步被不同语言文化读者接受的过程。无论是汉学家的推介还是本土译家的传播，都使得异质文明的读者能够了解、想象这位跨越时空的诗人和其富有魅力的人生经历与人格品质。

随着诸多译本的翻译传播，建立于其上的翻译研究也纷至沓来。如阿瑟·韦利（Arthur Waley）在其文章 *Mr. Waley on the T'ao Ch'ien Poem* 中对 Mrs Ayscough 所译陶诗从道家文化层面提出学术性修改意见；欧阳桢（Eugene Eoyang）翻译了陶诗《时运》并撰写文章 *Tao Ch'ien's "The Seasons Come and Go：Four Poems"*，突出了陶诗独具田园风格与内涵的道家思想，表现了陶渊明顺时、顺势、顺境的思想境界。整体而言，各种理论观照下的陶渊明诗文翻译探究、书评介绍、学术争鸣从不同的维度体现了中国古典文学在异域世界的重要地位和影响，同时也折射出现代世界对于这位隐逸诗人的思想憧憬。尤其是进入 21 世纪后，陶诗翻译研究越来越受到重视，研究范围包括译本述评、译者研究、译本比较、策略探讨、语言学与跨文化分析等等，研究"量""质"兼具。

陶渊明满腹诗情才意，是中国文化精神和文学艺术特色的典型代表，更是古代江西人文史上的一颗璀璨明珠。著名翻译家汪榕培先生曾说道，"陶渊明的诗歌是西方读者了解古代中国的一面镜子，缩短东西方距离的一座桥梁"。翻为镜，译为桥，翻译要映射与沟通的是关于真、善、美的要义。因此，翻译陶诗在体现出古典韵律和意境文雅的同时，还需要向译语读者传递其所蕴含思想文化的真切与善意。

二、鉴赏·评析

谈及陶渊明，无人不识其名篇《桃花源记》。该作品风格清新独特，亦幻亦真，借景抒情、以诗言志，兼具时代感、个人化与超然性。因此，诸多名家也选译此篇，将其作为推介陶公的代表作。以下选取 Owen 与 Birch 译文作为鉴赏与评析的文本。

【原文】

桃花源记

晋太元中，武陵人捕鱼为业①。缘溪行，忘路之远近。忽逢桃花林，夹岸数百步，中无杂树，芳草鲜美，落英缤纷。渔人甚异之。复前行，欲穷其林。

林尽水源，便得一山。山有小口，仿佛若有光，便舍船从口入。初极狭，才通人；复行数十步，豁然开朗。土地平旷，屋舍俨然，有良田、美池、桑竹之属。阡陌交通，鸡犬相闻。其中往来种作，男女衣着，悉如外人。黄发垂髫②，并怡然自乐。见渔人，乃大惊，问所从来③，具答之。便要还家，设酒杀鸡作食。村中闻有此人，咸来问讯。自云先世避秦时乱，率妻子邑人来此绝境，不复出焉，遂与外人间隔。问今是何世，乃不知有汉，无论魏晋。此人一一为具言所闻，皆叹惋。余人各复延至其家④，皆出酒食。停数日，辞去。此中人语云："不足为外人道也。"

既出，得其船，便扶向路⑤，处处志之。及郡下，诣太守⑥，说如此。太守即遣人随其往，寻向所志，遂迷，不复得路。

南阳刘子骥⑦，高尚士也，闻之，欣然规往，未果，寻病终⑧。后遂无问津者。

（选自［清］吴楚材、吴调侯选注：《古文观止》）

【注释】

① 太元：东晋孝武帝年号。武陵：郡名，属湖广常德府，旁有桃源县。

② 黄发：旧说是长寿的象征，故借指老人。垂髫：小孩头上垂下的发，用

以指小孩。

③ 所从来：从什么地方来。

④ 延：邀请。

⑤ 向路：老路。向：原来。

⑥ 诣：拜见。

⑦ 刘子骥：南阳（今河南南阳市）人，名骥之，好游山泽，高尚不仕。一次到衡山采药深入忘返，他想回家又迷了路。回去后打算再去寻找石仓仙药，已不知石仓的所在了。

⑧ 规往：计划前去。寻：不久。

【译文】

Tao Qian's "Account of Peach Blossom Spring" remains one of the most beloved stories in the ancient Chinese Litterature . By Tao Qian's time, the tension between the state and the individual had developed fully. The "Account" offered the image of a third and idyllic possibility, that of a small farming community cut off from history and the larger state.

An Account of Peach Blossom Spring

During the Tai-yuan Reign of the Jin (376-396), there was a native of Wuling who made his living catching fish. Following a creek, he lost track of the distance he had traveled when all of a sudden he came upon forests of blossoming peach trees on both shores. For several hundred paces there were no other trees mixed in. The flowers were fresh and lovely, and the falling petals drifted everywhere in profusion. The fisherman found this quite remarkable and proceeded on ahead to find the end of this forest. The forest ended at a spring, and here he found a mountain. There was a small opening in the mountain, and it vaguely seemed as if there were light in it. He then left his boat and went in through the opening. At first it was very narrow, just wide enough for a person to get through. Going on further a few dozen paces, it spread out into a clear, open space.

The land was broad and level, and there were cottages neatly arranged. There were good fields and lovely pools, with mulberry, bamboo, and other such things. Field paths crisscrossed, and dogs and chickens could be heard. There, going back and forth to their work planting, were men and women whose clothes were in every way just like people elsewhere. Graybeards and children with their hair hanging free all looked contented and perfectly happy.

When they saw the fisherman, they were shocked. They asked where he had come from, and he answered all their questions. Then they invited him to return with them to their homes, where they served him beer and killed chickens for a meal. When it was known in the village that such a person was there, everyone came to ask him questions.

Of themselves they said that their ancestors had fled the upheavals during the Qin and had come to this region bringing their wives, children, and fellow townsmen. They had never left it since that time and thus had been cut off from people outside. When asked what age it was, they didn't know of even the existence of the Han, much less the Wei or Jin. The fisherman told them what he had learned item by item, and they all sighed, shaking their heads in dismay. Each person[①] invited him to their homes, and they all offered beer and food.

After staying there several days, he took his leave. At this people said to him, "There's no point in telling people outside about us."

Once he left, he found his boat; and then as he retraced the route by which he had come, he took note of each spot. On reaching the regional capital, he went to the governor and told him the story as I have reported. The governor

---

① 此处主语应为 All the people，与后面的 their 保持一致。

immediately sent people to follow the way he had gone and to look for the spots he had noticed. But they lost their way and could no longer find the route.

Liu Zi-ji of Nan-yang was a gentleman of high ideals. When he heard of this, he was delighted and planned to go there. Before he could realize it, he grew sick and passed away. After that no one tried to find the way there.

(Translated by Stephen Owen)

Peach Blossom Spring

During the reign-period T'ai yuan (326-97) of the Chin dynasty there lived in Wu-ling a certain fisherman. One day, as he followed the course of a stream, he became unconscious of the distance he had travelled. All at once he came upon a grove of blossoming peach trees which lined either bank for hundreds of paces. No tree of any other kind stood amongst them, but there were fragrant flowers, delicate and lovely to the eye, and the air was filled with drifting peachbloom.

The fisherman, marveling, passed on to discover where the grove would end. It ended at a spring; and then there came a hill. In the side of the hill was a small opening which seemed to promise a gleam of light. The fisherman left his boat and entered the opening. It was almost too cramped at first to afford him passage; but when he had taken a few dozen steps he emerged into the open light of day. He faced a spread of level land. Imposing buildings stood among rich fields and pleasant ponds all set with mulberry and willow. Linking paths led everywhere, and the fowls and dogs of one farm could be heard from the next. People were coming and going and working in the fields. Both the men and the women dressed in exactly the same manner as people outside; white-haired elders and tufted children alike were cheerful and contented.

Some, noticing the fisherman, started in great surprise and asked him where he had come from. He told them his story. They then invited him to their home[①], where they set out wine and killed chickens for a feast. When news of his coming spread through the village everyone came in to question him. For their part they told how their forefathers, fleeing from the troubles of the age of Ch'in, had come with their wives and neighbors to this isolated place, never to leave it. From that time on they had been cut off from the outside world. They asked what age was this : they had never even heard of the Han, let alone its successors the Wei and the Chin. The fisherman answered each of their questions in full, and they sighed and wondered at what he had to tell. The rest all invited him to their homes in turn, and in each house food and wine were set before him. It was only after a stay of several days that he took his leave.

"Do not speak of us to the people outside," they said. But when he had regained his boat and was retracing his original route, he marked it at point after point ; and on reaching the prefecture he sought audience of the prefect and told him of all these things. The prefect immediately dispatched officers to go back with the fisherman. He hunted for the marks he had made, but grew confused and never found the way again.

The learned and virtuous hermit Liu Tzu-chi heard the story and went off elated to find the place. But he had no success, and died at length of a sickness. Since that time there have been no further "seekers of the ford".

(Translated by Cyril Birch)

【评析】

(一) 英译策略之"逻辑显化"

汉语和英语分属汉藏和印欧两大语系，两种语言客观上存在着很大差

---

① 此处应为 homes.

异。从词汇层面来看，汉语与英语的词汇意义并不完全对等，一种语言中的某个词在另一种语言中可能对应多个词汇。从句子层面来看，汉语重意合，英语重形合。汉语注重意念连贯，以意役形，以神统法，而英语注重形式接应，严密规范。形合和意合是语言的两种基本组织手段，是王力先生在《中国语法理论》中提出的两个概念。所谓形合（Hypotaxis），指的是通过使用从属从句、附加成分或者其他语法结构来建立句子中的层次结构和逻辑关系。在形合结构中，有一个主句，其余的成分则作为从属或附加于主句之中，从而形成了层级关系。形合通常用于构建复杂的句子，以表达更多的信息、关系和逻辑。在形合结构中，主句通常包含主要的信息，而从句则提供额外的说明、解释、条件或其他相关信息。这种结构有助于语言的表达丰富和复杂化。

英语具有明显的形合特征，即英语句式常用各种连接词、分句或从句，注重显性连接和句子形式，注重结构完整，注重以形显意。因此，英语中起连接作用的词语特别多，从语法角度讲，连接词分为并列连词和从属连词，它们犹如胶水，可将纸张黏合起来。从意义上讲，连接词起着衔接各类逻辑语义的作用。以介词为代表，据20世纪早期的一位语言学家G.Curme统计，英语中各类介词约286个，是英语里较活跃的词类之一，是连接词语、从句的重要手段。除了介词以外，英语中还存在其他的连接手段，如形态变化，包括词缀变化，动词、名词、代词、形容词和副词的形态变化（如性、数、格、时、体、语态、语气、比较级、人称变化等）。

所谓意合（Parataxis），是将句子的不同成分或短语简单并列，不使用从属关系或其他复杂的语法结构来表达逻辑关系。在意合结构中，各个成分之间通常是通过逗号、分号或者其他标点符号来分隔的。意合结构通常用于表达简单、直接的思想或者观点，或者在表达时不需要详细的逻辑关系或修饰。这种结构在许多口语和书面语言中都很常见，特别是在叙述、陈述或者描述事物时。与形合相比，意合结构更加直接，不需要建立复杂的层级关系，因此可以使句子更为简洁明了。

汉语具有明显的意合特征，即汉语连词成句，注重隐性连贯，少用甚至不用连接手段，注重逻辑事理顺序，注重以神统形，结构简练明快。举例来说："她走进房间，坐下来，开始读书。"在这个句子中，各个动作被简单地并列，没有使用从属关系或其他复杂的语法结构。

汉语的形合手段比英语少很多，没有英语中常用的那些关系词和连接词。就介词数量而言，汉语中介词的数量大约只有30个，且多是从动词中借来的，并且汉语中的介词往往被省略，特别是在口语中，不省略反而使句子冗长累赘。在汉语中，词语或短句之间的关系自在不言中，语法意义和逻辑关系往往隐藏于字里行间，人们可以根据语境自然推断出来，故而汉语中短小精悍的四字格成语常常是意合的佳作。

总而言之，英语注重句子形式，连接手段和形式数量大、种类多、使用频繁，而汉语句式简明紧凑，分句之间的语法关系和逻辑关系是隐含的。

因此，汉译英时为了保证译文语法正确、语义明确，显化策略是必不可少的。在翻译《桃花源记》时，两位译者多处使用显化策略，如：

"林尽水源，便得一山。山有小口，仿佛若有光。"原文前三组皆是四字格短语，彼此的语义不需要借助过多的介词就可呈现。但是英文则需要将逻辑显化，Stephen译文以"and here""and it vaguely seemed as if there were light in it"等形式呈现语义和逻辑关系；Birch以"and then""in the side of the hill""which"等形式呈现语义和逻辑关系。

"复行数十步，豁然开朗"这句原文中并没有使用逻辑连接词，但如果仔细推敲就会发现原文中隐含的逻辑关系：虽然前面空间狭窄，但是走几步后便豁然开朗。Birch译文："It was almost too cramped at first to afford him passage; but when he had taken a few dozen steps he emerged into the open light of day."使用转折词"but"将原文隐含的逻辑关系显化，使译入语读者能更好地体会桃花源的神秘感。

"既出，得其船"，结合语篇分析可知，虽然桃花源中人希望捕鱼人不要告知外界桃花源的存在，但是捕鱼人并未遵守承诺，一出外界便告知太守。Birch 的译文 "'Do not speak of us to the people outside,' they said. But when he had regained his boat and was retracing his original route, he marked it at point after point",使用转折词"but"将原文逻辑关系显化出来,这不仅符合英语形合的特点,也将捕鱼人受人之托却不守承诺的行为凸显出来,与朴实的桃花源中人形成鲜明对比。

"欣然规往,未果。"刘子骥得知桃花源的消息后"欣然规往",但是没有实现这个计划便病逝了。虽然原文没有逻辑关联词,但是 Birch 的译文 "Liu Tzu-chi heard the story and went off elated to find the place. But he had no success",同样使用转折词"but"将逻辑梳理显化,语义清晰,同时也留下"出师未捷身先死"式的惋叹,令人回味无穷。

此外,正因为汉语是意合语言,因此在句子中,时常会出现主语缺失的情况。而英语是形合语言,需要将主语明确翻译出来。补充主语这一翻译策略在本文两位译者的作品中也有多处体现:

原文"便舍船从口入""见渔人,乃大惊……问所从来,具答之。便要还家……问今是何世""既出,得其船……及郡下,诣太守说如此"等皆是无主句,但是两个译文皆补充了主语,使译入语更符合目的语读者的阅读习惯。

(二)文本鉴析

词性转换是汉英翻译实践中常见的一个策略。"晋太元中,武陵人捕鱼为业"中"捕鱼"是动词,Birch 译成名词"fisherman"。Birch 把原文的动态过程名词化,增添名词短语的信息量。英语是静态性语言,多使用名词、介词、词组等,而中文是动态性语言,动词居多,故此处的翻译策略很好地体现出中英文的语言特性,使译文更符合英语的表达习惯。

"桃花林"一词 Stephen 选用"forests of"与原文的"忽逢"——"all of a sudden"相结合,不仅将捕鱼人眼前景色突变为浓密桃林的视觉冲击展现出来,且体现了捕鱼人当时内心的诧异与好奇,与后面"渔人甚异之"——

"The fisherman found this quite remarkable and proceeded on ahead to find the end of this forest"保持逻辑连贯。

四字短语"中无杂树"意思是说桃花源两岸没有别的树，遍布桃树，突出桃花源的美丽以及桃花源的神秘，Stephen 的译文"there were no other trees mixed in"精准又简洁。

"芳草鲜美，落英缤纷"的意思是"芬芳的青草鲜嫩美丽，落花纷纷"。Stephen 省略了原文"草"的形象，但是"falling petals drifted everywhere in profusion"中的"falling"和"drifted"却使画面至此活跃起来，充分译出"缤纷"二字所体现出的凌乱、丰富，以及花瓣轻盈飘落时的动态美。Birch 的译文"but there were fragrant flowers, delicate and lovely to the eye, and the air was filled with drifting peachbloom"不仅体现了桃花林浓郁茂密，还让读者明白了桃花源让人惊叹的不仅仅是它带来的视觉盛宴，还有沁人心脾的花香，这种嗅觉的体验也会让人流连忘返，愈加沉醉。Birch 将视觉和嗅觉描写相结合，生动形象地给读者展现出"花落纷纷，花香四溢"的动态画面，结合感官体验给读者一种身临其境的感觉，引起读者的阅读兴趣。同时，为了保持句子间的逻辑合理性，Birch 将"芳草"理解成"花香"，同 Stephen 一样省略了"草"的形象，译为"fragrant flowers"，保持了译文的逻辑连贯，避免读者产生疑惑。

"黄发"旧说是长寿的象征，故借指老人。无论是 Stephen 选用的"graybeards"还是 Birch 的"white-haired elders"，都实现了色彩上与原文相对应的效果，同时也采取了与原文一致的修辞手法——转喻（Metonymy），即以个人的特征代表整体。但是值得注意的是，"beard"通常是成年男性的特征，因此这里的翻译实际上缩小了所指的范畴。

"往来"是指居民在道路上往来行走，而"种作"是其他居民在路边田间耕种劳作，相较于 Birch 的译文"People were coming and going and working in the fields"，Stephen 将"往来种作"译为"going back and forth to their work planting"，即在田间来回劳作，对语义进行了删减。

"阡陌交通，鸡犬相闻"的原文意思是"田间小路四通八达，鸡鸣狗叫清晰可闻"。其中"鸡犬相闻"出自《老子》："甘其食，美其服，安其居，乐其俗。邻国相望，鸡犬之声相闻，民至老死不相往来"，意指人口稠密。两版译文"field paths crisscrossed"与"linking paths led everywhere"皆保留了"阡陌"的形象，省略了人口稠密之意。

"男女衣着，悉如外人"从字面意思看很容易理解为"桃花源中人的穿着与外界一样"，但是仔细分析我们会发现此处实际是指人们的衣着打扮在捕鱼人看来比较奇特，不同于世俗世界的人。渔人发现桃花源时是"晋太元中"，是晋孝武帝在位时期。桃花源中人因"先世避秦时乱"且"不复出焉，遂与外人间隔"，因此推断他们的祖先最初所穿衣服为秦朝服饰。《桃花源诗》中有两句："俎豆犹古法，衣裳无新制。"意思为：祭祀还是先秦的礼法，衣服没有新的款式。因此桃源内的人穿着仍然为秦时服饰。据《宋书·周郎传》记："凡一袖之大，足断为两，一裾之长，可分为二。"东晋上至王公名士，下及黎民百姓，均以宽衣大袖为风尚，由此看来秦朝百姓的服饰和东晋百姓的服饰是不同的（孙拥军，2022）。如此，桃花源中人才会"见渔人，乃大惊"。两版译文"men and women whose clothes were in every way just like people elsewhere"与"both the men and the women dressed in exactly the same manner as people outside"皆表示捕鱼人发现桃花源中人与外面世界的人穿着并无二致，体现不出桃花源中人与世隔绝的特点，存在逻辑不通，语义与原文有出入。

造成理解偏差的原因可能是多重的，较直接的原因或许是中文的"外人"存在一词多义的可能，即究竟是相对于捕鱼人而言的外人，还是相对于桃花源中人而言的外人呢？从叙事视角来看，捕鱼人初入桃花源，见良田美池，看人来人往，不由感叹"男女衣着，悉如外人"。这里是用捕鱼人的视角在记叙，所以"内、外"应该是针对捕鱼人而言。因此这里的"外人"应该是和捕鱼人所生活的世俗世界之人相对。捕鱼人所生活的世界与桃源世界不同，捕鱼人世界为"内"，桃源世界为"外"。因此"外人"应该为区别于世俗世界之人而言的。再如，文章中还有两次出现"外人"之词，"遂与外人间隔"，"不足为外人道也"。这些话语是桃花源中人所言，因此叙述的视角自然是桃花源中人，对他们而言，桃源生活为"内"，世俗生活为"外"，故此"外人"自然指的是桃花源外之人了。

另外，两位译者虽是著名的汉学家，中文造诣颇深，但是中外文化不同，历史不同，这也增加了语义理解的难度。从写作背景来看，《桃花源记》约作于永初二年（421），即南朝刘裕弑君篡位的第二年，这时作者陶渊明已归隐田园十六年。他虽归隐，但"猛志固常在"，仍旧关心国家政事。元熙二年六月，刘裕废晋恭帝为零陵王，改年号为"永初"。次年，刘裕用毒酒杀害晋恭帝。这些事件不能不激起陶渊明思想的波澜。他从固有的儒家观念出发，产生了对刘裕政权的不满情绪，只好借助创作来抒写情怀，塑造了一个与污浊黑暗社会相对立的美好境界，以寄托自己的政治理想与美好情趣。因此桃源中的生活应该是对立于世俗生活而存在的，这里寄托着陶渊明的理想与情怀。既然陶渊明塑造的是一个世俗之外的理想世界，他完全没有必要非让桃花源内的人穿着与世俗世界的人一样的衣服。此外，陶渊明的思想以儒道为主，深受魏晋玄学影响。道家注重"无为"，特别是老子的思想对陶渊明的影响更大，所以后期陶渊明选择了避世。陶渊明在《五柳先生传》的最后也是借黔娄之妻谈道："不戚戚于贫贱，不汲汲于富贵。其言兹若人之俦乎？衔觞赋诗，以乐其志，无怀氏之民欤？葛天氏之民欤？"无怀氏、葛天氏都是上古帝王，传说在他们的治理下，民风淳朴。陶渊明理想中的社会应该是上古时期那种无为而治的淳朴社会。桃花源中的人无非是理想的载体，他们承载的应该是上古社会的淳朴生活。因此陶公又怎能让其桃源之人的穿着打扮都如世俗之人呢？

语言是文化的载体，当译者在两种语言之间穿梭时，要时刻保持文化敏感性，透过字词看到背后博大精深的文化底蕴，方能更好地传词达意。

"见渔人，乃大惊"指桃花源中人见到捕鱼人时非常吃惊。从段落衔接来看，两位译者皆补充了主语，但是 Stephen 译文的"they"指代的是上文的"men and women"还是"Graybeards and children"呢？无论是二者中的哪一个，都将主语具体化了，同原文语义有偏差。Birch 则选择"some"这样一个相对模糊的代词作主语，避免了上述语义偏差。

"设酒杀鸡作食"可以体现桃花源中人对这个外来人的热情，是桃花源中人朴实好客的写照，所以"feast"这样一个带有节日气氛与款待之意的词或许比"meal"这个表日常饮食的词更具有表现力。

"见渔人，乃大惊……无论魏、晋。"本段的视角已经发生转换，从捕鱼人转为桃花源中人。"村中闻有此人"很明显就是从桃花源人的视角出发。Stephen 的译文"When it was known in the village that such a person was there"采用了被动态，相较于 Birch 的"When news of his coming spread through the village"的主动态，视角更远，有了一种疏离感，无法将桃花源中人的视角体现出来。

"咸来问讯"体现出与世隔绝的桃花源中人对这个突然出现的外面世界的人感到好奇，我们甚至可以视觉化出捕鱼人被桃花源中人团团围住、七嘴八舌打听情况的画面。所以 Birch 的"question him"比 Stephen 的"ask him questions"更能把捕鱼人面对众多问题应接不暇的状态展现出来。

"来此绝境，不复出焉，遂与外人间隔"中的"绝境"在本句中至关重要，体现出桃花源远离世俗、与世隔绝。因此相较于 Stephen 的"come to this region"，Birch 的"to this isolated place"更好地传达出了所处之地与外界隔绝、成为世外桃源的语义。

"遂与外人间隔"，根据上下文可知这是桃花源中人的主动选择，他们为避乱世来此地，主观上选择不再与外界保持联系，但是两版译文"thus had been cut off from people outside"和"they had been cut off from the outside world"皆采用被动句式，失去了原文的主动性。

"问今是何世"，通过分析原文可知此处是桃花源中人问捕鱼人如今是什么朝代，但是 Stephen 的被动句式"When asked what age it was, they didn't know of……"是指捕鱼人问桃花源中人如今朝代，语义与原文有出入。

"皆叹惋"是指桃花源中人对于外面世界朝代更迭、世事沧桑的一种感慨，是一种很复杂的情绪，但是 Stephen 的译文"they all sighed, shaking their heads in dismay"更多的是一种感伤情绪，较消极，不及 Birch 的"they sighed and wondered at what he had to tell"丰富，与原文相比有情感缺失之憾。

"不足为外人道也"表现了桃花源中人不愿意被外界发现他们的存在从而扰乱他们的清净与安宁，因此他们希望这个误闯入他们的世界、得到他们热情款待的外人可以保守秘密，故此处是严肃认真地交代与期盼，并非无足轻重、随口一说。如此看来，Birch 以祈使句"do not speak of us to the people outside"的方式更好地表达了桃花源中人的态度，也与捕鱼人一回到外面世界就食言形成明显对比。

"说如此"意指"说了这番经历"。Stephen 此处突然切换视角，将作者陶渊明这样一个一直以第三视角客观描述整个事件的人物拉入叙事之中。这种视角的转换增加了全文的真实性，但同时也易造成突兀，使读者产生疑惑。

"太守即遣人随其往"意指"太守立即派人跟着他去"。与 Birch 的"go back with the fisherman"相比，Stephen 译文"the governor immediately sent people to follow the way he had gone"缺失"随其往"的部分。

"高尚士也"意指刘子骥是南阳一位志向高洁的隐士。为帮助译入语读者理解，Stephen 采用归化译法，使用"gentleman"一词来表达"隐士"这一信息；而 Birch 为了更好地表达桃花源的神秘性，采用异化翻译策略，使用了含有宗教意味的"hermit"一词。

"后遂无问津者"的"问津"指打听渡口，在本文实际指问路。Stephen 采用归化翻译策略，将原文实际语义以目的语读者理解的方式传达出来。Birch 采用异化翻译策略，使用与汉语"津"对应的英文"ford"一词，虽然有助于译文充满异国情调色彩，但语义层面上或许与原文有一定的出入。

三、译论·比较

文字美、意境美、情感美，这是散文的价值所在，也是散文翻译的重点难点。许渊冲先生曾提出翻译实践应当遵循"三美论",认为求"美"是诗歌、散文等翻译的最高境界。作为文学的基本体裁之一,散文翻译也须求"美"。译者在翻译时要凸显散文的文字灵韵、意境内涵与情感表现,这是一种过程经历的挑战,也是一份结果达成的欣喜。

刘宓庆教授(2005)曾认为,在词语层面,原文承载审美的基本手段可以涵盖在"用词"中。文字之美内嵌于"词"这一基本的语言表达单位,其作为音义结合的整体能够升华文章思想感情,其美学价值也体现为"词"的甄选与揣摩。

以字表意、以词显情,译"意"、译"情"在散文翻译中至关重要。传统的"信、达、雅"与"美而不忠""信而不美"等论调使得译者从心理上觉得散文翻译中"情""意"并举难以实现。其实,基于斟词酌句后的抒"情"与表"意"是存在契合点的。前者是追求美的韵律与修辞,后者是实现美的形式与风格,"情"中有"意"、"意"中有"情",二者的辩证统一共促对于"美"的艺术追求。因此,散文翻译就是"词""情"与"意"之间的斟酌、徘徊、踟躇乃至彷徨,最终使三者呈现出一种"美"的统一。

鉴于此,可按照以下要点对林语堂所译《桃花源记》进行文本比较分析:

(1)林语堂其人其事以及翻译风格;
(2)从"文字美、意境美、情感美"三方面分析该译本;
(3)将林译本与 Owen 及 Birch 译本进行横向对比。

The Peach Colony

During the reign of Taiyuan of Chin, there was a fisherman of Wuling. One day he was walking along a bank. After having gone a certain distance, he suddenly came upon a peach grove which extended along the bank for about a hundred yards. He noticed with surprise that the grove had a magic effect, so singularly free from the usual mingling of brushwood, while the beautifully grassy ground was covered with its rose petals. He went further to explore, and when he came to the end of the grove, he saw a spring which came from a cave in the hill. Having noticed that there seemed to be a weak light in the cave, he tied up his boat and decided to go in and explore.

At first the opening was very narrow, barely wide enough for one person to go in. After a dozen steps, it opened into a flood of light. He saw before his eyes a wide, level valley, with houses and fields and farms. There were bamboos and mulberries; farmers were working and dogs and chickens were running about. The dresses of the men and women were like those of the outside world, and the old men and children appeared very happy and contented. They were greatly astonished to see the fisherman and asked him where he had come from. The fisherman told them and was invited to their homes, where wine was served and chicken was killed for dinner to entertain him. The villagers hearing of his coming all came to see him and to talk. They said that their ancestors had come here as refugees to escape from the tyranny of Tsin Shih-huang (builder of Great Wall) some six hundred years ago, and they had never left it. They were thus completely cut off from the world, and asked what was the ruling dynasty now. They had not even heard of the Han Dynasty (two centuries before to two centuries after Christ), not to speak of the Wei (third century) and the Chin (third and fourth centuries). The fisherman told them, which they heard with great amazement. Many of the other villagers then began to invite him to their homes by turn and feed him dinner and wine.

After a few days, he took leave of them and left. The villagers begged him not to tell the people outside about their colony. The man found his boat and came back, making a mental note of the direction of the route he had followed. He went to the magistrate's office and told the magistrate about it. The latter sent someone to go with him and find the place, but they got lost and could never find it again. Liu Tsechi of Nanyang was a great idealist. He heard of this story, and planned to go and find it, but was taken ill and died before he could fulfill his wish. Since then, no one has gone in search of this place.

[*Translated by Lin Yutang*（林语堂）]

四、实践·译笔

1. 归去来兮，田园将芜胡不归？既自以心为形役，奚惆怅而独悲？
2. 云无心以出岫，鸟倦飞而知还。
3. 羁鸟恋旧林，池鱼思故渊。
4. 方宅十余亩，草屋八九间。
5. 开荒南野际，守拙归园田。

五、阅读·延展

美的问题

第三，翻译与艺术文——以上所论翻译之忠实与通顺问题，系单就文字上立论，求译文必信必达的道理。但是还有翻译艺术上之问题，也不能不简略考究一下。翻译于用之外，还有美一方面须兼顾的，理想的翻译家应当将其工作做一种艺术。以爱艺术之心爱它，以对艺术谨慎不苟之心对它，使翻译成为美术之一种（translation as a fine art），且所译原文，每每属于西洋艺术作品，如诗文小说之类，译者不译此等书则已，若译此等书则于达用之外，不可不注意于文字之美的问题。

（摘自林语堂《论翻译》）

关于翻译的"美的标准"，林氏认为："翻译于用之外，还有美一方面须兼顾的，理想的翻译家应当将其工作做一种艺术。以爱艺术之心爱它，以对艺术谨慎不苟之心对它，使翻译成为美术之一种"。尤其是翻译文学作品，更"不可不注意于文字之美的问题"。

他同意真正的艺术作品是不可翻译的说法，"因为作者之思想与作者之文字在最好作品中若有完全天然之融合，故一离其固有文字则不啻失其精神躯壳，此一点之文字精英遂岌岌不能自存。"他认为翻译艺术作品"应以原文之风格与其内容并重"，因其风格本有独立的欣赏价值。"凡译艺术文的人，必先把其所译作者之风度神韵预先认出，于译时复极力发挥，才是尽译艺术文之义务。"他并把作品的"体裁"分作"外的"与"内的"，"外的体裁"即句之长短繁简区诗之体格等，"内的体裁"即作者之风格文体，如理想、写实、幻想、幽默等等。他的这一分类是否科学，那是另一回事；他指出翻译时必须注意这些方面，则是很正确的。

（《林语堂的〈论翻译〉》，摘自陈福康的《中国译学史》）

Translation as an art form

In the 1920s, Otokar Fischer, the Czech scholar and translator, defined translation as an activity at the interface between science and art. Some scholars have emphasized the philological or academic nature of translating (translation from classical and oriental languages has been considered a scholarly activity), yet others have pointed to its artistic nature (Goethe's translation of *Hasanaginica* and Herder's translations of folk songs etc. are considered an integral part of these poets' works). Accordingly, translation theory is considered to be either a linguistic or a literary discipline. A relevant branch of linguistics is contrastive analysis of the two language systems concerned; knowledge of its findings is an essential pre-requisite of the translator's craft. The search for linguistic equivalents is certainly the translator's main preoccupation, but there is more to it than that; notably, the artistic dimension of his activity goes beyond the mere practical application of contrastive grammar or stylistics. For example, critical assessment of the potential impact of the values of the source work in respect of issues of life in the recipient culture, the adoption of a specific interpretative position, the transposition of the artistic realities represented in the work and the transposition of its stylistic levels to the target culture and its language system, and so on. It is with this interrelationship between the concretizations of the work in the original and in the translation, the hybrid structure of the translated work and its function in the target culture, inter alia, that literary analysis is concerned.

In order to establish a sounder theoretical position for the analysis of artistic issues in translation than what can be derived from a purely practical approach, it will be necessary to define the relationship between translation and other arts.

The translator's goal is to preserve, capture and convey the original work, and not to create a new work having no precedent in the source. Therefore, the goal of translation is reproduction. In practice, the procedure involves substituting one set of verbal material for another—this entails autonomous creativity involving all the artistic means of the target language. Translation is therefore an original creative process taking place in a given linguistic environment. A translation as a work of art is artistic reproduction, translation as a process is original creation and translation as an art form is a borderline case at the interface between reproductive art and original creative art. In this respect, acting is the closest parallel to translation amongst all the arts, even if the original creative aspect is more prominent in acting than in translation, because the actor creates a work of a quite different category, transposing a literary text materialized in language into a stage performance materialized by a human being, the actor. The translator, on the other hand, merely transposes a work from one type of verbal material to another within the same category.

(Excerpts from *Chapter* 3 *of Translation Aesthetics* by *Jiří Levý* in *The Art of Translation*)

第三单元

豫章一阁·初唐王勃

一、译事·译研

王勃（650—676），字子安，"初唐四杰"之首。其诗歌具有雄杰之气象、革新之自觉，是引领唐诗发展的巨擘。王勃年少显才华，有建功立业之志，"高情壮思，有抑扬天地之心；雄笔奇才，有鼓怒风云之气"（《游冀州韩家园序》)，且早得功名，"年未及冠，应幽素举及第"（《旧唐书·文苑传上·王勃》)，可惜赍志以殁，令人唏嘘。王勃最负盛名的乃其骈文佳作《滕王阁序》，深受历代极评。

《滕王阁序》历时千余载，经久不衰，是文学传播的成功范例。北京大学罗经国教授编译的《古文观止精选（汉英对照）》中包含了《滕王阁序》，其英译典雅，对于弘扬中国传统文化具有重大现实意义，同时也具有很高的传播与研究价值。

二、鉴赏·评析

【原文】

滕王阁序（节选）

豫章故郡，洪都新府①，星分翼轸，地接衡庐。襟三江而带五湖，控蛮荆而引瓯越②。物华天宝，龙光射牛斗之墟③；人杰地灵，徐孺下陈蕃之榻。雄州雾列，俊采星驰。台隍枕夷夏之交，宾主尽东南之美。都督阎公之雅望，棨戟遥临；宇文新州之懿范④，襜帷暂驻。十旬休假⑤，胜友如云；千里逢迎，高朋满座。腾蛟起凤，孟学士之词宗；紫电青霜，王将军之武库。家君作宰，路出名区；童子何知，躬逢胜饯。

时维九月，序属三秋⑥。潦水尽而寒潭清，烟光凝而暮山紫。俨骖騑于上路，访风景于崇阿。临帝子之长洲，得仙人之旧馆。层峦耸翠，上出重霄；飞阁流丹，下临无地。鹤汀凫渚，穷岛屿之萦回；桂殿兰宫，列冈峦之体势。披绣闼⑦，俯雕甍⑧，山原旷其盈视，川泽纡其骇瞩。闾阎扑地，钟鸣鼎食之家；舸舰迷津，青雀黄龙之轴。虹销雨霁，彩彻云明。落霞与孤鹜齐飞，秋水共长天一色。渔舟唱晚，响穷彭蠡之滨；雁阵惊寒，声断衡阳之浦。

遥吟俯畅，逸兴遄飞。爽籁发而清风生，纤歌凝而白云遏。睢园绿竹，气凌彭泽之樽；邺水朱华，光照临川之笔。四美具，二难并。穷睇眄于中天，极娱游于暇日。天高地迥，觉宇宙之无穷；兴尽悲来，识盈虚之有数。望长安于日下，指吴会于云间。地势极而南溟深，天柱高而北辰远。关山难越，谁悲失路之人？萍水相逢，尽是他乡之客。怀帝阍而不见，奉宣室以何年？

呜呼！时运不齐，命途多舛；冯唐易老，李广难封。屈贾谊于长沙，非无圣主；窜梁鸿于海曲，岂乏明时？所赖君子安贫，达人知命。老当益壮，宁移白首之心？穷且益坚，不坠青云之志。酌贪泉而觉爽，处涸辙以犹欢。北海虽赊，扶摇可接；东隅已逝，桑榆非晚。孟尝高洁，空怀报国之心；阮籍猖狂，岂效穷途之哭？

勃三尺微命，一介书生。无路请缨，等终军之弱冠；有怀投笔，慕宗悫之长风。舍簪笏于百龄，奉晨昏于万里。非谢家之宝树，接孟氏之芳邻。他日趋庭，叨陪鲤对；今晨捧袂，喜托龙门。杨意不逢，抚凌云而自惜；钟期既遇，奏流水以何惭？

（节选自［清］吴楚材、吴调侯选注：《古文观止》）

【注释】

① 豫章故郡，洪都新府：豫章是汉朝设置的，治所在南昌，所以说"故郡"。唐初把豫章郡改为"洪州"，所以说"新府"。"豫章"一作"南昌"。

② 瓯越：古越地，即今浙江地区。古东越王建都于东瓯（今浙江省永嘉县），境内有瓯江。

③ 龙光射牛斗之墟：龙光，指宝剑的光辉。牛、斗，星宿名。墟、域，所在之处。

④ 懿范：好榜样。

⑤ 十旬休假：唐制，十日为一旬，遇旬日则官员休沐，称为"旬休"。

⑥ 三秋：古人称七、八、九月为孟秋、仲秋、季秋，三秋即季秋，九月。

⑦ 绣闼：绘饰华美的门。

⑧ 雕甍：雕饰华美的屋脊。

【译文】

A Tribute to King Teng's Tower（节选）

Nanchang, which was the capital of Yuzhang Prefecture during the Han Dynasty, now falls under the jurisdiction of Hongzhou. It straddles the border of the influence of the Ye and the Zhen constellations, and is adjacent to the Heng and the Lu mountains. The three rivers enfold it like the front part of a garment and the five lakes encircle it like a girdle. It controls the savage Jing area and connects Ou and Yue, and its products are nature's jewels. The radiance of its legendary sword shoots directly upward between the constellations *Niu and Dou*. Its talented people are outstanding, and the spirit of intelligence pervades the place. This was the place where Xu Ru spent the night on his visit to Chen Fan. The mighty Hongzhou spreads out immensely amid the fog, and the intellectual luminaries are as numerous as meteors chasing one another. It borders both the uncultured and the civilized areas, and its host and guests are all prominent people from the East and the South. Under the escort of the guard of honor with halberds in their hands. Governor Yan, a man of high repute, comes to attend this event from afar. Prefect Yuwen, a model of virtue, stops his carriage on the way to his new appointment. On this official holiday, which falls on every tenth day, good friends gather together, and a galaxy of distinguished guests from distant places fill the hall. Also present at the gathering are Master Meng, whose literary grace is as imposing as a dragon soaring and a phoenix dancing, and General Wang, who has weapons as sharp as the famous swords "Purple Lightning" and "Blue Frost" in his armory. I, an ignorant boy, have the good fortune to take part in this grand banquet on my journey to visit my father, who is a magistrate of a county.

　　It is September, the third month of autumn. The puddles on the ground have dried up, and the water in the pond is cool and translucent. At dusk the rays of the setting sun, condensed in the evening haze, turn the mountains purple. In the stately carriages drawn by the horses we make our way ahead, visiting the attractive scenic spot in the mountains. Soon we arrive at the river bank, where the King Teng's Tower beckons. Then we ascend the tower where the fairy once dwelled. Ranges upon ranges of green mountain rise as high as the sky. The red glow in the water is the reflection of the richly painted tower that seems hovering in the air. From its heights no land is visible. Circling around are numerous islets on which the cranes rest on the sandy beaches and the wild ducks on the sand-bars. Cassia-wood courts and orchid-wood halls rise and fall like mountain ranges. Pushing open the door carved with decorative patterns, I look down upon endless waves of brightly tinted roof tiles, each elaborately engraved with lovely etchings. A panorama of mountains and plains stretches beneath me, and I am mesmerized by the mighty scene of the winding rivers and big lakes. In the city there are houses everywhere. There are families of great affluence, whose meals are served with many cooking tripods of food and to the accompaniment of music. Massive ships and fierce war vessels are densely moored at the ports. On the stems of many ships are carved designs of blue birds and brown dragons. The rain has just let up and the rainbow has vanished. The sunlight shoots through the rosy clouds. A solitary wild duck flies alongside the multi-colored sunset clouds, and the autumn water is merged with the boundless sky into one hue. The fishermen can be heard singing the evening songs, their voices drifting as far as the banks of the Poyang Lake. Even the wild geese feel the chill of dusk settling upon them, and they cry all the way while flying southward, disappearing around the south bend of the Heng Mountain.

Looking afar and chanting, and then looking downward and singing, I feel a sudden rush of ecstasy soaring up in me. The music of the panpipe is like a gentle cool breeze. The soft singing lingers on ; it is so soothing that even the passing white clouds seem to come to a halt. The gathering here can be compared to the banquet in the bamboo garden hosted by Prince of Xiao of the Liang State, and many a guest is a greater drinker than Tao Yuanming. It is also like the feast at River Ye where Cao Zhi composed the poem in praise of the lotus flower. Present are many talented scholars who are as gifted as Xie Lingyun of Linchuan. It is not an easy thing to have four excellent things all at once, that is, good weather, beautiful scenery, full enjoyment and heartfelt happiness, and it is even more difficult to have a generous host and honored guests. I look into the vast expanse of the sky and amuse myself to my heart's content on this festive day. The sky is high and the land is boundless ; I cannot but feel the immensity of the universe. Sadness follows happiness. I am aware that success and failure are predestined. I look into the distance, but Chang'an, the capital of the country, is far beyond the setting sun in the west, and Wuhui is unapproachable somewhere amid the clouds. At the farthest end of the south are the depths of the South Sea, and far away in the north is the pillar that upholds the sky, but the Polestar is still farther. Since the mountains and passes are hard to travel over, who would sympathize with the disappointed ones? The people I meet here are all politically frustrated, drifting together like duckweeds. I pine for the Emperor but am not summoned. How long should I wait before I am called to the court again like Jia Yi?

Alas! I am ill fated, and my life is full of frustrations. Feng Tang grew old quickly and Li Guang had difficulty getting promoted. Jia Yi was unjustly exiled to Changsha. Was it because there was no wise emperor on the throne? Liang Hong had to seek refuge at the seaside. Was it because there was no good government in his time? Fortunately what supports one is the belief that a man of noble character always reconciles himself to poverty and a man with a philosophical view is always contented with his lot. Old as one is, he gains vigor with age and by no means wavers in his aspiration. Poor as one is, he is all the more determined in adversity and by no means gives up his ambition. One keeps his integrity even if he has drunk the water of the spring of Avarice? and is cheerful even if he is confronted with misfortune. Though the North Sea is far away, one can still get there with the help of the strong wind. Though the morning is gone, it is not too late to make up the loss in the evening. Meng Chang was noble and honest, but his devotion to the country was futile. Ruan Ji was unruly and untrammeled, but he burst out crying when in dire straits. How can we learn from him?

I am an insignificant scholar of a low official position and am of the same age as Zhong Jun, but unlike him, I have no opportunity to serve in the army. I will follow the example of Ban Chao, who threw aside the writing brush to enlist in the armed services and I admire Zong Que who made up his mind to seek a military career by braving the wind and waves. I am determined not to accept the offer of a lifelong government position by wearing a hair dress and holding a tablet before the chest as court officials do. Rather, I will travel thousands of li to go home to wait on my parents, paying respect to them morning and evening. As a son I am not as good as Xie Xuan but in my early years I had the fortune to have men of virtue as my neighbors. In a few days I will be with my father and I will take care of him and receive instructions from him as did Kong Li. On this day I have the honor to be invited by Governor Yan to this grand occasion. I am as blissful as if I had leaped over the Dragon's Gate. Since I do not have someone like Yang Yi to recommend me. I can only sigh with grief and caress this piece of writing which expresses my lofty aspiration. Now that I have met a bosom friend like Zhong Ziqi, why should I be ashamed of presenting this writing of mine?

[Translated by Luo Jinguo（罗经国）]

【评析】

（一）翻译策略之归化（Domestication）与异化（Foreignization）

施莱尔马赫（Friedrich Schleiermacher）是德国哲学家、神学家、著名翻译理论家，也是现代解释学的创始人。1813年，施莱尔马赫发表了长篇论文《论翻译的不同方法》。他指出："译者要么尽量不打扰原文作者，让读者靠近作者；要么尽量不打扰读者，让作者靠近读者。"（Either the translator leaves the author in peace, as much as possible, and moves the reader towards him; or he leaves the reader in peace, as much as possible, and moves the author towards him.）

"让读者靠近作者"的形象说法是译者带读者去异国他乡旅行，带领读者去见识异域风光中的他者，反而能更清楚地看清自我。将读者引向作者的过程中，译者要努力填补读者不能理解的语言真空，把自己的印象传递给读者。就像导游一样，带领读者到陌生的异国他乡去观光，使本国读者能够像外国读者一样，理解原作的风貌，外国的原汁原味由读者品尝。虽然读者不需要时刻想到自己的母语，但还是明显感受到文化之间的差异，这也就是异化（Foreignization）。简言之，异化是指在生成目的语文本时，通过保留原文中某些异国情调的东西，故意打破目的语习惯的语言和文化规范。

"让作者靠近读者"是使外国作者像本国作者那样写作、说话并与目的语读者直接对话。作者就像移民一样，入乡随俗地成为当地人，这也就是归化翻译（Domestication）。概言之，归化是指译文采用明白晓畅的风格，把目的语读者对外国文本和文化的陌生感降到最低程度，使得译文通顺易懂。

《滕王阁序》是骈文发展史上成就最高的作品之一，其语言优美，句式多变，善于用典。其典故来源广，用法灵活多变且贴切。据统计，本文典故多达37个，主要分为三类：神话传说、语典和事典。这些典故表达了躬逢胜饯的喜悦之情、怀才不遇的苦闷之情和建功立业的渴望之情等。因此，如何在译文中体现这些典故，让英语读者领会到用典之妙，集切题、隽永、典雅、和谐之美于一炉便成为让译者煞费心神之处。本文译者罗经国先生为了行文明白晓畅，同时尽量传递中文之美，在翻译典故时大量使用了异化与归化的策略，如：

"星分翼轸，地接衡庐"。中国古人用天上的二十八星宿来对应地上的区域，"翼轸"所属为南朱雀一宫，主要对应的是古时楚的分野，大约接近现湖南大部分、湖北、安徽、江西等地。译文"It straddles the border of the influence of the Ye and the Zhen constellations"中"straddles"体现了南昌横跨"翼轸"对应区域的雄伟气势，同时符合原文的空间叙事视角。译者虽然没有解释天上"翼轸"对应地上的南方，但"straddles the border of"保全了"星分翼轸"表地理位置的功能；同时译者补充的"the influence of"以及选用的"constellations（星座）"可以帮助英文读者联想到西方的星象学说。星象学连结的是宗教与巫术，和中国的天兆观念不能全然类比，但二者都是古人将星宿与凡世相连接的体现，可以实现文化的类比相通，这便是"让作者靠近读者"，以归化的方式把目的语读者对外国文本和文化的陌生感降低到最低程度，以便在外国文本中找到自身文化的身影。

"闾阎扑地，钟鸣鼎食之家"是说住户众多且富有，"钟鸣鼎食"指古代贵族吃饭时击钟列鼎而食，形容排场豪华。译文"There are families of great affluence"已经传达出原文的语义，但译者还是增加了"whose meals are served with many cooking tripods of food and to the accompaniment of music"进行文化补充。此处便是异化翻译策略的体现，英文读者不仅能接收到原文的语义，还能明显感受到文化差异和古老东方的异国情调，使那些对中国古代文化感兴趣的读者加深对古代贵族的理解。

"睢园绿竹，气凌彭泽之樽"一句有用典，"睢园"指西汉梁孝王刘武在睢阳建造的菟园，园中多绿竹，为集文士饮酒赋诗之处。此处借指滕王阁。"彭泽之樽"指陶渊明，他曾任彭泽县令，以善饮酒著称。译文"The gathering here can be compared to the banquet in the bamboo garden hosted by Prince of Xiao of the Liang State, and many a guest is a greater drinker than Tao Yuanming"为英语读者补充了睢园的背景知识，同时点明陶渊明所代表的饮酒文化。同样，"邺水朱华，光照临川之笔"涉及曹植与谢灵运两位人物，他们在中国文坛上赫赫有名，但是译者没有为便于读者理解而花大量笔墨予以介绍，而是同"a greater drinker"一样，使用"composed the poem"与"talented scholars who are as gifted as"点出与曹植、谢灵运相关的文化关键词。这种异化的方式既不妨碍读者理解原意，同时也保留了原汁原味的异国文化。

"兴尽悲来，识盈虚之有数"这一句中的"盈虚"是中国特有的概念，古人仰望明月，见月亮有盈有亏，正如阴阳此消彼长，植物有枯有荣、人生有得有失。不像西方人比较注重结果，中国人似乎始终生活在过程之中，这个过程没有开始也没有终结，有的只是盈亏交替，岁月沉淀。当然，在翻译这句的时候是不可能就着"盈虚"去浓墨重彩讲月亮的。译者在此处不仅抓住了王勃含蓄表达的核心——成败，也抓住了西方人需要理解的要点。于是将"盈虚"译为了"success and failure"，这种归化策略的使用符合译文读者的习惯，增加了译文的可读性。

"天柱高而北辰远","天柱"是指传说中的天之柱,出自《山海经·神异经》:昆仑之山有铜柱焉,其高入天,所谓天柱也。围三千里,圆周如削。下有回屋焉,壁方百丈。此处翻译为"the pillar that upholds the sky"。在西方文化中也有相似的概念,如在希腊神话中,阿特拉斯(Atlas)是擎天神,他被宙斯降罪用双肩支撑苍天。这种归化的方式使译文靠近读者,让读者在异国文化中找到熟悉的感觉。

"喜托龙门"。译者采用异化的策略,保留了原汁原味。由于西方的"dragon"不同于中国的"龙",故此处英文读者阅读起来会有一些疑惑:为何在他们文化里代表残暴的"dragon"在这里却是"as blissful as"呢?这种文化冲突乍看之下会影响英文的可读性,但对中国文化感兴趣的读者来说却能引起他们的思考与探索,有助于他们进一步了解中国的"龙"文化。

(二)译文评析与鉴赏

《滕王阁序》的"序"是文体的一种,有书序、赠序、宴集序等。书序是著作或诗文前的说明性或评价性文字,本文是饯别序,即临别赠言,属于赠序类的文章。译者并没有按照原意翻译,而是以英文读者所喜闻乐见的方式译为"a tribute to";滕王在这里指唐朝滕王李元婴,他是李渊的第二十二个儿子,唐太宗李世民的弟弟,并不是皇帝或者国王,因此他并不是英语的"king"。故而改成"prince"或许语义更准确。

"豫章故郡,洪都新府"。豫章是汉朝设置的,但是原文并没有直接写明,译文为了使英语读者更好地理解南昌在不同时代下的称呼与辖属,补充了原文没有的背景信息"during the Han Dynasty",并通过时态"were"和"now falls"将"故"与"新"体现出来,是为南昌的时代变迁。

"襟三江而带五湖,控蛮荆而引瓯越"。古时认为长江经过江西鄱阳湖分成三道入海,故而称"三江",又一说指太湖的支流松江、娄江、东江,泛指长江中下游的江河;"五湖"一说指太湖、鄱阳湖、青草湖、丹阳湖、洞庭湖,又一说指菱湖、游湖、莫湖、贡湖、胥湖,皆在鄱阳湖周围,与鄱阳湖相连。"蛮荆"：古楚地，今湖北、湖南一带。"瓯越"：古越地，今浙江地域。古东越王建都于东瓯（今浙江省永嘉县），境内有瓯江。译文此处运用比喻的修辞手法，同时使用头韵法，如用"garment"和"girdle"来体现语言的音乐美和整齐美，具有很高的审美价值，增添了人们欣赏语言艺术的情趣。"蛮荆"与"瓯越"两处作者采用直译的策略，并未解释这两处当今所指，这对于不熟悉中国历史与地理的读者来说理解起来比较困难。

"物华天宝，龙光射牛斗之墟"：龙光，指宝剑的光耀。牛、斗，星宿名。墟、域，地址之处。据《晋书·张华传》，晋初，牛、斗二星之间常有紫气照射。张华求教懂天象的雷焕，雷焕称这是宝剑之精，上彻于天。张华命雷焕为丰城令寻剑，公然在丰城（今江西省丰城市，古属豫章郡）监狱的地下，掘地四丈，得一石匣，内有龙泉、太阿二剑。后这对宝剑入水化为双龙。"人杰地灵，徐孺下陈蕃之榻"：徐孺是徐孺子的略称。徐孺子名稚，东汉豫章人，其时隐士。据《后汉书·徐稚传》，东汉名人陈蕃为豫章太守，不接来宾，唯徐稚来访时，才设一睡榻，徐稚去后又悬置起来。这两句文化背景丰富，译者并没有花大量笔墨补充背景，而是直接干脆地翻译中心意思，用一个"legendary"概括了背后的故事。另外，"pervades"（弥漫、遍布之意）用得极妙，传神地表达出南昌人才辈出、人杰地灵的特点，与"this was the place where"一起将重心拉回对地点的描述。但是译者没有解释徐孺下榻的典故，对于不熟悉中国文化的读者来说无法理解王勃此处想借赞扬南昌之机，夸赞本次宴会主人洪州都督阎伯屿礼贤下士的用心。

"棨戟"指外有赤玄色缯作套的木戟，古代大官出行时用。译者虽没有描述它的外形，但是用"the guard of honor with halberds"表达了此物的功能，即此处代指仪仗。"都督阎公之雅望，棨戟遥临；宇文新州之懿范，襜帷暂驻。"这句骈文讲究对仗的工整和声律的铿锵，是一个对偶句，译文采用"Governor Yan, a man of high repute"与"Prefect Yuwen, a model of virtue"的形式，两句相同的句式还原了原文的对仗，可谓精彩。

"腾蛟起凤，孟学士之词宗；紫电青霜，王将军之武库。"这句意指在座贵宾皆是文武奇才，译者以"as imposing as"和"as sharp as"直译"腾蛟起凤"和"紫电青霜"两大比喻，"a dragon soaring and a phoenix dancing"中的"ing"韵律使译文颇具音律之美，同时从视觉和听觉的角度生动地呈现出文客做文章有气吞山河之势。

"童子何知，躬逢胜饯。"中国人讲究谦虚，谦辞的精髓就是"压低自己，抬高他人"。而英美文化在人与人的交流中会比较直接，直接赞扬对方的好，直接表达自己的喜悦与感激，而不会刻意地贬抑自我。这种文化差异非常考验译者的功底。本文涉及三处礼貌谦辞，分别是：

（1）家君作宰，路出名区；童子何知，躬逢胜饯。

译文：I, an ignorant boy, have the good fortune to take part in this grand banquet on my journey to visit my father, who is a magistrate of a county.

（2）勃，三尺微命，一介书生。

译文：I am an insignificant scholar of a low official position.

（3）他日趋庭，叨陪鲤对。

译文：In a few days I will be with my father and I will take care of him and receive instructions from him as did Kong Li.

翻译（1）时，译者运用换序译法，更换了前后文的次序，将"童子何知"（an ignorant boy）置于前，通过顺序的调整来体现自谦的语气。

翻译（2）时，译者采用解释的方式，"三尺微命"指地位卑下，"一介书生"指身份普通无奇，且给人文弱之感。这句话就意义层面来讲并没有突出作用，属于可有可无的表达，而这种可有可无的表达在中国人的习惯中是不可缺少的。译者在翻译这个句子的时候果断地运用意译手法，省去了"一""三"这样让西方读者不解的数词，用"insignificant""low"等词语将原文进行语义脱壳，直接干脆，简洁明快。

翻译（3）时，译者采用了省略与增补。省略了"趋庭"——快步走过庭院，这是表示对长辈的恭敬，和"叨"——惭愧的承受，表示自谦，用"be with my father"和"take care of him"替代了这种文化功能。增加了"鲤对"——在父辈面前接受教诲的背景故事，即 "receive instructions from him as did Kong Li"。

"潦水尽而寒潭清，烟光凝而暮山紫。"译者并未直译"寒潭"，而是进行重组表达为 "the water in the pond is cool"，此乃触觉；接着 "at dusk the rays of the setting sun, condensed in the evening haze, turn the mountains purple" 将"烟光凝而暮山紫"解释为落日的余光透过层层雾霭，重重山岭披覆着云烟氤氲，层林尽染落日紫光。虚与实之间，一幅静谧美好的秋景如画面一般呈现在读者眼前，这两句译文从视觉上和触觉上将读者带入深秋，对应下一句 "visiting the attractive scenic spot in the mountains"。

"临帝子之长洲，得仙人之旧馆。"此处译者以"beckons"一词体现了滕王阁雄踞江边，成为游人必访之美景，随后译者补充原文没有体现的逻辑 "then we ascend the tower"，从而才能看到登阁之后的壮丽景色，即"层峦耸翠，上出重霄；飞阁流丹，下临无地。鹤汀凫渚，穷岛屿之萦回；桂殿兰宫，列冈峦之体势"。但是山峦重叠，青翠的山峰耸入云霄，此处 "green mountain" 若是复数形式或许更符合语境。此外，"帝子"与"仙人"都是指滕王李元婴，而译者在这里采取直译的方法，将"仙人"译为 "the fairy"，虽增加了诗歌的意境和趣味性，但对于不清楚文言文写作手法的读者而言略有突兀且存在语义偏差。

"飞阁流丹"是指凌空的楼阁，飞檐涂饰红漆，红色的阁道犹如飞翔在天。但是译者这里处理得极妙，他将"流丹"译为 "the red glow in the water is the reflection of the richly painted tower"，即凌空的红色楼阁倒映在江水中，熠熠生辉，为画面增加了灵动之感。"下临无地"一词作者选用 "visible" 营造出滕王阁高耸云端之势，配合前文的"飞阁"（that seems hovering in the air），体现出唐代建筑"以势壮美"的美学思想。

"俯雕甍"指俯视彩饰的屋脊，译者在这里用 "endless waves of" 增补了原文没有的信息，但正是借此表达出了滕王阁屋顶上的瓦片压得密如鱼鳞、此起彼伏。

"山原旷其盈视,川泽纡其骇瞩。"译者巧用"panorama""stretches""beneath"营造出了"旷""盈"所体现的气势,让读者仿佛身临其境,站在滕王阁上极目望去将美景尽收眼底。

"舸舰迷津,青雀黄龙之轴":指船只泊满渡口,渡口尽是雕上青雀黄龙花纹的大船。"舸舰"均指大船,但是这里译者采用直译的策略,将"舰"译为"fierce war vessels",充斥有军事色彩,容易使英语读者误解为在为军事做准备,且留下好斗的印象,与文章此处描绘的繁荣宏伟气势不符。

"落霞与孤鹜齐飞,秋水共长天一色"是一句千古名句,王勃写到此处时,高朋满座对他赞不绝口。这两句在句式上不但上下相对,而且自成对偶,形成"当句对"的特点。如"落霞"对"孤鹜","秋水"对"长天",这是王勃骈文的特点。从这里开始,王勃的描写也渐渐从近景转向远景。对这两句的英译,译者综合考虑了各个部分。首先,译者为"落霞"补充了"multi-colored",增添了色彩,将落日余晖洒向江面泛起粼粼霞光之景呈现给英文读者。其次将"飞""色"组成的动静结合的画面感通过"flies alongside"和"is merged with"表现出来,而"solitary wild duck"不仅表明鹜的形单影只之孤,更是赋予其一种秋天独有的忧郁之感。只是或许用"one solitary wild duck"与"multi-colored"更易形成反差与对比,能更好地传达出作者此时心境的转变。最后,下文的"drifting as far as""chill"与"they cry all the way while flying southward, disappearing around the south bend of the Heng Mountain"等将画面拉向远方,先前形容建筑时的雄伟豪壮之情开始消散,一股悲凉之意悄然爬上心头。"autumn water"平静又安谧,与"boundless sky"形成水天一色。"alongside"和"merged with"将画面中的和谐之感完美诠释,让读者不禁在脑海中勾勒出一幅秀丽的风景图。

"纤歌凝而白云遏":指柔软的歌声吸引了白云,译者用一个"so…that"句式栩栩如生地描绘出了歌声的柔细,好似缭绕云端,连飘动的白云也为之驻足。译者在白云前加了一个修饰词"passing",增加了画面的动感,与"halt"形成对比。

"望长安于日下,指吴会于云间。地势极而南溟深,天柱高而北辰远"的意思为:西望京都,远在夕阳之下;东指吴越,隐现在云雾之间。陆地的尽头是深不可测的大海,北极星辰高悬,天柱山高不可攀。作者在翻译长安时补充了"the capital of the country"的知识,有助于英文读者理解作者为什么后面会讲到"the people I met here are all politically frustrated"。但是"吴会"是吴地的古称,读音为"Wukuai"而非"Wuhui"。这一句中的"南溟"指的是南方的大海,典出《庄子·逍遥游》,原句是"是鸟也,海运则将徙于南冥(溟),南冥者,天池也。"译者翻译为"the South Sea",容易使西方读者将之与"the South China Sea"的地理概念混淆。而《逍遥游》中南边的大海应该是指大地南面的大海(庄子的时代还没有形成精确的地理概念,人们对世界的认识还停留在天圆地方、大地四面环海的层面),故此处不宜作为专有名词来翻译,而应使用更宽泛的描述性语句"the sea in the south"来代替。

"萍水相逢"的原意是浮萍因水而四处流荡,聚散不定,比喻人本来素不相识,因机缘巧合偶然相逢。译者采用异化的策略翻译为"drifting together like duckweeds"。对于英语读者来说,"浮萍"不具备代表"流荡"的象征意义,他们难以从逻辑上理解这句话,更无法理解原文所体现的流离飘荡之意,因此此处不如采用归化策略,译为"gathering together by coincidence"。

"奉宣室以何年":奉宣室,代指入朝做官。贾谊迁谪长沙四年后,汉文帝复召他回长安,于宣室中问鬼神之事。宣室,汉未央宫正殿,为天子召见大臣议事之处。译者用"like Jia Yi"使译文"called to the court"与贾谊相结合,使英文读者更好地了解宣室与贾谊这一典故。

"冯唐易老,李广难封":冯唐,汉文帝时任中郎署长,景帝时出为楚相。武帝即位时匈奴犯边,武帝求贤良,有人举荐冯唐,而他已是九十多岁的老人,后人便用冯唐来形容老来难以得志。李广,西汉名将,多次参与抗击匈奴战争,战功赫赫,但始终未予封侯。这句话译者直译为:"Feng

Tang grew old quickly and Li Guang had difficulty getting promoted",没有背景知识的补充,"Feng Tang grew old quickly"在英语中容易让读者产生疑惑(难道变老的速度还因人而异吗?)。在翻译"李广难封"时作者巧妙地避开封侯二字,直接采用归化的策略,译为"getting promoted",降低了读者的阅读难度,但同时也失去了向外介绍古代中国的爵称和爵位制度的契机。欧洲同样也有爵位制,此处本可以引起读者思考这样两个问题:在中国的历史文化长河中,以公、侯、伯、子、男为主的爵位制度,其底蕴可谓是非常的深厚,那么在西方国家,他们的爵位制度又有什么样的深意呢?中西方的五等爵制有什么联系吗?此外,若是能补充李广战功赫赫(despite glorious achievements on the battlefield)或许更有助于英语读者体会到其中的辛酸,也呼应前文的"I am ill fated, and my life is full of frustrations"。"非无圣主"一词译者化主动为被动,与下一句"岂乏明时"相对应,既保持了句型的一致,又增强了语气。

"老当益壮,宁移白首之心?穷且益坚,不坠青云之志。"原文中"老"对"穷","壮"对"坚","白首之心"对"青云之志"。译文中将每一句的前半句处理为一个由"as"引导的让步状语从句,并为原文的"老"和"穷"添加了主语。在这两句的英译中,罗先生分别将前半句译为"old as one is"和"poor as one is",对仗工整,且在后面的句子中分别加入主语"he",符合西方人的行文习惯,注重句子逻辑结构。"宁知"译为"by no means wavers"一方面表明王勃在逆境中也不消沉的决心,另一方面用介词短语表"绝不"这一坚定的态度。"白首之心"对应"青云之志",都是指远大的志向,罗将其处理为"aspiration"和"ambition",句式对应,巧妙地押了尾韵。

"酌贪泉而觉爽,处涸辙以犹欢。"这一句中王勃运用了两个典故:"酌贪泉"和"处涸辙"。"酌贪泉"的典故是说晋人吴隐之上任途中,经过一处名为"贪"的泉水,传说喝了这水的人会变得很贪心。吴隐之不信,就取来泉水喝了,并赋诗一首,"古人云此水,一歃怀千金。诚使夷齐饮,终当不易心。"(见《晋书·吴隐之传》)大意是说人要没有贪心,喝了这水也不会变贪，内心纯正的人不会因为受到外界环境的污染而堕落。他到任后也非常廉洁。此句中翻译"贪泉"时使用的短语"the spring of Avarice"的形式与西方文化中"the tree of wise""the tree of life"之概念的词语很像，这似乎也为中文名为"贪"的泉水增加了一些寓意。"处涸辙"是说庄子向监河侯借粮食，监河侯答应等赋税征收到手后就借给他一大笔钱。庄子听了很生气，说车辙中的鲋鱼需要的是斗升之水，如果拖延时间去取西江之水，那不就等于将鲋鱼置于枯鱼之肆即卖干鱼的市场吗？译者在此处索性摒弃这个冗长又弯弯绕绕的故事，而只是用"misfortune"一词挑明了"处涸辙"的处境，非常符合英语读者的阅读习惯。这两处运用归化策略使译文流畅简洁，体现了语言的交际功能，有利于读者顺利领会原文作者的意图。

"无路请缨，等终军之弱冠"：终军，汉武帝时谏大夫，二十岁时请求去缚南越王，事见《汉书·终军传》。古代男子二十岁行冠礼，称"弱冠"。古代中国的年龄称谓非常丰富，如"豆蔻""而立""花甲"等等，这里译者省掉了"弱冠"的具体信息，采用归化的策略将之翻译为"of the same age as Zhong Jun"，虽然利于英语读者理解，但是失去了古代中国关于年龄称谓的丰富文化内涵。

"舍簪笏于百龄，奉晨昏于万里"：簪笏，古代官员所用的冠簪、手板，此处借指官职。这里译者其实翻译到"accept the offer of a lifelong government position"时就已经表达出了原文的语义，但是译者不满足于此，补充了"by wearing a hair dress and holding a tablet before the chest as court officials do"，使译文更加生动形象，加深了英文读者对古代官员制度的了解。

"非谢家之宝树，接孟氏之芳邻。"前句出自《晋书·谢安传》，谢安曾问子侄们，为何人们都望子弟好？其侄谢玄答："譬如芝兰玉树，欲使其生于庭阶耳。"以此喻家国栋梁之才。后句出自刘向《列女传·母仪篇》，孟轲母亲为使儿子有个良好的教育环境，曾三次迁居，选择有好名声的邻居，即"孟母三迁"的故事。译者并未直译"宝树"，而是用"as good as Xie Xuan"，简洁明了地概括了谢玄的典故，同时以"have men of virtue as my neighbors"

概述孟子的典故，陈词达意，短小精悍，干净利落。

"钟期既遇，奏流水以何惭？"锺期，即钟子期，春秋时楚人，善听琴。古代文学典故中，俞伯牙和钟子期的故事被奉为知音难觅的典范。这里王勃以赋诗作文代奏"高山流水"，表示既遇知音阎公，就在宴会上赋诗作文，也不以为愧。译文为"now that I have met a bosom friend like Zhong Ziqi"，虽然"a bosom friend"点出了伯牙、钟子期所代表的"高山流水遇知音"的情谊，但是英文读者不熟悉中文这样含蓄的表达方式，无法理解此处王勃以伯牙自比，以钟子期喻本次宴会主人阎公，表示既然机缘巧合幸遇阎都督这样的知音，才愿作此序赋此文。另外，"杨意不逢，抚凌云而自惜;钟期既遇，奏流水以何惭"这句话中存在假设和复合因果的逻辑关系，在英译时应予以体现。因此译者在前半句加上了"since"，后半句加上了"now that"，使译文看上去更完整也更好理解。

三、译论·比较

施莱尔马赫对后来的翻译研究学者如劳伦斯·韦努蒂（Lawrence Venuti）等人产生了很大的影响。1995年美国翻译理论家韦努蒂在《译者的隐形》一书中进一步论述了这两种翻译策略：归化论认为翻译应该遵循"何处去"的原则，采取认同目的语文化的策略；异化论强调"何处来"，认为翻译就是传播陌生的文化，因此在翻译的作品中应保留原语文化的风格。归化追求最大程度的等效，而异化则追求最大程度的等值。因此，归化翻译和异化翻译具有不同的社会语用价值和文化构形特征。在归化与异化之间不存在绝对的鸿沟，不能处处将二者对立起来。选取一种策略而完全排除另一种策略的做法是不可取的，也是不现实的。

我们在翻译中，始终面临着异化与归化的选择，通过选择使译文在接近读者和接近作者之间找到一个"融会点"。这个"融会点"不是一成不变的"居中点"，它有时距离作者近些，有时距离读者近些，但无论接近哪一方，都要遵循一条原则，即异化时不妨碍译文的通顺易懂，归化时不失去原文的风格。译文作品可兼两策略之长而避其短，过度的异化或归化都有损译文的质量。作为两种翻译策略，异化和归化是辩证统一、相辅相成的，绝对的异化和绝对的归化都不存在，两者根据翻译的目的、文本类型的不同而显示为现实、具体、动态的统一。

总的来说，翻译中关于归化与异化的讨论多不胜数，有视其为对立统一的，也有视其为一体两面的，既可称其为"方法"，又可谓之为"策略"。实际上，如同直译意译，归化异化也是一种思考问题的二元论划分，本质上属于超越语言层面的话语政治，即这一组概念的提出源于对语言霸权或语言中心主义的思考。无论是归化还是异化，如果站在语言（原语或译语）的角度，这一二元划分并不能明示语言层面的内外之别。换言之，归化和异化在语言层面的界限是模糊的，这从词汇学中各种语言的交往互渗史中可见一斑。因此，归化和异化的区分更多是源于文化对比与社会反思后落实在语言层面的话术，在深层次上属于翻译的话语政治或话语政治的翻译体现。总之，从归化和异化的角度对翻译文本进行分析，往往需要考量各个文本所蕴含的政治背景、情感态度、文化取向等因素。

鉴于此，请按照以下要点对罗经国所译范仲淹《岳阳楼记》选段进行文本鉴析：

（1）对"选段"所体现的政治情怀进行文化思考；
（2）比较原文与译文，思考各自凸显的话语政治重点。

嗟夫！予尝求古仁人之心，或异二者之为，何哉？不以物喜，不以己悲，居庙堂之高则忧其民，处江湖之远则忧其君。是进亦忧，退亦忧。然则何时而乐耶？其必曰"先天下之忧而忧，后天下之乐而乐"乎！噫！微斯人，吾谁与归？

Ah! I have tried to study the minds of people of lofty ideals in ancient times. Perhaps they were different from the people I mentioned above. Why is this? The reason is that they were not thrown into ecstasies over their success[①], nor felt depressed over their failures. When they were in high positions at court, they were concerned about the people. When they were in remote places, they were concerned about their emperor. They worried when they got promoted or when they were sent into exile. Then, when were they happy? They would say, "To be the first in the country to worry about the affairs of the state and the last in the country to enjoy oneself." Alas! Who else should I seek company with save them?

[Translated by Luo Jinguo（罗经国）]

四、实践·译笔

呜呼！胜地不常，盛筵难再；兰亭已矣，梓泽丘墟。临别赠言，幸承恩于伟饯；登高作赋，是所望于群公。敢竭鄙诚，恭疏短引。一言均赋，四韵俱成：

> 滕王高阁临江渚，佩玉鸣鸾罢歌舞。
> 画栋朝飞南浦云，朱帘暮卷西山雨。
> 闲云潭影日悠悠，物换星移几度秋。
> 阁中帝子今何在？槛外长江空自流。

五、阅读·延展

我（瞿秋白）的意见是：翻译应当把原文的本意，完全正确的介绍给中国读者，使中国读者所得到的概念等于英俄日德法……读者从原文得来的概念，这样的直译，应当用中国人口头上可以讲得出来的白话来写。为着保存原作的精神，并不用着容忍"多少的不顺"。相反的，容忍着"多少的不顺"（就是不用口头上的白话），反而要多少的丧失原作的精神。

---

① 从语法角度而言，此处应为 successes。

……至于供给甲类的读者（指"有很受了教育的"）的译本，无论什么，我(鲁迅)是至今主张"宁信而不顺"的。自然，这所谓"不顺"，决不是说"跪下"要译作"跪在膝之上"，"天河"要译作"牛奶路"的意思，乃是说，不妨不象吃茶淘饭一样几口可以咽完，却必须费牙来嚼一嚼。这里就来了一个问题：为什么不完全中国化，给读者省些力气呢？这样费解，怎样还可以称为翻译呢？我的答案是：这也是译本。这样的译本，不但在输入新的内容，也在输入新的表现法。中国的文或话，法子实在太不精密了，作文的秘诀，是在避去熟字，删掉虚字，就是好文章，讲话的时候，也时时要辞不达意，这就是话不够用，所以教员讲书，也必须借助于粉笔。这语法的不精密，就在证明思路的不精密，换一句话，就是脑筋有些胡涂。倘若永远用着胡涂话，即使读的时候，滔滔而下，但归根结蒂，所得的还是一个胡涂的影子。要医这病，我以为只好陆续吃一点苦，装进异样的句法去，古的，外省外府的，外国的，后来便可以据为己有。这并不是空想的事情。远的例子，如日本，他们的文章里，欧化的语法是极平常的了，和梁启超做《和文汉读法》时代，大不相同；近的例子，就如来信所说，一九三五年曾给群众造出过"罢工"这一个字眼，这字眼虽然未曾有过，然而大众已都懂得了。

（摘自《鲁迅和瞿秋白关于翻译的通信》）

The violent effects of translation are felt at home as well as abroad. On the one hand, translation wields enormous power in the construction of national identities for foreign cultures, and hence it potentially figures in ethnic discrimination, geopolitical confrontations, colonialism, terrorism, war. On the other hand, translation enlists the foreign text in the maintenance or revision of literary canons in the target-language culture, inscribing poetry and fiction, for example, with the various poetic and narrative discourses that compete for cultural dominance in the target language. Translation also enlists the foreign text in the maintenance or revision of dominant conceptual paradigms, research methodologies, and clinical practices in target-language disciplines and professions, whether physics or architecture, philosophy or psychiatry, sociology or law. It is these social affiliations and effects—written into the materiality of the translated text, into its discursive strategy and its range of allusiveness for the target language reader, but also into the very choice to translate it and the ways it is published, reviewed, and taught—all these conditions permit translation to be called a cultural political practice, constructing or critiquing ideology-stamped identities for foreign cultures, affirming or transgressing discursive values and institutional limits in the target-language culture. The violence wreaked by translation is partly inevitable, inherent in the translation process, partly potential, emerging at any point in the production and reception of the translated text, varying with specific cultural and social formations at different historical moments.

The most urgent question facing the translator who possesses this knowledge is. What to do? Why and how do I translate? Although I have construed translation as the site of many determinations and effects—linguistic, cultural, economic, ideological—I also want to indicate that the freelance literary translator always exercises a choice concerning the degree and direction of the violence at work in any translating. This choice has been given various formulations, past and present, but perhaps none so decisive as that offered by the German theologian and philosopher Friedrich Schleiermacher. In an 1813 lecture on the different methods of translation, Schleiermacher argued that "there are only two. Either the translator leaves the author in peace, as much as possible, and moves the reader towards him ; or he leaves the reader in peace, as much as possible, and moves the author towards him" (Lefevere, 1977:74). Admitting (with qualifications like "as much as possible") that translation can never be completely adequate to the foreign text, Schleiermacher allowed the translator to choose between a domesticating method, an ethnocentric reduction of the foreign text to target-language cultural values, bringing the author back home, and a foreignizing method, an ethnodeviant pressure on those values to register the linguistic and cultural difference of the foreign text, sending the reader abroad.

(Excerpts from *The Translator's Invisibility* by Lawrence Venuti)

第四单元

词人宰相·北宋晏殊

一、译事·译研

晏殊（991—1055），字同叔，江南西路抚州临川县人，北宋时期著名的政治家、文学家与教育家。晏殊著述丰富，文章赡丽，应用不穷，闲雅有情思，是北宋第一个大量创作令词的词人。晏殊词在北宋极享盛誉，影响深远，有"晏元献小词为本朝之冠"（南宋曾季狸《艇斋诗话》）之称。晏殊身历富贵数十载，有身处富贵而超越富贵的高雅志趣和天然气韵，能以清雅笔墨写尽富贵之态，欧阳修称之为"富贵优游五十年"。因此，晏殊词具有"富贵气象"，即"公每吟咏富贵，不言金玉锦绣，而唯说其气象"（吴处厚《青箱杂记》）。可以说，其词雍容典雅，有"自然且富贵"的风格，被宋初词坛诸多词人奉为圭臬。

相比于其他宋词的对外译介，晏殊词的翻译传播可谓寥寥。以英译为例，对晏殊词的译介主要包含在一些译著中，如刘若愚在1974年出版的专著 *Major Lyrics of the Northern Sung*（《北宋六人词家》）中的第一章"Sentiment and Sensibility"就对晏殊词进行了译介。海陶玮和叶嘉莹在1998年出版的 *Studies in Chinese Poetry*（《中国诗歌论集》）中共译介了21首晏殊词。另外，晏殊词主要还有一些散译。如刘殿爵（D. C. Lau）在 *Twenty Selected Lyrics* 中翻译了《踏莎行》（"To the Tune of T'a so hsing"）；Stephen Owen 在

An Anthology of Chinese Literature：*Beginnings to 1911* 中英译了《破阵子》（"Breaking Through the Ranks"）和《浣溪沙》（"Washing Creek Sands"）。国内翻译家许渊冲也英译了部分晏殊词。据不完全统计（汪次昕，2000），晏殊词有 23 首被英译出版，其中被选译较多的是《浣溪沙·一曲新词酒一杯》（16 种）、《踏莎行·小径红稀》（10 种）、《蝶恋花·槛菊愁烟兰泣露》（8 种）、《山亭柳·赠歌者》（5 种）、《破阵子·春景》（4 种）、《清平乐·金风细细》（4 种）、《玉楼春·春恨》（4 种）。

总体而言，需要加强晏殊词的对外译介，尤其是其独特且自成一派、有别于其他宋词大家的"富贵气象"词风，这也是中国传统诗词文化翻译传播的沧海遗粟，值得翻译研究者与实践者传播与宣扬。

二、鉴赏·评析

【原文】

玉楼春·春恨

绿杨芳草长亭路，年少抛人容易去。
楼头残梦五更钟，花底离情三月雨。
无情不似多情苦，一寸还成千万缕。
天涯地角有穷时，只有相思无尽处。

【译文】

在杨柳依依、芳草萋萋的长亭古道上，年少的人总是能轻易地抛弃送别之人登程远去。楼头传来的五更钟声惊醒了离人残梦，花底飘洒的三月春雨增添了心中的愁思。

无情人哪里懂得多情的人的苦恼，一寸相思愁绪竟化作了万缕千丝。天涯地角再远也有穷尽终了那一天，只有那相思没有尽头，永不停止。

Tune: "Spring in the Jade House"

Green willows and fragrant grass by the posthouse road

Where the young man left me without a pang.

An unfinished dream at the fifth watch bell

The sorrow of parting under the blossoms in a third month rain.

Insensitive misses susceptible's bitterness,

Whose every inch turns into a thousand myriad strands.

The sky's edge, earth's corner—sometime they come to an end;

It's just this longing that is never done.

(Translated by James Robert Hightower)

(The lyricist, who was from Lin-ch'uan in Kiangsi, passed the Presented Scholar examination at an incredibly young age of fourteen and soon thereafter received an official appointment. By the age of forty-four, he had become Grand Councilor and was one of the few southerners to achieve such a high rank at the Northern Sung court. As a true statesman-poet, Yen sponsored a literary salon in his own home. He was particularly skilled in composing short lyrics and followed the tradition of the Southern T'ang lyricists.)

Tune: Spring in Jade Pavilion: Spring Grief

Farewell pavilion green with grass and willow trees!

How could my gallant young lord have left me with ease!

I'm woke by midnight bell from dim dream in my bower;

Parting grief won't part with flowers falling in shower.

My beloved feels no sorrow my loving heart sheds;

Each string as woven with thousands of painful threads.
However far and wide the sky and earth may be,
They can't measure the lovesickness overwhelming me.

[Translated by Xu Yuanchong（许渊冲）]

【评析】

当代翻译理论研究先后经历了几次转向，主要为语言学转向、文化转向和社会学转向，其中"文化转向"是由两大翻译研究主将安德烈·勒菲弗尔和苏珊·巴斯奈特共同提出的，即翻译研究不再把翻译看成是语言转换间的孤立片段，而是将翻译置于更广阔的历史文化语境中审视。本词的两位译者来自不同的文化背景，詹姆斯·罗伯特·海陶玮（James Robert Hightower）生前长期担任美国哈佛大学教授，是美国"第一位研究中国文学的学者"，被誉为"美国汉学界的泰斗"和"研究中国文学的权威"。但是海陶玮本人一开始的专业是化学，大学期间阅读到了埃兹拉·庞德（Ezra Pound）翻译的中国诗歌并对此产生了兴趣，而后开始学习中文，成为著名的汉学家。许渊冲早年毕业于西南联大外文系，译作涵盖中、英、法等语种，翻译选材集中在中国古诗词方面，形成韵体译诗的方法与理论，被誉为"诗译英法唯一人"。通过解读译文，我们可以窥见不同的文化背景对两位译者翻译实践的影响。

《玉楼春·春恨》是一首描绘闺阁幽思的词，整体风格凄婉哀怨，缠绵悱恻，意趣幽远。"春恨"二字点出词眼，是一个关键信息。不知出于何种原因，海陶玮并没有将这一"词眼"译出，而许渊冲的"Spring Grief"从一开始就为译作奠定了感情基调。

上阕首句"绿杨芳草"描绘出一派春意盎然的景象。但是"长亭"在中国文化里往往代表着离别，离别自然是伤感悲情的。"抛人"更是将故事主角被弃、徒留原地的这种伤感强化，而"容易"二字可以看出离别之人走得决绝、走得匆忙、走得轻而易举，头也不回，与"绿杨芳草"的春天形成鲜明的情感反差。海陶玮将"长亭"译为"posthouse"，英文释义为"an inn for exchanging post horses and accommodating riders"。从情感上来讲，这是一个中性名词，在英语文化中并不附带离别和依依不舍之情；从词义上来看，"长亭"是古时在城外路旁每隔十里设立的亭子，供行人休息或饯别亲友，并不是供行人借宿的场所。许渊冲从功能的角度将之译为"Farewell pavilion"，同时"pavilion"这一具有浓厚东方建筑色彩的词也为英文读者带来异域风情。海陶玮根据字面含义将"年少抛人容易去"中的"年少"一词解释为"young man"，情感意义上不及许译的"my gallant young lord"强烈，后者表明这是主角的"白马王子"，是女子倾慕的心上人，心爱之人离去，离别之情才更是催人断肠。同时，许渊冲用感叹句表达原文"容易"二字的情感，借助句式传递闺怨情绪，也对应了标题"spring grief"。

"楼头残梦五更钟，花底离情三月雨。"这一句对仗工整，情感幽咽婉转，色调轻浅幽渺，富有含蓄蕴藉、窈深幽约之美。在中国诗词文化里，"花""梦""雨"总是与"愁""怨"等情感交织，如"自在飞花轻似梦，无边丝雨细如愁"。残梦依稀，钟鼓伤情；细雨迷蒙，离情更苦。海陶玮对于这样一句具有典型中国古诗意象之诗词的处理颇有得庞德真传的意思。庞德在创作中十分注重意象的表达，语法的切断是他的一个特点，例如，庞德在翻译《送友人》中的诗句"浮云游子意，落日故人情"时，将原文处理为："Mind like a floating wide cloud, Sunset like the parting of old acquaintances."译诗中省略系词，没有主谓结构，而是以分词短语为中心组成诗行，形成陌生化的阅读效果，留下丰富的想象空间。而海陶玮将"楼头残梦五更钟，花底离情三月雨"译为"An unfinished dream at the fifth watch bell. The sorrow of parting under the blossoms in a third month rain"可以说是与庞德译文有异曲同工之妙，都是在理解原诗精神的基础上传递思想内容，重点是突出意象，寻求与诗人的情感共振。许渊冲的译文："I'm woke by midnight bell from dim dream in my bower; Parting grief won't part with flowers falling in shower."工整又押韵，亦是十分精彩。"五更"是寅正四刻，对应现在的时间是凌晨三点至五点。许渊冲在翻译李商隐的《无题四首》其一"来是空言去绝踪，月斜楼上五更钟"时，译为"You said you'd come but you have gone and left no trace ; I hear in the moonlit tower the fifth watch bell"。或许在本词中，许渊冲是为了押韵而淡化了具体时间，以"midnight"一笔带过。

"无情不似多情苦，一寸还成千万缕。"这句作者用白描的手法表达"多情自古伤离别"之意，与上阕意蕴脉脉相承。海陶玮采用反话正说的策略将原句"无情不似多情苦"的否定句转换为肯定句，采用平铺直叙、陈述事实的方式还原白描的手法。许渊冲的"Each string as woven with thousands of painful threads"以明喻的方式表达了"心似双丝网，中有千千结"之意，体现了爱情横遭阻抑的幽怨和坚定不移的信念，与最后一句的感情相呼应。"天涯地角有穷时，只有相思无尽处。"行文到此处，作者终于揭开本词最后的面纱，表明一直折磨女主人公的"恨"也好，"怨"也罢，其实都是相思之苦，所以许渊冲的"lovesickness overwhelming me"非常贴切，比海陶玮的"longing"感情更加强烈，表达更加直接。

值得一提的是海陶玮最后为读者做了加注，解释了词作者晏殊的生平。他借助这种副文本（paratexts），即介绍、脚注、书籍封面等文本以外的材料帮助读者补全翻译中的叙事框架。加注是海陶玮的风格，其很多译文都有加注，说明这位汉学家希望从文化大背景的角度为读者提供更多的线索和信息，进而帮助读者更好地理解译文。

【原文】

浣溪沙

一向年光有限身，
等闲离别易销魂，
酒筵歌席莫辞频。

满目山河空念远，

落花风雨更伤春，

不如怜取眼前人。

【译文】

人的生命将在有限的时间中结束，无端的离别也会让人觉得悲痛欲绝。不要因为常常离别而推辞酒宴，应当在有限的人生，对酒当歌，开怀畅饮。

到了登临之时，放眼辽阔河山，突然思念远方的亲友；等到风雨吹落繁花之际，才发现春天易逝，不禁更生伤春愁情。不如在酒宴上，好好怜爱眼前的人。

Washing Creek Sands (Huan xi sha)

Only a moment, this season's splendor, this body, a bounded thing;

to part now as if it didn't matter easily breaks the heart;

so don't be hasty, refusing the party's wine, the banquet's song.

Mountains and rivers fill our eyes, but care is wasted on things too far;

besides which, this grief at spring passing, at wind and rain that bring down flowers;

it is better by far to take as your love the person before your eyes.

（Translated by Stephen Owen）

Tune: Silk-Washing Stream

What can a short-lived man do with the fleeting year.

And soul-consuming separations from his dear?

Refuse no banquet when fair singing girls appear!

With hills in sight, I miss the far away in vain.

How can I bear the fallen blooms in wind and rain!

Why not enjoy the fleeting pleasure now again?

[Translated by Xu Yuanchong（许渊冲）]

【评析】

  这首词的两位译者，一位是英语母语者，一位汉语母语者。宇文所安（Stephen Owen）是北美当代著名汉学家，哈佛大学荣休教授，海外中国古典文学研究领域的巨擘。他给自己取了中国字中的姓氏"宇文"，是因为他觉得自己的血液里有"胡人"的因子。他又从最喜欢的《论语·为政篇》的"视其所以，观其所由，察其所安"中摘得"所安"两字，作为自己的身份符号。1946年宇文所安出生于美国密苏里州圣路易斯市，成长在美国南方小城，1959年移居巴尔的摩。在巴尔的摩公立图书馆，他沉湎于诗歌阅读，首次接触到庞德翻译的李白诗歌《长干行》，"遂决定与其发生恋爱"。许渊冲前文已有介绍，不再赘述。总之，两位译者都熟悉英语读者的价值观、信念和阅读方式，同时对中国文学作品的认同感都很高。通过分析两版译文，我们可以感受到不同文化在两位译者身上打下的烙印。

  "一向年光有限身"指人的生命将在有限的时间里结束，许渊冲选择使用"a short-lived man"作主语，而宇文所安使用"this season""this body"。相比许渊冲，宇文所安的译文充分体现了英语的特点，即多使用无灵句。根据施事主体与行为动作的搭配，句子可分为有灵句（animate sentence）和无灵句（inanimate sentence）。有灵句以人为施事主体；无灵句以无生命的事物为施事主体，而谓语部分是与人有关的动词。汉语中无灵句出现得比较少，在中国人看来人是行为动作的执行者，施事者应该在动作之前（冒国安，2004）；英语则多使用无灵句。

  宇文所安再现了原诗"等闲离别易销魂"中的描写，并力图加深读者对这些信息的印象；许渊冲则将原诗的陈述句变成疑问句，选择通过句式的改变来传递原诗的情感。"酒筵歌席莫辞频"一句，宇文所安通过说理，将本句与前两句逻辑串联起来，补充了逻辑连接词"so"，不仅语义明了，也体现了汉英语用差异原则："汉语语用重过程，英语语用重结果。"此外，

"酒筵歌席"在古代中国通常伴有女子歌舞助兴。母语为汉语的许渊冲当然明白其中所以然,因此补充了相关文化知识,译为"when fair singing girls appear"。而宇文所安则兼具多重文化身份,倾向于忠实地再现原诗中的场景,此处体现了两位译者文化身份认同上的差异。同样的差异也体现在"满目山河空念远"的译文中,宇文所安忠实地再现"山""河"景象,并补充"but"这一原文没有的逻辑词;而许渊冲仅用"hills"模糊化了原诗中的景象,注重整首诗的意境表达。

下阕原诗并没有凸显诗人的存在,对此两位译者采用不同的处理方式。宇文所安使用"your love""your eyes",以这样一种淡化诗人的存在、以客体身份出现的方式表达诗意,而许渊冲选择"I"这样一个极具主体性的词。这或许是因为,中国人重"心"(东方传统文化中的"心",不是解剖学上的"心"),西方人重"脑"(mind,主要指智慧)。因而中国人具有较强的主体意识和主观意识,西方人具有较强的客体意识和客观意识。这表现在:中国人在叙事和理解叙事时主体参与度高,会夹杂一些主观臆测,而西方人则倾向于陈述客观事实(王建国,2023)。

许渊冲的翻译重"美感",在翻译中国古典诗词时,他想翻出古诗词的韵律和美感。钱锺书先生都把许渊冲的翻译称作"不忠实的美人",可见确实是"美"的。但是宇文所安认为译者在翻译中国古典诗歌时不必强求押韵,因为这样的译作在美国很少有人愿意去读,而且还可能会产生反讽的效果(钱锡生、季进,2010)。这也是两位译者不同翻译风格的体现。

【原文】

踏莎行

小径红稀,
芳郊绿遍,
高台树色阴阴见。

春风不解禁杨花,

蒙蒙乱扑行人面。

翠叶藏莺,

朱帘隔燕,

炉香静逐游丝转。

一场愁梦酒醒时,

斜阳却照深深院。

【译文】

  小路旁的花儿日渐稀少,郊野却是绿意盎然,高高的楼台在苍翠茂密的树丛中若隐若现。春风不懂得去管束杨花柳絮,好似那蒙蒙细雨乱扑人面。

  黄莺躲藏在翠绿的树叶里,红色的帘子将飞燕阻隔在外,炉香静静燃烧,香烟像游动的青丝般缓缓上升。醉酒后从一场愁梦醒来时,夕阳正斜照着幽深的庭院。

Tune : Treading on Grass

Along the path red blossoms fade,

On fragrant fields green grass displayed,

By lofty tower trees spread out a dark, dark shade.

The vernal breeze knows not how to keep willow-down,

From running riot and making wayfarers frown.

Green leaves hide orioles from sight,

Pearl screens keep out swallows in flight,

Incense from burners wafts like the gossamer light.

When I awake from sorrowful dream and from wine,

In deep deep courtyard peeps the sun on decline.

[Translated by Xu Yuanchong（许渊冲）]

Tune："Treading on Fragrant Grass"

A path strewn with a sprinkling of red；

A broad plain carpeted all over with verdure.

Hue of trees, lush and dark, hazy around the high tower.

The spring breeze knows not how to stop,

Willow catkins blowing in a fine drizzle,

On the wayfarer's face.

Leaves emerald-green—the orioles are hidden from view；

Pearled blinds drawn--the swallows are denied entrance.

Incense smoke calmly ascends,

To whirl round with the floating gossamer.

Fumes of wine gone, I wake from a troubled dream,

To find the slanting sun,

Shining on a courtyard profoundly secluded.

[Translated by wang Jiaosheng（王椒升）]

【评析】

"译者的声音"（translator's voice）这一概念由韦努蒂（2004）首次提出。他认为，读者总是期望译文流畅地道，认为此时译作是透明的，译者是隐身的，他们从文本中听到的是作者的声音。但这实际上是一种源于文化自恋的幻觉，"只有当从外语文本中识别出自己的声音时，译者才会意识到自己与异域作者建立了亲密的情感认同"（周晓梅，2019）。通过这两首词的译文比较，我们可以发现译者通过各种方式表达自己的声音。

这首词将晏词"风流蕴藉，温润秀洁"的特点表现得异常鲜明。整首词多用动词，但是达到了以动显静的效果，因为词里描绘的场景，比如：树阴在地上投下的光影层次，藏在翠叶下的莺儿，挡在朱帘外的燕子，香炉中的烟安静上扬，追逐着空中的游丝慢慢地绕转，照进院中的斜阳一寸寸移动，越来越深，直到最后消失不见，暮色降临——这番景象，非得要长久地置身于安静之中，才能见到。这种以动衬静的方法不仅细到极致，更是突出了作者的闲愁之情。

"莎"（suō）：莎草，是一种常见的野草，广布于热带、温带，其块茎入药，叫"香附"，夏季开花。踏草是唐宋时期广为流行的活动，又叫踏青，北方一般在清明时节前后。所以，"踏莎行"调名本义为咏古代民间盛行的春天踏青活动。许渊冲忠实地译为"Tune：Treading on Grass"，Wang 译本增加原词没有的修饰词"fragrant"，在译诗中显现了自己的声音，并赋予了文本新的意义。

"小径红稀，芳郊绿遍，高台树色阴阴见。"原文这三句词从近到远，视野开阔，很有空间感，属于移步换形之法，具有典型的时序特征。作者以"红"来借代花，以"绿"来借代草，不仅抓住了花草各自的特点，而且使词作增加了色彩美的视觉效果。一个"遍"字刻画了芳草旺盛的生长气势。许渊冲的译文以"red blossoms""green grass"再现了原词的色彩美；Wang 另辟蹊径，以形容词"broad"和动词"carpeted"来表现原词展现出来的绿意盎然、绿草连绵。

"春风不解禁杨花，蒙蒙乱扑行人面。"本句将"春风"与"杨花"写得若有人性，最是空灵有味。许渊冲以"running riot"来表现"蒙蒙乱扑"的景象，同样颇具人性，好不热闹，而"making wayfarers frown"增加了原词没有的主观感受，在译诗中加入了自己独特的理解，译者的声音在此处得以清晰地显现。

"翠叶藏莺，朱帘隔燕"一句，Wang 通过两个破折号揭示下文，先是给读者"犹抱琵琶半遮面"之感，而后揭晓答案，从句式的角度给读者"藏""隔"的阅读体验，可谓是巧匠用心。

"一场愁梦酒醒时,斜阳却照深深院"一句,两版译文都通过自我提及(如"I")的方式强调了诗人的显性存在,将诗人推向中心位置,强调其伤感的心情,同时也表达了译者的声音,体现了译者的主体性。此外,英语语序倒置的现象比较多,许渊冲的译文"In deep deep courtyard peeps the sun on decline"便是出于修辞需要的韵律倒装(Metrical inversion),动词"peeps"描绘了斜阳西下,同时也刻画了诗人睡眼惺忪、醉眼蒙眬之态。纵观全词,许渊冲的译文"running riot""peeps"都为读者呈现了一副黄昏静中有动、愁中有活力俏皮的画面,不仅再现了原词的闲愁,还加入了自己对其内涵意义的独特理解,译者的声音得以传达。

三、译论·比较

纵览中国传统译论,无论是"形神说"还是"化境论",都和"风格"有关。简单而言,依据主客体之分,风格在翻译中可体现为译者风格和译作风格两个方面。如果添加历时的维度,还可分为不同时代的翻译风格等。译者风格指通过译文反映出的译者个体在语言使用或非语言手段方面的区别性特征,强调的是译者在诸多译作中所表现出来的共同翻译特征和规律(李德俊,2019);译作风格也称之为翻译风格,指具体某部译作所呈现的不同于其他译作的翻译个性(胡开宝、谢丽欣,2017),强调的是具体某部译作的独特性或显性特征。

目前关于翻译风格的研究主要还是基于语料库的模式探究,属于语料库翻译学的研究范畴。在词汇层面,翻译风格主要通过考查类符/形符比(TTR,反映的是语料库的词汇丰富程度,也称为词汇密度)、词长、关键词等方面的特征来确定;在句法层面,翻译风格主要通过考察平均句长(平均句长越长,语句的复杂程度越高)和句长标准差(句长标准差反映了语料库中句子长度与平均句长的差异,标准差越大,说明文本中句长差异越大,反之越小)方面的特征来确定。

不过,除却从语料库入手对翻译风格进行考察,我们还可以拓展研究思路，回归传统阐释，从社会、历史、文化、情感态度等方面切入，进行人文思想的反哺与填充。毕竟，翻译研究"也不能无限放大技术的作用……工具是用来为科研服务的，数据与技术图表只能说明现象，而它们背后的机理和思想脉络才是终极要义，犹如从地下开采出来的矿石，如不加工和提炼，或者加工和提炼不到位，它永远也只是矿石，不会成为稀有金属"（罗选民，2019）。

鉴于此，请按照以下要点对《浣溪沙》的两个译本进行文本比较分析：
（1）从文字、音韵、节奏、意象等层面鉴析原文风格与译文风格；
（2）指出翻译风格与原文风格的异同。

浣溪沙

一曲新词酒一杯，
去年天气旧亭台。
夕阳西下几时回？

无可奈何花落去，
似曾相识燕归来。
小园香径独徘徊。

【译文】

填一曲新词喝一杯美酒，还是去年的天气旧日的亭台，西落的夕阳何时才能回来？

花儿总要凋落让人无可奈何，似曾相识的春燕又归来，独自在花香小径里徘徊留恋。

Tune: Silk-Washing Stream

I compose a new song and drink a cup of wine,

In the bower of last year when weather is as fine.

When will you come back like the sun on the decline?

Deeply I sigh for the fallen flowers in vain,

Vaguely I seem to know the swallows come again.

Loitering on the garden path, I alone remain.

[Translated by Xu Yuanchong（许渊冲）]

Tune: "Sand of Silk-Washing Brook"

A Reminiscence

A goblet of wine.

A verse newly composed:

The same old terrace am pavilion,

The same weather,

As last year's.

The westering sun—

When will it be here again?

Swallows coming back seem to be old acquaintances;

Flowers fade away, do what one may.

Inside the small garden,

Up and down the scented footpath,

Alone I pace.

[Transbted by Wang Jiaosheng（王椒升）]

四、实践·译笔

破阵子

燕子欲归时节,高楼昨夜西风。求得人间成小会,试把金尊傍菊丛。歌长粉面红。

斜日更穿帘幕,微凉渐入梧桐。多少襟情言不尽,写向蛮笺曲调中。此情千万重。

五、阅读·延展

再谈风格。到底什么叫风格?风格的内容又是怎样?我认为,风格的具体内容不外乎下列四点:

甲、题材(Subject Matter)

乙、用字(Choice of Words)

丙、表达(Mode of Expression)

丁、色彩(Color)

题材有正有反,用字有难有易,表达有繁有简,色彩有浓有淡。这是内容的要素。此外,还有内容的标准。依据温契司脱(C. T. Winchester)在他的《文学批评原理》一书中的说法,风格的最高标准是:

甲、雄伟(Energy)

乙、优美(Delicacy)

他说,风格以雄伟为上乘,优美为次选。我们知道,韩愈和苏东坡是韩潮苏海,他们两人的文章风格,为后人所称道、崇拜,并且是模仿的对象。在英国文学史上,也有两个名家,一个就是上面所提的麦考莱,他以雄伟胜。另一个是贝德(W. H. Pater),他以优美胜。他们两人的文章风格,同样为后人所称道、崇拜,并且是摹仿的对象。

我现在提出一个问题：在中国到底有多少人学得像韩愈和苏东坡？在英国到底有多少人学得像麦考莱和贝德？这问题无从回答，因为我们不知道，同时，也没有听到过。足见风格不易摹仿，因为风格之不同，如人心之各异，而人心之各异，正如人面之各殊。

　　这样说，在同一语言的领域里，尚且不易摹仿一个作者的风格；在翻译方面，把原作译成另一种语言而要保持同一风格，这是更不易做到的工作。我认为，理解原作，包括风格的研究是读者的工作，也就是读者所应该做的工作；进一步要把理解所得，和研究风格的体会，用另一种语言，根据原作题材的正反，用字的难易，表达的繁简，色彩的浓淡，同时还要照顾到原作的雄伟的体势，或者是优美的格调，一字字，一句句，一段段，一章章翻译出来，既忠实原作，又合乎译文的语言规律，这是不可能也是不必要的工作，同时，也决没有人会敢于作这样的尝试。

（摘自张中楹《关于翻译中的风格问题》）

　　"Style is the result of choice—conscious or not," asserts Leo Hickey in his introduction to *The Pragmatics of Style* …… However, style itself is a very problematic concept. Roger Fowler rejects style as a technical term because of its imprecision and proposes instead "register" plus a range of other sociolinguistic terms such as "dialect" and "idiolect". Leech and Short in their groundbreaking and still seminal *Style in Fiction* themselves give a very general definition: "It refers to the way in which language is used in a given context, by a given person, for a given purpose, and so on" (Leech and Short, 1981:10). Despite such a broad definition, they go on to make several crucial points about the nature of style, or styles. In particular, style may refer to "the linguistic habits of a particular writer ... genre, period, school [...]" (ibid:11). Following this, style can thus be individual (specific to the particular author, such as García Márquez) or collective (specific to a genre, such as the novel) or refer to a period (such as the Latin American Boom of the 1960s). While we accept that style may be understood in these different ways, we follow Bakhtin in supposing that the individualistic element is always present in all genres:

> *Any utterance—oral or written, primary or secondary, and in any sphere of communication—is individual and therefore can reflect the individuality of the speaker (or writer) ; that is, it possesses individual style. [...] The most conducive genres [to reflecting the individuality of the speaker] are those of artistic literature ; here the individual style enters directly into the very task of the utterance, and this is one of its main goals.* (Bakhtin 1981 : 276, emphasis added)

The individual element in authorship is crucial. Each writer, and therefore each translator, has an individual style. This goes for any genre, although Bakhtin considers literary works, and thus literary authors, as possessing the greatest degree of individualism. If anything, this complicates matters for the analysis of style in literary translation since from the outset the translator is likely to be faced with a highly individual ST style. Analysis therefore has to take into account the markedness of the ST before determining the markedness and individuality of the TT. The task is facilitated if there is more than one TT of the same ST piece (such as the Borges translations in the Introduction), since the multiple TTs can be compared to each other, the controlled variable being the unchanging ST. Variations between the TTs must be due to translator choice and style. However, such comparison is not generally possible ; copyright restrictions permit only one translation. This is by far the most frequent scenario with modern Latin American literature. In such cases, examination of a broad range of related translations by the same translator, of the same author, of similar or different genres is one means of controlling the analysis. The variation of stylistic patterns according to the situational context may indicate the relative importance of the different variables.

(Excerpts from *Style and Ideology in Translation* by Jeremy Munday)

第五单元

万世文章·北宋欧阳修

一、译事·译研

一座现代城市的文化宣传定然离不开其历史上的名人、名言、名物、名迹。今南昌市"永叔路"正是以北宋欧阳修之字命名的,一条普通之路也自此具有了清晰而可感的人文形象及丰富而独特的文化蕴含。欧阳修(1007—1072),祖籍江西庐陵,字永叔,号醉翁(晚年别号六一居士),谥号"文忠"。其年少聪慧,"为诗赋,下笔如成人"(吴梅影,2019),宋仁宗天圣八年(1030)取进士功名,后在洛阳、夷陵、滁州等多地任职理政,历经波澜起伏(三起三落),但也荣辱不惊、泰然自若。欧阳修还是北宋正统儒家代表、文坛巨擘,其追求"内圣外王","达则兼济天下,穷则独善其身",提倡平实文气,引领了北宋"道德文章"之风,象征着一代士大夫凝练厚重、守正持中的性情与精神。

欧阳修诗文传入日本、朝鲜约在十四世纪中期。如唐宋八大家的作品室町时期(1336—1573)已在日本流传开来,到了江户时期(18—19世纪)研习"欧苏"可谓蔚然成风。古贺侗庵(1788—1847)认为"欧苏二子,宗韩柳祖秦汉,一洗唐末五代之陋,导一世于正轨,厥功卓矣"。欧阳修诗文进入西方世界则到了19世纪后期,其译介语言主要包括英语、法语、德语、西班牙语、俄语等。限于篇幅与主题,以下主要是欧阳修散文之英译与法译梗概。

欧美译研欧阳修主要通过其散文，尤其是其名篇《醉翁亭记》。如英国著名汉学家翟理斯（H. A. Giles）在《中国评论》（*Chinese Review*，1877—1878年卷）上将其英译为 *The Old Drunkard's Arbour*，并收入其专著《历史的中国与其它故事》（*Historic China and Other Sketches*，1882）。另外，翟理斯还英译了欧阳修的其他散文，如 *Tsang Ch'iu Lun*(*Releasing Prisoners*)(《纵囚论》), *Fellness and Decay* (《伶官传序》), *An Autumn Dirge* (《秋声赋》), *At A Grave* (《泷冈阡表》), 收录于译著《古文珍选》（*Gems of Chinese Literature*）。同为英国著名汉学家、翻译家的亚瑟·韦利（Arthur Waley）分别在其译著《中国古诗选译续集》（1919）中收入所译 *Autumn*, *Chiu Shen Fu* (《秋声赋》)、译著《郊庙歌词及其它》（1923）中收入所译 *The Cicada*, *Ming Ch'an Fu* (《鸣蝉赋》)，译文精雕细琢，颇受学界褒扬。此外，国内学者刘师舜教授的英文译著《中国古典散文：唐宋八大家》（*Chinese Classical Prose：the Eight Masters of the T'ang-Sung Period*，1979）收有欧阳修散文英译14篇；美国哈佛大学教授罗纳德·伊根（Ronald C. Egan）在其专著《欧阳修的文学作品》(1984)中收有欧阳修散文英译16篇，译文严谨而不乏生动。

对译介欧阳修进行爬梳可发现，欧阳修的文学地位在译介过程中得到了再次巩固与提升。以中国古代文学散文在法国的翻译与研究为例，从20世纪上半叶留学法国的中国学者徐仲年（Hsu Sung-Nien）、曾任法国国立东方语言文化学院图书馆馆长的俄罗斯裔法国汉学家马古烈（Georges Margouliès）到中国文学教授班文干（Jacques Pimpaneau）等，欧阳修及其文章译介皆出现在他们编纂的中国文学史著作和文学选集当中。如徐仲年在《中国古今文选》中称，"正是得益于欧阳修，宋朝才形成了自己的文学"，其为"宋朝最杰出的文学大师"。他评价欧阳修的散文风格"具有古风的质朴流畅，而且毫无迂腐做作之气"，而且"欧阳修也是一位历史学家，我毫不犹豫地将其置于班固之上"。因此，他节译了欧阳修所撰的《新五代史》中的名篇《伶官传》片段，入选文选中的"历史著作"部分。同样，马古烈一方面称赞欧阳修的史学成就，认为其"步法班固之《汉书》，是班固当之无愧的继承者"，另一方面也褒扬其散文折射出的艺术品格，"能于平易自然中追求婉曲有致"，文辞"纡余委备、声韵和谐"。因此，他在《中国古文选》中翻译收录了《朋党论》《纵囚论》《醉翁亭记》等八篇散文。班文干也对欧阳修的诗文革新给予了高度评价，认为其散文风格"平易婉转"。他在译介过程中有意提醒西方读者摆脱文化上的刻板印象，着重推介了《醉翁亭记》，传递其中所表达的游赏宴饮之乐，而非神秘呆滞的古板形象。班文干精心选译了《送徐无党南归序》《朋党论》《释秘演诗集序》《与高司谏书》《醉翁亭记》《卖油翁》等名篇，涉及序文、政论、书信、游记、寓言等体裁，收入《中国古代文选》中。可以说，对于欧阳修的译介是文学散文与史论散文并重。

总的来说，欧阳修其人其文在世界文坛享有盛名，其思其想也被视为精神瑰宝与重要的学术研究资源。尤其是《醉翁亭记》等兼具艺术性和思想性的古典散文，其描绘的寄情于山水的美丽画卷不仅深深镌刻在中国的文化记忆中，也在全世界范围内光彩耀眼。

二、鉴赏·评析

欧阳修作为北宋时期的文坛领袖，创作了许多高质量的古文文章，是名副其实的古文学家。其传世文章达几千篇，书信、争论、史论、叙事、抒情、序跋等各体兼备，尤其是在谪贬滁州时，写下千古名篇《醉翁亭记》，寄情山水，与民同乐，有"天下莫不传诵"之美誉。滁州时期的"醉翁"，其自放山水间无论是真实还是虚写，都有明显的超越谪贬穷愁形象的积极作用（陈湘琳，2010）。

【原文】

醉翁亭记

环滁皆山也。其西南诸峰，林壑尤美，望之蔚然①而深秀者，琅琊也。山行六七里，渐闻水声潺潺，而泻出于两峰之间者，酿泉也。峰回路转，有亭翼然临于泉上者，醉翁亭也。作亭者谁？山之僧智仙也。名之者谁？太守自谓也。太守与客来饮于此，饮少辄醉，而年又最高，故自号曰醉翁也。醉翁之意不在酒，在乎山水之间也。山水之乐，得之心而寓之酒也。

若夫日出而林霏②开，云归而岩穴暝；晦明③变化者，山间之朝暮也。野芳发而幽香，佳木秀而繁阴，风霜高洁，水落而石出者，山间之四时也。朝而往，暮而归，四时之景不同，而乐亦无穷也。

至于负者④歌于途，行者休于树，前者呼，后者应，伛偻提携⑤，往来而不绝者，滁人游也。临溪而渔，溪深而鱼肥；酿泉为酒，泉香而酒洌；山肴野蔌，杂然而前陈者，太守宴也。宴酣之乐，非丝非竹⑥；射⑦者中，弈者胜；觥筹交错⑧，起坐而喧哗者，众宾欢也。苍颜白发，颓乎其中者，太守醉也。

已而夕阳在山，人影散乱，太守归而宾客从也。树林阴翳，鸣声上下，游人去而禽鸟乐也。然而禽鸟知山林之乐，而不知人之乐；人知从太守游而乐，而不知太守之乐其乐也。醉能同其乐，醒能述以文者，太守也。太守谓谁？庐陵⑨欧阳修也。

（选自［清］吴楚材、吴调侯选注：《古文观止》）

【注释】

① 蔚然：草木茂盛的样子。

② 林霏：树林中的雾气。

③ 晦明：指天气阴晴明暗。

④ 负者：背着东西的人。

⑤ 提携：指搀扶着走的小孩子。

⑥ 非丝非竹：不在于音乐。

⑦ 射：这里指投壶，宴饮时的一种游戏，把箭向壶里投，投中多的为胜，负者按照规定的杯数喝酒。

⑧ 觥筹交错：酒杯和酒筹交互错杂。形容喝酒尽欢的样子。觥，酒杯。筹，酒筹，宴会上行令或游戏时饮酒计数的筹码。

⑨ 庐陵：庐陵郡，就是吉州。今江西省吉安市，欧阳修先世为庐陵大族。

【译文】

The Old Drunkard's Pavilion

Ch'u has mountains all around it, but the forests and valleys in the southwestern range are particularly attractive. There is one that even from a distance appears to be the most lush and elegant; that is Lang-yeh Mountain. If you walk a few miles into its hills, you gradually become aware of the sound of gurgling water flowing out from between two peaks; this is Wine-brewing Brook. The road winds past veering heights, and soon you come to a pavilion that spreads out beside the spring; this is the Old Drunkard's Pavilion. Who was it that built this pavilion? A monk of the mountains, Chih-hsien. Who named it? The Governor, who named it after himself. The Governor and his friends go there often to drink. The Governor gets drunk on even a small amount of wine, and he is also the oldest in the group; that is why he calls himself the Old Drunkard. However, the Old Drunkard's real interest is not the wine but the mountains and streams. Having captured the joys of the mountains and streams in his heart, he lodges them in wine.

When the sun rises the forest mists vanish, and when the clouds return the crags and grottos fall into shadows; these alternations of light and darkness mark the mountain's dawns and dusks. As the wild flowers blossom they send forth subtle fragrance, as tall trees bloom they yield deep shade; then the winds and frost are lofty and pure, the rivers dry up and their stones are exposed; these are the four seasons in the mountains. If one spends the day walking in the mountain, one finds that the scenery changes with each season, and the pleasure it provides likewise has no end.

Men carrying heavy loads sing in the valleys, travelers rest under the trees. Those in front call out, and those behind yell back. From old men with crooked backs to children led by the hand - people pass back and forth continuously ; these are the natives of Chu moving along the paths. One may fish in the brook, which is deep and filled with meaty fish, or one may brew wine from the brook, whose water is fragrant and whose wine is clear. To have, in addition, mountain fruits and wild herbs arrayed before one ; this is the Governor's feast.

The pleasures of the feast are not those of strings nor flutes. One man shoots and hits the target while another wins at a game of chess. Goblets and tallies are strewn about in the chattering hubbub of men, some sitting and others standing ; these are the enjoyments of the guests. Then there is one man with a wrinkled face and white hair who sprawls on the ground ; this is the drunken Governor. Later, the setting sun touches the mountains and the men's shadows overlap ; this signals the Governor's departure, with the guests close behind. Then the forest lies in darkness, with no sound but the chirping of birds ; the revelers have left and the birds now are joyous.

But although the birds know the joys of the mountain forest, they do not know the joys of the guests. And although the guests know the joy of accompanying the Governor, they do not know the Governor's joy in their joy. While drunk he shares in their joy, and when he sobers up, he records it all in writing ; this is the Governor. Who is the Governor? Ou-yang Hsiu of Lu-ling.

(Translated by Ronald C. Egan)

An Account of the Pavilion of the Drunken Old Man

　　Encircling Chu-zhou all around are mountains. The wooded gorges of the various peaks to the southwest are overwhelmingly lovely. The one that stands out in the view, rising thick with dense growth, is Lang-ya Mountain. Going six or seven miles into the mountain, you gradually begin to hear the sound of flowing water ; and the watercourse that spills out from between the two peaks is Brewer's Stream. As the path turns with the bend of the cliff, there is a pavilion, its wings outspread, standing beside the stream ; and this is the Pavilion of the Drunken Old Man.

　　Who was it who built the pavilion? It was the mountain monk Zhi-xian. Who was it gave the pavilion its name? This was the governor himself. The governor would come with his guests to drink here ; and when he had gotten a little drunk, he, being the eldest of the company, gave himself the nickname "Drunken Old Man." The Drunken Old Man's interest was not in the wine itself but in being here amid the mountains and waters. The delight in mountains and waters was first found in the heart and then lodged temporarily in the wine.

　　When the sun comes out and the forest haze lifts, or when the clouds come back to the hills and the caves in the cliffs grow dark, all the transformations of light and shadow are the passages from dawn to dusk in the mountains. Wildflowers spring up and give off secret fragrances ; then the cassia trees rise high and form dense shade ; then winds blow high up and the frost gleams in purity ; then the waters sink and stones appear : these are the four seasons in the mountains. At dawn we go there and at dusk return ; and as the scenery of the four seasons is never the same, so our delight too is limitless.

　　And as for those who carry burdens along the paths and travelers who rest under the trees, the ones in front shout and those behind answer ; hunched over with age or with children in tow, they go back and forth without ceasing. These are the travels of the people of Chu-zhou. By the creek, we fish ; the creek is deep and the fish are plump. We use the stream's water in brewing wine ; and since the water smells sweet, the wine is sharp and clear. Pieces of fish and game from the mountains and vegetables from the wilds are served to us in varying dishes ; and these are the banquets of the governor. Our delight when tipsy at these banquets does not come from the music of harps and flutes. Someone playing toss-pot makes his throw ; someone playing chess wins ; horn-cups and wine tallies are all jumbled together amid the noisy chatter of people getting up and sitting down ; and these are the pleasures of the assembled guests. And the person with his face darkened by age and white-haired, lying passed out in the middle, is the governor, drunk.

Then the evening sun is in the mountains and the shadows of people scatter in disarray ; this is the governor going home and his guests following. As the woods become veiled in shadow, there is a singing above and down below, and this is the delight of the birds at the departure of the human visitors.

And yet the birds may experience the delight of the mountain forests, but they do not experience the delight of the people. The other people may experience the delight of coming to visit this place with the governor, but they do not experience the governor's delight in their delight. The person in drunkenness can share their delight and who, sobering up, can give an account of it in writing is the governor. And who is the governor? Ou-yang Xiu of Lu-ling.

(Translated by Stephen Owen)

【评析】

（一）英译策略之"直译与意译"

直译（literal translation）与意译（free translation）是在实际翻译过程中

应用最普遍、最常见的两种翻译方法。两者之间存在相异点，各有独特之处。所谓"直译"是指在翻译过程中按原文逐字逐句地翻译。人们关心的是语言层面的技术处理问题，即如何在保持原语形式的同时，不让其意义失真。所谓"意译"是指根据原文的大意来翻译，不作逐字逐句的翻译（区别于"直译"），通常在翻译句子或词组（或更大的意群）时使用较多。意译主要在原语与译语呈现出巨大文化差异的情况下被采用。也就是说，"意译"主要从意义出发，只要求将原文大意表达出来，不需过分注重细节，但要求译文自然流畅。如汉语"得陇望蜀"的直译是"covet Sichuan after capturing Gansu"，对西方人来说不太好理解，但是意译"The more one receives, the more one desires"在功能上与原文是对等的。特别要注意的是，"意译"也不等于"信口开河、不着边际地翻译"。直译与意译这两种翻译方法的共同点在于：目的相同。无论是直译还是意译，都是要准确地表达原作者的本意，没有好坏之分。直译与意译在本文两个译本中多有体现，比如：

关于"酿泉"，两位译者分别用了"Wine-brewing Brook"和"Brewer's Stream"。从语义上来讲，"酿"在此处做动词，Ronald 采取直译的办法，还原语义；而 Stephen 进行词性转换，将动词换为名词"酿酒者"。同时"Brewer"在英语中亦可作人名使用，如著名篮球运动员 Corey Brewer（科里·布鲁尔）和 Ronnie Brewer（罗尼·布鲁尔），这样的译法虽更符合英语使用习惯，但是存在语义偏差。

"太守与客来饮于此"：本文多次提到"乐"，其中一乐便是与民同乐，这是作者欧阳修作为当地的行政长官爱民情怀的体现，也是在他治下滁州政通人和的写照。相较于 Stephen 将"客"直译为"guests"，Ronald 意译为"朋友"更能体现欧阳修与民相亲、与民为友的形象。

"醉翁之意不在酒，在乎山水之间也。"这是一句千古名句，流传至今。山水之乐是一种自然之乐。"山水"不仅仅是山与水，更是旖旎秀丽的自然风光的代名词。Ronald 将"水"意译为"streams"，Stephen 将"山水"直译为"mountains and waters"，其实本质上都没有体现自然的整体性。

若是将 Stephen 的译文补充为"in being here amid the mountains and waters, carried away by the breathtaking nature",或许语义更完整。

"朝而往,暮而归"一句,Stephen 直译为"at dawn we go there and at dusk return",一来一回,符合文义;Ronald 意译为"if one spends the day walking in the mountain",将这句话理解为一天都在山中"walking",虽然呈现了在山中探索其乐无穷之意,但是"walking"这样的具体行为弱化了作者一行人摆宴会流觞曲水、觥筹交错的环节,无法与后文形成观照。

"至于负者歌于途,行者休于树"的意思是"至于那些背着东西走在路上唱着歌的,在树下稍作休息的行人"。本句有唱有憩,有动有静,也从侧面反映出当时当地在欧阳修的治理下人们安居乐业,对生活积极乐观。Ronald 采取直译的方法将动词"歌"译为英语动词"sing",实现语义对等;而 Stephen 省略了"歌"的动作,破坏了中文描绘出的动静结合场景,也无法传达"歌"背后的社会状态,造成语义缺失。

(二)文本鉴析

"环滁皆山也":五个字简明有力地概括了滁州的地理环境,两版译文也同样简洁。但是 Stephen 的"encircling"将"环"表现得非常贴切,且重心落在了"mountains"上,符合原文的"皆山也"。

"其西南诸峰,林壑尤美,望之蔚然而深秀者,琅琊也":滁州西南方向的深林山谷草木繁茂,尤为秀美,而远远望去收入眼帘的幽深秀林便是琅琊山。这里有一种电影的叙事感,画面一点点拉近,Ronald 用一个"but"引导的转折句和一个最高级"even from a distance appears to be the most",辅以副词"particularly"来表现这种视觉的层次感,且"from a distance"呈现了"望"的视角;相较于 Ronald 的"the forests and valleys",Stephen 的"the wooded gorges of the various peaks"弱化了"林"的形象,使"林"成了"壑"的修饰,在一定程度上损失了原文的美感。

"山行六七里,渐闻水声潺潺,而泻出于两峰之间者,酿泉也。峰回路转，有亭翼然临于泉上者，醉翁亭也。"这句话呈现了渐进式听觉和视觉效果，浑然一体。刚上山感受到的是树林静谧，六七里以后渐渐可以听到潺潺的流水声，且水流声不断增强，然后直接看到水流的位置，这是突然出现的视觉效果。酿泉水从两峰之间倾泻而下，而后随着山路折弯，又见一座亭子坐落在泉水边，亭子顶部四角向上翘起像飞鸟展翅一般。短短几句话，远处是山，深处是林，近看是泉，抬头见亭，好似走进一幅山水画。

原文是一篇"记"，故而不难看出这是作者本人的经历，"山行"的动作发出者也是作者一行人。原文没有主语，两版译文为符合英语行文习惯增添了主语。Ronald 补充的主语是"you"，Stephen 补充的主语是"we"。仔细分析原文我们会发现，从一开始作者欧阳修就在"卖关子"，直到文章最后"太守谓谁？庐陵欧阳修也"才点明上文所述为本人亲历。故而 Ronald 并没有在这里点明"山行"的动作发出者为作者本人，而是与原文保持一致，直到最后一句才揭秘，保持了原文营造的神秘感，吊足了读者的胃口。

Ronald 将"六七里"处理为模糊的数据，但实际上从滁州古城到琅琊山的确也就六七公里，因此 Stephen 的"going six or seven miles into the mountain"实现了语义等值。

"渐闻水声潺潺"一句，相较于 Stephen 省略的做法，Ronald 用一个拟声词"gurgling"对应了原文拟声词"潺潺"，从音美上实现对等。

关于"泉"的翻译，"stream"包含"brook"，并且"stream"有河岸，受水流侵蚀，即使溪水干涸也能清晰看到原溪水的流经路线，而"brook"没有这般冲刷力。从文义出发，尤其是"泻"字体现出来的力量，此处"stream"更贴切，因而"酿泉"若是结合两位译者的译法，译为"Wine-brewing Stream"或许语义更准确。

Stephen 将"渐闻水声潺潺，而泻出于两峰之间者"译为"you gradually begin to hear the sound of flowing water; and the watercourse that spills out from between the two peaks is Brewer's Stream"，前半句描写了听觉，后半句描写了视觉，符合原文的行文顺序。但是 Ronald 将这两句话整合为一句，

省略了看到"酿泉"的视觉描写。同样,"有亭翼然临于泉上者",Ronald 也省略了"翼然",没有对中国建筑的美予以刻画;Stephen 描写流水时的"flowing water",加上描写"亭"时的"standing beside the stream",动静结合,相得益彰。

"作亭者谁?山之僧智仙也。名之者谁?太守自谓也。"这两句话都是问句起,答句收,自问自答,读起来朗朗上口。第一句语义非常明确:"建造这个亭子的人是谁呢?是居住在这座山里的智仙和尚"。在翻译"僧"这一文化意象词时两位译者采用模糊策略译为"monk",但"monk"扩大了原词的语域。根据《朗文当代高级英语辞典》第五版,"monk"也可指修道院里的男性教徒,包含了除佛教以外的其他宗教教徒,若是译为"Buddhist monk",或许能更准确地传达原文的文化内涵。佛教法号的含义非常深刻,它代表着佛教徒的修行成就和精神追求。对于"智仙"这一称呼,两位译者皆采取音译,并不能体现这一名字所承载的意义。"山之僧"单单从字面理解不容易知晓这位僧人是住在山里的,两位译者分别译为"A monk of the mountains"和"the mountain monk",虽体现了僧人与山的所属关系,但不及"who lived in the mountain"解释到位。

"太守自谓也"意为"正是太守用自己的别号给这亭子命名的"。但是原文问的是谁,回答也应该是谁,而不是命名的行为,这是一种问答信息错位,因此我们采用中华书局版《古文观止》的译法,译为"自号醉翁的滁州太守"。在意合的中文里,既问答相对,又体现出"醉翁"以其名为亭子命名的语义。两版译文均注意到需问答一致,都回答为"人",但是 Ronald 用一个定语从句体现原文"醉翁"以其号命名的语义,非常机智。"太守"是中国古代的一种地方官衔,又称郡守。而在西方文化里是没有"太守"这一称谓的,这时就出现了词义空缺。为了使目标语读者能够更好地理解原文,两位译者皆采用了归化策略,即译为"governor"(地方长官),虽符合目的语表达习惯,但未能体现这一中国文化所特有的官职名称,因此不利于文化间的充分交流。

"得之心而寓之酒也。"本文中多次出现"……而……也"句型表示递进与承接,如:"太守归而宾客从也"和"游人去而禽鸟乐也",两位译者对此类句型的处理并不一致。Ronald 的译文"Having captured the joys of the mountains and streams in his heart, he lodges them in wine; the revelers have left and the birds now are joyous",通过时态——现在完成时与一般现在时体现出递进的逻辑。而"this signals the Governor's departure, with the guests close behind"一句借助状语从句体现逻辑。但是 Stephen 除了"得之心而寓之酒也"一句借助"was first""and then"等顺序标志词体现外,便没有关注这一特殊句式了。

"若夫日出而林霏开,云归而岩穴暝,晦明变化者,山间之朝暮也。"中国古代散文以骈体文居多,"骈四俪六"是骈体文的重要特征。在《醉翁亭记》中,"骈四俪六"结构较多。"骈四"如"峰回路转""风霜高洁""临溪而渔";"俪六"如"云归而岩穴暝""野芳发而幽香""佳木秀而繁阴"。在准确理解原文的含义,用目的语再现原文时,不单要考虑词汇与内容的对等,还需要注重"形似",即译文在形式上追求与原文相对等,体现原文的形式美。本句是一个非常优美的句子,意思是"要说太阳出来而树林里的雾气散了,云烟聚拢起来而山谷洞穴昏暗了",两位译者都有兼顾原文的形式美,采用主谓形式。但是 Stephen 的"the passages from dawn to dusk"更能体现山中时光在缓缓流淌,体现时间的流动感,好似一幅延时摄影作品在读者眼前播放,也从反面衬托出了林中之静谧。

"野芳发而幽香,佳木秀而繁阴":指遍地的野花开放,散发着清幽的香气,秀美的树木繁茂成荫。原文是一个对偶句,Ronald 用两个"as"引导的状语从句来兼顾"形美","blossom"与"bloom"形成押韵。同时,相对于 Stephen 将"佳木"理解为桂树,Ronald 的"tall trees"更符合文义。

"水落而石出者,山间之四时也。""……者……也"是文言判断句最常见的形式。主语后用"者",表示停顿,有舒缓语气的作用。谓语后用"也"结句,是对主语加以肯定的判断或解说。本文这样的判断句数量较多,如:

"望之蔚然而深秀者，琅琊也""而泻出于两峰之间者，酿泉也""晦明变化者，山间之朝暮也""往来而不绝者，滁人游也""杂然而前陈者，太守宴也""起坐而喧哗者，众宾欢也""颓乎其中者，太守醉也"以及"醉能同其乐，醒能述以文者，太守也"。通过比较可以发现，Ronald 通过"主 + 系 + 表"的结构对应原文的这种句型，如："that is Lang-yeh Mountain""this is Wine-brewing Brook""these are the four seasons in the mountains""these are the natives of Chu moving along the paths""this is the Governor's feast""these are the enjoyments of the guests""this is the drunken Governor"以及"this is the Governor"，充分说明 Ronald 注意到了文言文这种判断句式，且尽量在全文中呈现这种句式；虽然 Stephen 也使用"主 + 系 + 表"的结构，但是在翻译个别句子的时候，他为了行文流畅，舍弃了这种句式对应，牺牲了形式美。

"朝而往，暮而归，四时之景不同，而乐亦无穷也。"中文指清晨前往，黄昏归来，四季的风光不同，乐趣也是无穷无尽的。这句话原文没有主语，两位译者为使译文符合英文习惯都加上了主语，Ronald 采用第三人称，Stephen 使用第一人称复数。阅读原文不难发现，本文就是欧阳修记录他本人与朋友游玩时的所见所闻、所感所想，因此采用第一人称复数更符合原文的视角和身份。

"酿泉为酒，泉香而酒洌，山肴野蔌，杂然而前陈者，太守宴也。"对于"泉香而酒洌"的文意理解，历来众说纷纭，代表性的主要有三说：一是照语序直译说，如新课标人教版《教师教学用书》中译为"泉水甜酒水清"；二是互文见义说，如《语文学刊》2001 年第 4 期所载束荣柱之《互文见义例析》中译为"泉水和酒味香甜，泉色和酒色清洌"；三是倒文说或交错说，如钱伯城在主编的《古文观止新编》（上海古籍出版社 1988 年版）中译为"泉水清因此酒也香"。无论为何种解释，"酒洌"都没有"烈酒"之意，故而 Stephen 的"the wine is sharp and clear"有过度翻译之嫌。"杂然而前陈者"中的"杂然"意在突出宴会品类丰富，Stephen 通过"served to us in varying dishes"实现语义对等。但是对于"山肴野蔌"即野味野菜，Stephen 直译为"game from the mountains and vegetables from the wilds"，虽然实现了语义对等，但是东西方饮食文化存在差异。在自然条件、生存需要、文化习惯等多种因素的共同作用下，古代中国一些地方有吃野味的风俗习惯。但是西方或许是受宗教的约束，对食物的来源，特别是肉食做了严格规定，使得西方并不热衷于野味。所以 Ronald 的译文使用归化的策略，以"mountain fruits and wild herbs"规避了可能存在的文化冲突。

"宴酣之乐,非丝非竹,射者中,弈者胜,觥筹交错"是说宴会喝酒的乐趣，不在于弹琴奏乐，投壶的人投中了，下棋的赢了，宴会上酒杯和酒筹交互错杂。纽马克将文化定义为"使用某种特定语言的特定群体的生活和表现方式"。在两个版本中，对"丝竹"的翻译反映出不同的文化背景。中国的"丝竹"是弦乐器与竹管乐器的总称，也指音乐。这里使用了借代的修辞手法。Ronald 采用直译的手法，译为"strings"和"flutes"，因为英文也有借代这一修辞手法，"strings"和"flutes"可以理解为弦乐器与管乐器，从而代表音乐。故而直译使英文也保留这一修辞手法，实现形式对等。但是 Stephen 以"the music of harps and flutes"借代音乐，同时他将"丝"解释为目的语读者耳熟能详的"harps"（竖琴），这有助于目的语读者直接明了地理解文义。

"颓然乎其间者"：颓然，原意是精神不振，这里形容醉态，指倒下的样子。由原文可知，太守并未醉到失去意识，只是四肢发软，醉醺醺地瘫坐在地。Ronald 的"sprawls on the ground"用得极妙，惟妙惟肖地刻画出人酒醉后四肢无力瘫软的样子；Stephen 的"passed out"指酒后断片，失去意识，存在过度翻译之嫌。

"树林阴翳，鸣声上下"：树林里的枝叶茂密成荫，可以听见鸟儿四处啼鸣。此时为黄昏，夕阳西下，树林里的光线也渐渐褪去，但并未到 Ronald 的"the forest lies in darkness"的程度；林中小鸟鸣叫，Stephen 的"singing above and down below"刻画出一幅鸟儿欢欣雀跃、上下欢歌的生动画面，也呼应了后文的"游人去而禽鸟乐也"（the delight of the birds at the departure of the human visitors)。

三、译论·比较

翻译作为一种话语利器，可以雕琢语言、形塑文化、构建认同。霍米·巴巴（1994）曾视翻译为一项爱国主义行为。相应地，译者应当具备民族文化身份意识，不能简单地、机械式地传递信息，而应受到自身文化身份的制约和影响（蒋林，2008）。换言之，译者的职责不仅仅停留于语言层面的文本意义再现，而是要继续拓展至社会历史文化层面的文化意义构建。因此，译者的文化自信、身份认同直接触及原作在异语文化中的生成与建构，也反向影响到本民族翻译话语体系。

著名翻译家、外国文学研究专家、诗人杨宪益先生生于1915年，从小熟读中国文史经典，深谙传统文化要义，又时逢乱世，心系民族安危。他（2010）曾明言："在我这个时代，一上来就碰到了一个抗日战争。做中国人怎么能不爱国呢？……我不能够耍枪杆子，只能够帮着摇旗呐喊……"于是，他怀揣"愿得身化雪，为世掩阴霾"的爱国志气，奋力握紧"笔杆子"，与妻子戴乃迭终身致力于翻译中国的事业。这对学术伉俪为中国经典作品外译作出了巨大贡献，践行了"翻译了整个中国"的译者使命。

杨宪益的翻译原则可谓"求信求真"（许钧，2019），这主要源于其译介中国经典著作的初衷，即保护原作的"经典性、异质性、文化性"。因此，杨译文本更多秉持了民族身份意识及其责任，从具体翻译实践层面再现中国经典作品中的文化风格、文化内涵与文化记忆。可以说，杨宪益的生平经历与爱国情怀极大地影响乃至左右着其作为一名译者的潜在价值引导与身份认同，而这也对现今"构建中国翻译领域话语体系"（王倩，2018）具有重要指导意义与借鉴价值。

鉴于此，请按照以下要点对杨宪益与戴乃迭所译的《醉翁亭记》进行文本比较分析：

（1）杨、戴其人其事以及翻译风格；

(2) 从"求信求真"的层面分析该译本；

(3) 将该译本与 Owen 及 Egan 译本进行横向对比。

The Roadside Hut of the Old Drunkard

The District of Chu is enclosed all around by hills, of which those in the southwest boast the most lovely forests and dales. In the distance, densely wooded and possessed of a rugged beauty, is Mt. Langya. When you penetrate a mile or two into this mountain you begin to hear the gurgling of a stream, and presently the stream—the Brewer's Spring— comes into sight cascading between two peaks. Rounding a bend you see a hut with a spreading roof by the stream, and this is the Roadside Hut of the Old Drunkard. This hut was built by the monk Zhixian. It was given its name by the governor, referring to himself. The governor, coming here with his friends, often gets tipsy after a little drinking ; and since he is the most advanced in years, he calls himself the Old Drunkard. He delights less in drinking than in the hills and streams, taking pleasure in them and expressing the feeling in his heart through drinking.

Now at dawn and dusk in this mountain come the changes between light and darkness : when the sun emerges, the misty woods become clear ; when the clouds hang low, the grottoes are wrapped in gloom. Then in the course of the four seasons, you find wild flowers burgeoning and blooming with a secret fragrance, the stately trees put on their mantle of leaves and give a goodly shade, until wind and frost touch all with austerity, the water sinks low and the rocks at the bottom of the stream emerge. A man going there in the morning and returning in the evening during the changing pageant of the seasons can derive endless pleasure from the place.

And the local people may be seen making their way there and back in an endless stream, the old and infirm as well as infants in arms, men carrying burdens who sing as they go, passersby stopping to rest beneath the trees, those in front calling out and those behind answering. There the governor gives a feast with a variety of dishes before him, mostly wild vegetables and mountain produce. The fish are freshly caught from the stream, and since the stream is deep and the fish are fat; the wine is brewed with spring water, and since the spring is sweet the wine is superb. There they feast and drink merrily with no accompaniment of strings or flutes; when someone wins a game of touhu or chess, when they mark up their scores in drinking games together, or raise a cheerful din sitting or standing, it can be seen that the guests are enjoying themselves. The elderly man with white hair in the middle, who sits utterly relaxed and at his ease, is the governor, already half drunk.

Then the sun sinks towards the hills, men's shadows begin to flit about and scatter; and now the governor leaves, followed by his guests. In the shade of the woods birds chirp above and below, showing that the men have gone and the birds are at peace. But although the birds enjoy the hills and forests, they cannot understand the men's pleasure in them; and although men enjoy accompanying the governor there, they cannot understand his pleasure either. The governor is able to share his enjoyment with others when he is in his cups, and sober again can write an essay about it. Who is this governor? Ouyang Xiu of Luling.

(Translated by Yang, X.Y. and Yang, G.)

四、实践·译笔

夫秋，刑官也，于时为阴；又兵象也，于行用金。是谓天地之义气，常以肃杀而为心。天之于物，春生秋实。故其在乐也，商声主西方之音，夷则为七月之律。商，伤也，物既老而悲伤；夷，戮也，物过盛而当杀。

(节选自欧阳修《秋声赋》)

【注】刑官：执掌刑狱的官。《周礼》把官职与天、地、春、夏、秋、冬相配，称为六官。秋天肃杀万物，所以司寇为秋官，执掌刑法，称刑官。

五、阅读·延展

……我不但不反对新的表现方法，而且要求这种新的表现方法能够容纳到广大的群众生活里去。我的前一封信说：

  一般的说起来，不但翻译，就是自己的作品也是一样，现在的文学家，哲学家，政论家……要想表现现在中国社会已经有的新的关系，新的现象，新的事物，新的观念，就差不多人人都要做"仓颉"。这就是说，要天天创造新的语言，新的句法……可是，这些新的字眼和句法的创造……要遵照着中国白话的文法公律。

所以这个问题是很清楚的。我和你同样主张要输入新的表现法，可是，我主张根本不要"容忍多少的不顺"的态度。

你的来信说："中国的文或话，法子实在太不精密了……译本不但要输入新的内容，而且还要输入新的表现法。"这里，要输入新的表现法，当然是不成问题的，问题是在于严格地分别中国的文还是话。中国的文言和白话的分别，其实等于拉丁文和法文的分别。我们先要认清这一点。中国的文言文，这是"士大夫民族"的国语，与我们小百姓不相干。这种文言文里面还须要输入什么新的表现法，或者不须要，这是另外一个问题，这是老爷们的问题，不是我们的问题。至于现代的中国文（就是白话），那么，我上次的信也已经说过：

  翻译——除了能够介绍原本的内容给中国读者之外——还有一个很重要的作用：就是帮助我们创造出新的中国的现代言语。中国的言语（文字）是那么穷乏，甚至于日常用品都是无名氏的。

中国的言语简直没有完全脱离所谓"姿势语"的程度——普通的日常谈话几乎还离不开"手势戏"。自然，一切表现细腻的分别和复杂的关系的形容词，动词，前置词，几乎没有。宗法封建的中世纪的余孽，还紧紧的束缚着中国人的活的言语（不但是工农群众）。这种情形之下，创造新的言语是非常重大的任务。

....

固然，这些新的字眼和句法之中，也许仍旧有许多要淘汰掉的；然而，假使个个翻译家都预先存心等待自然的淘汰，而不每一个人负起责任使他所写出来的新的字眼和句法尽可能的能够变成口头上的新的表现法，那么，这种翻译工作就不能够帮助中国现代文的发展。

现在不但翻译，甚至于一般欧化文艺和所谓"语体文"，都有这种病根——就因为这种不负责任的态度，所以不但不能够帮助中国现代白话文的发展，反而造成一种非驴非马的骡子话，半文不白的新文言。

（摘自瞿秋白《再论翻译——答鲁迅》）

LANGUAGE is an indispensable element in the realization of the verbal act. It is a necessary precondition for communication. As Jakobson observes, "the message requires…a Code fully, or at least partially, common to the addresser and addressee (or in other words, to the encoder and the decoder of the message)." Translation is a dual act of communication. It presupposes the existence, not of a single code, but of two distinct codes, the "source language" and the "target language." The fact that the two codes are not isomorphic creates obstacles for the translative operation. This explains why linguistic questions are the starting-point for all thinking about translation. A basic premise of translation theory is the famous "prejudicial objection" dismantled by Mounin, piece by piece, in one of the first works to elevate translation to the status of a quasi-scientific area of scholarship. Translation is a unidirectional operation between two given languages. The target language is thus, every bit as much as the source language, *a sine qua non* of the translative operation. If the target language remains elusive, the act of translation becomes impossible. This is true even in the hypothetical case in which a text must be translated into a language that has no writing system. Throughout history, translators have had to contend with the fact that the target language is deficient when it comes to translating the source text into that language. Such deficiencies can be clearly identified as, for example, lexical or morpho-syntactic deficiencies or as problems of polysemy. More often, however, the deficiency in the receiving code has to do with the relation between signs and their users, a relation that reflects such things as individuality, social position, and geographical origin of the speakers: "thus the relatively simple question arises, should one translate or not translate argot by argot, a patois by a patois, etc…" Here, the difficulty of translation does not arise from the lack of a specific translation language. It arises, rather, from the absence in the target language of a subcode equivalent to the one used by the source text in its reproduction of the source language. How should the cockney dialogue in *Pygmalion* be translated? What French-language dialect equivalent should be used to render the lunfardo of Buenos Aires in translations of Roberto Arlt's novels? What variety of French would correspond to the Roman dialect of the Via Merulana in a translation of Carlo Emilio Gadda's *Quer pasticciaccio brutto de via Merulana*? What is the French equivalent of the English of the American South in Faulkner's novels? Such are the questions ritually posed by the translator, torn between the source text and the target language. These problems become more complex when historical time is factored in. Should the translator recreate the feeling of the time period of the text for the contemporary reader? Or, conversely, should the archaic form of the language be modernized to make the text more accessible to the contemporary reader? Should Dante, Shakespeare, Cervantes, or Chaucer be translated into archaic language? Should Cicero's style be rendered by the style of a well-known politician of modern times? The choice of a target language becomes even more difficult when the text to be translated is a parody of a variety of the source language. *Gaweda*, a "museum language" of Great Poland, reproduced and parodied by Gombrowicz in his *Trans-Atlantyk*, is a case in point. Translation problems can arise not only from deficiencies in the receiving society but also from a surfeit of linguistic options. For example, in certain societies, the language of men is different from that of women, and these differences are governed by particularly strict constraints. Charles Taber and Eugene Nida have discussed the problem of whether the Scriptures should be translated into the language of men or of women. Writings on the translative operation abound with such questions. Translators address these issues in prefaces to their work, outlining the deficiencies of the target language, deficiencies arising from sociological, geographical, or historical variation in the source language.

(Excerpts from *The Search For a Native Language : Translation and Cultural Identity* by Annie Brisset)

第六单元

宰相诗人·北宋王安石

一、译事·译研

王安石（1021—1086），字介甫，今江西抚州人，世称临川先生，生于官宦之家，其个性鲜明，信念坚定，是北宋一朝杰出的政治家、文学家、改革家、思想家，荣居"唐宋八大家"之列。王安石有着精深的思想体系，主导了"荆公新学"这一极具影响力的学术派别，致力于天人合一、革故鼎新、通经致用等思想研究。著名宋史研究专家刘子健曾试图重评王安石及其时代，强调其作为一名改革家，不仅是中国历史上的杰出思想者，而且其改革理念已然具有了超前的现代性色彩，"成为现代世界的灵感来源之一"，理应在世界史上占有一席之地。

从学术史来看，清代文学家、史学家蔡上翔（《王荆公年谱考略》），近代学者梁启超（《王安石传》）、柯昌颐（《生前事与身后名：王安石评传》）等人都对王安石其人、其事、其思、其想进行了多层次（历史、政治、经济、思想等）分析与品评，暂且按下不表。本章重点强调的是西方对于王安石及其作品的译研情况。整体而言，西方对于王安石的译介并不多见，主要有1735年杜赫德在《中华帝国全志》中法译王安石的《上时政疏》《复仇解》两篇文章以及1932年福兰阁德译《上仁宗皇帝言事书》。直到1937年英国传教士、汉学家亨利·雷蒙德·威廉森（Henry Raymond Williamson, 1883—

1966) 完成两卷巨著 *Wang An Shih, a Chinese Stateman and Educationalist of the Sung Dynasty*，可谓当时关于王安石研究的最为详细之作（萧公权，2014）。该巨著第二卷最后一章英译了王安石的多篇诗文，部分篇目如下：

On Original Nature	《原性》	*Discussion of Human Nature*	《性说》
Human Nature and Disposition	《性情》	*The Possibility of Repentance*	《原过》
On Ceremonies and Music	《礼乐论》	*Further Discussion on "The Nature" and "The Decree"*	《对辨》
Discussion on the Canons of Human Relationships	《礼论》	*On the Superiority of Confucius to Yao and Shun*	《夫子贤于尧舜》
On Great Men	《大人论》	*On Seeking to apply One's Principles to Affairs of State*	《行述》
On the Attainment of Unity	《致一论》	*Tzu Kung*	《子贡》
The Highest Form of Love	《荀卿》	*Love and Wisdom*	《仁智》
Courage and Generosity. "Right" the Universal Standard of Action	《勇惠》	*The "Mean"*	《中述》
Knowledge of Men	《知人》	*Devolution of Responsibility*	《委任》
On Taking Up Office	《进说》	*The True Educational Method*	《原教》

到了 20 世纪末，Stephen Owen 在其著作 *An Anthology of Chinese Literature: Beginnings to 1911* 中译介了王安石多首诗作，如 *My Brother Wang Chun-fu Brings Out a Painting by the Monk Hui-chong and Engages Me to Write a Poem on It*（《纯甫出释惠崇画要予作诗》）、*Climbing Bao-gong Pagoda*（《登宝公塔》）等。在译介之余，该书也发表了一些对于人物的品评观点，如"王安石是一个不修边幅的儒家政论者，有极权主义倾向，笃定自信，认为其治国理念是当时治理大宋所迫切需要的。而且其'新法'措施不幸（misfortune）被神宗采纳并付诸实施，这使他立即遭到保守派和实用主义者的反对"。颇有意思之处在于，该书认为王安石作为一个富有集权主义色彩的政治家，"有点不协调的（somewhat incongruously），也最为人所知的是一位讲究四行诗和律己诗的文体家，还是杜甫的狂热崇拜者"。这种埋伏在字里行间的"不

协调"主要还在于世人对其印象或评价的两分化,即对于"作为一个政治家的王安石"之微词和"作为一个诗人的王安石"之称道。

纵然"无论当时,还是现代,王安石不能被人完全理解,甚至往往遭受彻底的误解",但这也仅限于政治领域的互为驳斥。在后世中国学者眼中,王安石是一位多产的散文家与诗人,其作品颇受赞誉。很多人对其政见嗤之以鼻,但对其文学创作则赞不绝口,认为其早期的散文在文风与形式层面堪称典范,"晚期作品更可谓名垂青史的经典"。正如 Burton Watson 在译介王安石时所说,"其早年的诗文充满了儒学理念,表达了忧国忧民的政治关怀;而他受世人所钦佩的更多是他退隐政坛后的反思性(reflective)诗作"(Watson, 1984)。

二、鉴赏·评析

在所有文学体裁的翻译中,诗歌翻译由于其特殊性,被研究和讨论得最多,古今中外,概莫能外。美国诗人罗伯特·弗罗斯特(Robert Frost)说"诗者,翻译所失也"(Poetry is what gets lost in translation),诗人雪莱也曾把诗歌翻译比作种下种子,却不能开花。这都说明了诗歌存在某种程度的不可译性。在文化翻译学派的领军人物苏姗·巴斯奈特(Susan Bassnett)看来,理解诗歌的灵或魂(spirit),是诗歌翻译的关键所在。她认为翻译诗歌首先要读懂原文和文本以外的因素,其次还要抓住原作的灵魂。

作为诗歌译者,诗歌的形式、结构、功能都是需要思考的。此外,诗歌意蕴的多义性,也要求译者是个有较强审美能力和阐释能力的读者。不仅如此,翻译诗歌对译者的写作能力也提出了非常高的要求,翻译的过程是经过语义理解和重组之后,再创造性地编织另一个语言文本。译者此时不仅是个读者,更重要的是一名作者。高明的诗歌翻译者能够使原诗歌投胎转世,延续生命或再生,拙劣的译者只会模仿。

美国诗人埃兹拉·庞德(Ezra Pound)总结了诗歌翻译的三条标准:

(1) 音乐性(Melopoeia);

（2）视觉性（Phanopoeia）；

（3）直接意义和双关（Logopoeia）。

这三个词的后缀"poeia"来源于希腊语的拉丁词，意指"制造、创作"（making，creating）。庞德总结的三种诗学特性，与刘勰《文心雕龙·情采》中所论述的"形文、声文和情文"极其相似。译"形"和"声"易，而译"情"难。

音乐性是指词汇的形式充满音乐特性。音乐性很难翻译，全靠神来之笔。在庞德看来，一个本土人很难从译文中欣赏到外国诗歌的音乐性。

视觉性可以完全不受损失地翻译，语言意象的创造就是证明。中西诗歌意象契合甚多，或者可以创造性地移植。视觉意象是庞德诗学的关键所在，因此，他在翻译中竭尽所能，予以全译，甚至增加原文中没有的意象。

直接意义和双关则几乎不可译，因为直接意义和双关必须受历史性（时间）、地点色彩（地域）和意识形态（社会文化因素）的局限。语汇中智力的闪现只能通过释义翻译，只有身临其境才能把握其个中三昧。

诗歌，尤其是中国古典诗歌，与其他文学体裁的显著区别之一，就是诗歌的语言有节奏性和韵律性。庞德在翻译理论中特别强调音韵和节奏的重要性，认为一首好诗没有了节奏就是一个空壳。诗歌翻译只有在音韵与节奏上与原文对等，才能保留原诗的韵味，才能达到形式的契合，最终实现真正的对等。巴斯奈特非常赞同庞德翻译诗歌提出的原则，这是她提倡的诗歌翻译的"有机过程"（Organic Process）。诗歌的形式、内容以及音韵、节奏都是一个有机的整体，翻译时要充分考虑到这几个因素，缺一不可。巴斯奈特也用"有机形式""有机结构"来指翻译中音义形的统一。

巴斯奈特非常重视重现诗歌翻译中的意义阐释，而意义的获得通常是诗人兼译者的"神来之笔"（divinely inspired）。她认为："柏拉图式的诗歌灵感的提法明显对译者产生了影响，译者身上可能灵光一现，使他能够在另一种文化语境中再现原作的精神和语气。译者因此寻求的是原文的'投胎转世'，他在技术层面上和形而上学层面上接近原文，在技术上对原作者和读者担负起责任来。"

巴斯奈特相信译诗需要有灵性,从她反复使用"复活"(resurrection)"神性的"(divine)等宗教词汇可以证明这一点。她强调,译者既是作者又是译者的共生关系。一言以蔽之,"盖诗者,非翻译所失者;诗者译之所得者也"(Poetry is not what is lost in translation, it is what we gain through translation and translators)。译诗虽然不可为,但毕竟又可为。可译的是原文的某些部分,不可译的也是原文的某些部分,但可译的部分远远超过不可译的那部分(刘军平,2009)。

本部分所选取的鉴赏篇目为王安石所作诗文《浣溪沙》《夜直》《南乡子》,学习者可以在感受其词韵魅力的同时,通过汉英对照,鉴析"他者"视角下王安石的文学形象。

【原文】

浣溪沙

百亩中庭半是苔,
门前白道水萦回。
爱闲能有几人来。

小院回廊春寂寂,
山桃溪杏两三栽。
为谁零落为谁开。

【释义】

百亩大的庭院有一半是青苔,门外沙子铺满了整条路,还有蜿蜒的小溪流。喜欢悠闲,有空来的人有几个呢?

春天到了,院子里曲折的回廊非常的安静。山上的桃花、溪边的杏树,三三两两地种在一起。不知道它们是为谁开放,为谁凋零?

【译文】

Lyrics for the Tune "Huan Xi Sha"

The courtyard, a hundred acres half under moss,

out in front a pale stream lingers leisurely.

How few love idleness enough to come this way!

A winding hall around a small courtyard in a lonely silent spring,

mountain peach and riverside almond, two or three in all,

for whom do they blossom, for whom do they fall?

(Translated by J. W. Walls & Y. L. Walls)

Tune: Silk-Washing Stream

Half moss-hidden is my courtyard a hundred acres wide,

Before my gate a winding path by riverside.

Who would visit one fond of leisure and free hours?

Spring in my courtyard girt with corridors is still;

Two or three peach and apricot trees stand near the hill.

For whom are they blooming and then fall in showers?

[Translated by Xu Yuanchong（许渊冲）]

【评析】

这首词为王安石在政治上二度失意后，退隐江宁（今南京），在府城东与钟山间的一所"半山园"所作。此时王安石的政治地位发生了极大变化，对于这种遭际的改变，表面上看他似乎采取了一种安然自适的态度，如这首词里描写的大都是周围清幽的景色，颇有村野情趣，渲染出一种淡泊宁静的生活环境，但最后一句透露出他无法彻底遮蔽内心的孤独寂寞以及淡淡哀愁。

浣溪沙，原为唐教坊曲名，后用为词牌名。据南朝宋孔灵符《会稽记》载，"勾践索美女以献吴王，得诸暨罗山卖薪女西施、郑旦，先教习于土城山。山边有石，云是西施浣纱石"。今浙江省诸暨市南近郊的苎萝山下浣纱溪畔有浣纱石，上有传为东晋王羲之所书"浣纱"二字，相传这里是春秋时越国美女西施浣纱处。一说浣纱溪即浙江绍兴南二十里的若耶溪。总之，调名"浣溪沙"的本意即咏春秋越国美女西施浣纱的溪水（左晓婷，2012）。

浣溪沙词调有五种格式，分别为：

正体，双调四十二字，上片三句，三平韵，下片三句，两平韵，过片二句用对偶句的居多。变体一，双调四十二字。上片三句，三平韵；下片三句，两平韵。

变体二，双调四十四字。上片三句，三平韵；下片五句，两平韵。

变体三，双调四十六字。上片五句，三平韵；下片五句，两平韵。

变体四，双调四十二字。上片三句，三仄韵；下片三句，两仄韵。

本词韵律为：仄仄平平仄仄平，平平平仄仄平平，仄平平仄仄平平。仄仄平平平仄仄，平平平仄仄平平，仄平平仄仄平平，属正体。

中文单从词牌名就可以得出如此多的信息，这种蕴含丰富文化底蕴的词牌名便是诗歌翻译的不可译性之体现。无论是 J. W. Walls 和 Y. L. Walls，还是许渊冲先生，皆无法用英文将中文所蕴含的典故、韵律等信息对等地表达出来。Walls 采用解释加拼音的方式，增加 "Lyrics for the Tune"，点明这是曲调的歌词，发音为 "Huan Xi Sha"，如此一来，英语读者便可了解这个标题的功能与发音；许先生同样增加了 "Tune" 来点明标题的属性，不过相较于 Walls，许先生将浣溪沙直译为 "Silk-Washing Stream"，从中可以窥见许先生传播中国文化的用心。

本词 "苔" "来" "栽" "开" 等构成 "ai" 韵，正如上文所提到的，本词属正体，第四字的平仄和第二字相反，第六字又与第四字相反，如此反复就形成了节奏感。但是逢单却可反可不反，这是因为重音落在双数音节上。

相比而言，单数音节就显得不重要了，平仄交错，才不至于单调。本词结尾用了平声，声音延续出去，也延续了对"为谁零落为谁开"的思考，意味绵长。两首译文的译者都注意到了韵律与节奏，以诗译诗，保证了原文与译文文体的一致性，Walls 下片"all"与"fall"形成韵律，许先生上片的"wide"与"riverside"、下片的"still"与"hill"以及三六句的"hours"与"showers"使全诗形成 aab、ccb 的韵律，可谓精彩。从节奏角度而言，英诗没有平仄之分，但是我们可以根据音步中重/非重音节的位置即韵律（Metre）来体现节奏。许先生的译文以抑扬格四音步（Iambic tetrameter）来传达原诗的节奏美，富于音乐性。Walls 译文通过状语前置及逗号的使用使诗句明显地分为两部分，这是通过外在形式加强内在节奏。

第一句"百亩中庭半是苔"，偌大的庭院有一半都长满了青苔，苍苔密布浸润着清新自然。这也可以看出主人公无心打扫，无意照看小院才致青苔丛生。结合创作背景，这句也从侧面表现出作者的庭院由以前的门庭若市变成现在的无人问津、门庭冷落，不禁显出几许苍凉和寂寞，营造了萧条空冷之感，衬托了作者的落寞孤寂。原文"百"表示"大""多"之意，"百亩"可显庭院之大，衬托庭院的幽静与荒芜。但是两版译文都直译为"a hundred acres"，与现实相去甚远；相较于"under moss"，许先生的译文"moss-hidden"更能凸显庭院青苔生长之旺盛，整个小院似乎都要隐匿在这青苔之下了。青苔的肆意蔓延、野蛮生长，恰恰让读者感受到主人无心打理，不仅很好地再现了原文的荒芜之意，也从侧面提示译文读者原作者的心境。

"门前白道水萦回，爱闲能有几人来。"这两句词里有两个景——道和水，门外沙子布满整条小路，一条小溪潺潺流过，这是一幅动静结合的画面，静谧清闲，本能吸引很多人的来访，但是却没有多少人到来，可见晚年的王安石从那些空虚的繁华中逐渐坠入落寞孤独的境地，那种落差感带来的惆怅可想而知。Walls 的"pale"可谓一语双关，既是水"pale"，何尝又不是人"pale"呢？但是 Walls 失去了"道"这个景，失去了中文视觉性与听觉性相辅相成、以动衬静、"鸟鸣山更幽"般的效果；"lingers leisurely"赋予水生命，生动形象地将"萦回"二字的意境勾画出来；"爱闲能有几人来"一句实为问句，却以句号收尾，更能增添作者面对门庭冷清时淡淡的无可奈何之意，是无奈如此美景无人共赏呢？还是无奈随着自己政治地位的变化而人走茶凉呢？我们不得而知。这是一种微妙的情感表达，Walls 注意到了这种情绪，但是他放大了这种情绪，以感叹句的形式强烈地表达出一种不甘之意。许先生采用问句形式，这种面对面提问的方式拉近了作者与读者的距离，"Who would visit one fond of leisure and free hours"意指谁会来看我这样一个钟爱闲情之人呢？许先生将"爱闲"之人设定为作者本人，虽然原词表达出了一种知音难寻之意，那么无论是作者还是来访者应该都是"爱闲"之人，但是原词问的应该是"爱闲"的来访者，正是没有同道中人与作者一同欣赏这静谧闲适的乡野景致，才更显作者的落寞。

"小院回廊春寂寂"一句巧妙化用了杜甫《涪城县香积寺官阁》中的"小院回廊春寂寂，浴凫飞鹭晚悠悠"。春天已经到来了，春天本是热闹的、繁华的、簇拥的，可是我们丝毫感受不到春天的气息——曲曲折折的回廊寂静得吓人，正好与前面的无人造访相互照应。"寂寂"这个叠字既渲染了气氛，又赋予词音乐性。Walls 通过"silent spring"头韵的方式再现了原词的艺术性，以"lonely"拟人的修辞手法突出寂无一人之冷清；许译版的"spring""corridors""is""still"等词的 /s/ 音也赋予了译文音乐性，但是缺少了 Walls 译文呈现出的寓情于景、情景交融之意境。

"山桃溪杏两三栽"一句化用唐代雍陶的《过旧宅看花》中的"山桃野杏两三栽，树树繁花去复开"。此时的王安石身在自然之中，感受着完全不同于官场的气息。

"为谁零落为谁开"则是化用了唐代严恽《落花》中的"尽日问花花不语，为谁零落为谁开"。不同于上一句的写景，这里运用托物言志的手法，表面上写"山桃溪杏"为了谁飘零落下，又为了谁盛开，其实何尝不是在说这个阶段孤独寂寞的自己无人问津呢。这里作者以山桃溪杏自喻，反映环境的零落荒寂诚然令人唏嘘，但一场惊天动地的"变法"，其中酸苦，用"为谁零落为谁开"之问的哀叹也顿时将作者内心的惆怅不平表现了出来。这些正说明了政治家兼文学家的王安石，晚年虽身在山林，但他的内心世界却并未完全平静。悠闲的环境使王安石得到了一时的心理平衡，却不能使他彻底忘怀过去的政治生涯，以至于他在山桃和溪杏身上还可以发现自己的影子。词以问句结束，引导读者思考词外之意，深化了词的内涵，扩大了词的表现空间。

Walls 译文 "for whom do they blossom, for whom do they fall" 只改变了最后一个单词，完美地再现了原词的形式；许先生的译文采用现在进行时与 "fall in showers" 使画面充满动态美，以 "then" 连接 "are blooming" 与 "fall in showers"，加上时态的变化，细致地将花开荼蘼、热烈绽放之后是零落的叹惋之心表现出来。这不正是王安石本人从身居高位到变法失败后罢相退居江宁的写照吗？

【原文】

夜直

金炉香尽漏声残，翦翦轻风阵阵寒。
春色恼人眠不得，月移花影上栏干。

【释义】

夜已经深了，香炉里的香早已燃尽，漏壶里的水也将漏完。夜风轻柔却也带着点点寒意。

夜晚的春色美得令人难以入睡，只见花影随着月亮的移动，悄悄地爬上了栏杆。

【译文】

Night Watch

Incense burnt in the golden urn, water-clock run dry,

a light breeze swishes time and again cool upon cool.

The luster of spring provokes me, keeps me awake,

and the moon moves flower shadows up the banister.

(Translated by J. W. Walls & Y. L. Walls)

The golden bowl's incense burns to ashes,

the sound of the water-clock fades;

Snip, snip goes the light breeze with its gusts of chill.

Spring's hues tease me, and I cannot sleep;

While the moon moves the shadows of the flowers up the balustrade.

(Translated by Robert Kotewall)

The incense-stick is burnt to ash, the water-clock is stilled,

The midnight breeze blows sharply by and all round is chilled.

Yet I am kept from slumber by the beauty of the spring,

Sweet shapes of flowers across the blind the quivering moonbeams fling!

(Translated by Giles)

【评析】

本诗创作于皇帝宋神宗决定采纳作者王安石的意见推行新法之际。此时的作者幸遇得伯乐，得以施展自己的政治抱负，内心自是激荡澎湃。

"夜直"的"直"通"值"，"夜直"即晚上值班。据宋代制度，翰林学士每夜轮流一人在学士院值宿。又据《容斋随笔》，宋制翰林学士每晚留一人于学士院值夜，以备皇帝随时召对，或咨询政务，或草拟制诰，或收发当夜外廷呈送的紧急封奏，转呈皇帝。王安石于宋英宗治平四年（1067）九月为翰林学士，因他当时正在江宁知府任上，没有立即到职。宋神宗熙宁元年（1068）四月，才奉诏进京，越次入对，从此才有资格到内廷值宿。此诗写于春天，为进京后的次年。本诗把政治上的际遇与自然界的春色融为一体，体现了中国诗词一贯含蓄的作风，要不是《夜直》这个题目略点主题，甚至会让读者以为这只是一首歌咏春色的诗,故而对于读者来说,结合创作背景正确理解这首诗的主题非常重要。但是三个译本,只有 Walls 对标题进行了翻译,或许这也是 Walls 意在帮助读者理解主题的用心之体现。

本诗是一首七言绝句。全诗四句,每句七言,在押韵、粘对等方面有严格的格律要求。由于篇幅短小,故语句精练含蓄,多言外之音。按平仄律,七言绝句有四种标准句型:

一、平起首句入韵式:可平可仄仄平平,可仄平平仄仄平。可仄可平平仄仄,可平可仄仄平平;

二、平起首句不入韵式:可平可仄平平仄,可仄平平仄仄平。可仄可平平仄仄,可平可仄仄平平;

三、仄起首句入韵式:可仄平平仄仄平,可平可仄仄平平。可平可仄平平仄,可仄平平仄仄平;

四、仄起首句不入韵式:可仄可平平仄仄,可平可仄仄平平。可平可仄平平仄,可仄平平仄仄平。

其平仄粘对具有一定的灵活性,即所谓的"一三五不论,二四六分明",但也要避免犯孤平和三平调。

如此可见,本诗属于第一种,韵脚为"残""寒""干",三版译文皆通过逗号赋予译文节奏。但是 Walls 牺牲了原诗的韵律;Robert Kotewall 借助 "fades"与"balustrade"形成押韵;Giles 在韵律上更为考究,形成 aabb 的韵律,使译文富有音乐性。

"金炉香尽漏声残,翦翦轻风阵阵寒。"寥寥几字却汇集了视觉、嗅觉、听觉和触觉,形象地表达了深夜里对时间与环境的感受。"金炉香尽""漏声残"都表现出长夜时光的流逝。此句是作者感受到的凉意和清新。Kotewall 通过"golden""burns""sound"和"gusts of chill"再现了这些感官体验,并通过重复使用"snip"再现原诗"翦翦"与"阵阵"两个叠词的效果;Walls 通过"cool upon cool"再现叠词效果,使用"swishes time"非常巧妙地点明时间之流逝,采用以动衬静的手法以微风沙沙作响显深夜之沉静,引申开来为下文作者心绪澎湃难以入眠作铺垫；Giles虽然没有使用重复的方法，但是他借助"breeze blows"这个头韵的方法使译文朗朗上口，以一个"midnight"点明此时夜已深，对应上文的"金炉香尽""漏声残"。

"春色恼人眠不得，月移花影上栏干"中的"恼人"可谓诗眼所在。"恼"字是反义正用，不能作恼恨的"恼"理解，应作"撩"解，意为春色撩人。此外"眠不得"不仅仅是因为春色留人醒，更是作者心中因君臣际遇，即将大展宏图而激动兴奋无法成眠。王安石久蓄改革之志，曾向仁宗皇帝上《万言书》，倡言改革，未被采纳。神宗即位，才使他获得了实现抱负的机会。此外，"春色"一词有时含有政治意义，如杜甫《奉和贾至舍人早朝大明宫》："五夜漏声催晓箭，九重春色醉仙桃。"《宋史·乐志》："回龙驭，升丹阙，布皇泽，春色满人间。"此情此景，自然是无法心绪寡淡酣然入睡的。"月移花影"与前文的"香尽""漏声残"相呼应，表明深夜时光悄声流淌；同时这画面感极强的文字，像电影一般让读者感受到一种东风相借、时来运转的故事感，仿佛下一幕便是东方肚白，也是王安石新法下的河清海晏、政治昌明。

对于诗眼"恼人"，Walls选择"provokes"这样一个很有主动性甚至攻击性的词。这种强烈的情感表达，使作者情难自抑，无法入眠的形象跃然纸上。Kotewall选择"tease"这样一个愉快的、具有互动性的词，从另一个角度表达了作者此时愉悦的心情。"tease"带给读者一种轻松感，没有沉吟多年、一朝得愿后的沉重释怀，而是一种年少得志的松弛感，美则美矣，却略失稳重。Giles没有正面处理"恼人"和"眠不得"，而是采用反话正说的方式，"slumber"可作一语双关之解，不仅是人无眠而"kept away from slumber"，死气沉沉的（slumber）政坛是否会因作者的新政而焕发生机呢？或许下文的"Sweet shapes of flowers across the blind"便是作者给的答案吧。

【原文】

南乡子

自古帝王州,

郁郁葱葱佳气浮。

四百年来成一梦,

堪愁。

晋代衣冠成古丘。

绕水恣行游。

上尽层城更上楼。

往事悠悠君莫问,

回头。

槛外长江空自流。

【释义】

　　这里曾是历代帝王建都之所,周围树木葱茏繁茂,山环水绕,云蒸霞蔚。可是,四百年来的繁华隆盛已像梦一般逝去,使人感叹。那晋代的帝王将相,早已是一抔黄土,被历史遗弃。

　　绕着江岸尽情地游行游赏。登上一层楼,再上一层楼。往事悠悠,早已不值一问,不如早回头。往事如烟,就像这槛外无情的江水空自东流。

【译文】

Lyrics for the Tune "Nan Xiang Zi"

For ages, the land of kings,

floating in a blessed aura

of fullness and plenty,

four hundred years, and now

nothing but a dream.

So sad !

Jin Dynasty caps and gowns

now burial mounds.

I wander at will along a winding stream,

and climb to the top of a city wall

and to the top of its tower.

The past is so remote,

don't even ask where it goes,

just turn around :

beyond the railing, only the Yangtze

River still flows.

(Translated by J. W. Walls & Y. L. Walls)

Tune : A Southern Song

The capital was ruled by kings since days gone by.

The rich green and lush gloom breathe a majestic sigh.

Like dreams has passed the reign of four hundred long years,

Which calls forth tears.

Ancient laureates are buried like their ancient peers.

Along the river I go where I will ;

Up city walls and watch towers I gaze my fill.

Do not ask what has passed without leaving a trail!

To what avail?

The endless river rolls in vain beyond the rail.

[Translated by Xu Yuanchong（许渊冲）]

【评析】

关于这首词的创作时间，高克勤《王安石诗文选评》定于治平四年（1067）前后，李德身《王安石诗文系年》定于治平元年（1064），皆在变法（1069年）之前。同《浣溪沙》一样，《南乡子》也是词牌名，讲究格律，原为单调，始自后蜀欧阳炯，直至南唐冯延巳始增为双调。以欧阳炯《南乡子·画舸停桡》为正体，单调，二十七字，五句两平韵、三仄韵。单调有二十八字、三十字等变体，平仄换韵。双调有五十四、五十六、五十八字等变体。本词为双调五十六字，韵脚为"州""悠""丘""游""楼""头""流"。从韵的角度看，许渊冲先生的译本形成 aabbb、ccccc 的韵，尤其是下阕一韵到底，可见许先生译诗功底之深厚。

原词上阕以宏大的气势开篇，点明金陵的古都气场，郁郁葱葱，龙盘虎踞。Walls 将"浮"直译为"floating"便描绘了一片气象万千、王气浮盛之地。许先生同样不甘示弱，"breathe a majestic sigh"同样给读者呈现了一种气吞万里的古都气势。

而后原文笔锋一转，由描写绮丽的景色转为嗟叹王朝兴亡更迭，"堪愁"两字，寄托了作者深沉的忧思。东晋时代煊赫一时的豪门世族，如今都化为累累古坟荒冢，仅此一点，就可想见六朝霸业已矣，表达了作者对历史变迁的感慨怅惘之情。而对于这种感情，Walls 的"nothing but"向读者表达了对如烟如梦的四百年已逝、兴衰荣辱终究都成过往的慨叹。"Jin Dynasty"和"now"这种时间对比也勾起读者的怀古之情。金陵依然岿然不动，但风流人物已湮没在时光洪流之中，如今只剩一抔黄土。许先生将"晋代衣冠"做了解释性处理，他并没有选择直译，而是将原文"衣冠"代指"人"这个功能清晰化，以"ancient laureates are buried like their ancient peers"表达了一种"俱往矣"的感叹,也颇有"旧时王谢堂前燕,飞入寻常百姓家"所表达的世事嬗变之情。

上阕写景怀古,下阕进入"伤今"情绪。作者绕着河岸恣意漫步,爬上城头又更上一层楼。中国古诗中"上尽层楼"含有"登高怀远""登高而愁"的情感,也暗含了作者思绪不宁、心事难遣之情。此时的宋朝积贫积弱,作者希望朝廷能够励精图治,实现国富民强,这也是王安石要辅佐宋神宗变法革新、挽救日益衰弱的北宋王朝的原因。眼见时光流逝,事业未竟,面对着滔滔江水,他不禁发出了"往事悠悠君莫问"的感慨。以"槛外长江空自流"作结,形成了一个高远深邃而又生生不息的意境。Walls 使用两个"top"传递"上尽层楼"之意,结合时代背景,也暗示了作者要想实现其政治抱负依然是任重道远,颇有"一山放过一山拦"的意味。但译者明白作者不是悲观的,结尾的"still"便是很好的证明。虽然一时无法实现政治愿望,但是江水悠悠,从古流到今,这样的活力何尝不是蕴蓄着希望呢?这样的处理方式再现了原文传递的意境,即莫问往事,带着热切的期盼向前看。

下阕许先生的"I gaze my fill"可以说是掌握了"登高怀远"的文化密码,登上高处,满腹报国精忠之心更显得壮志难酬。或许许先生是同情王安石的,同情他才华没有得到施展,同情他虽然渴望兼济天下,忧国忧民,但是宏业未竟,忧思难遣,所以在"roll"这样一个体现奔腾生命力的词后,加了一个"in vain",两者形成剧烈反差,这种无穷的凄凉让人喟然长叹。

三、译论·比较

作为中华文明的宝贵遗产,古诗凝聚着集体文化记忆,凸显着民族的历史叙事、文韵与气节,正所谓"以诗述史、以诗叙情、以诗显志"。相应地,古诗外译成为向世界讲好中国故事的最佳切入点之一,其富含有中国叙事的话语色彩,能够在传译中充分体现中国智慧。因此,古诗英译或可遵循一些宏观要旨:

首先，秉持传播思维，立足国情，积极围绕现实所需进行译介。西学东渐以降，很长时段内主要是非本土译者在进行古诗外译。我们一方面要认可其所作出的传播贡献，另一方面也应反思其译介立场往往也是非本土的。如此一来，传播过程中亦然发生了文学形象的偏离甚或造成了国家形象的歪曲。现如今，国家外译推崇"本土译者+外国译者"联合进行，但限于条件，"本土译者仍是古诗英译的主力军。他们在翻译选材上更加有针对性，在翻译理念上更能体现'文以载道'的文学传统……那些充满家国情怀、仁爱精神、和平愿望、生活智慧，以及使人明理悟道的古诗，已成为重点译介和阐释的对象"（严晓江，2023）。因此，在评价译作时也应当审视古诗中所蕴含的中华民族精神和中华传统美德是否得到了尊重、理解与认同。

其次，坚守话语阵地，鉴往知来，运用"反向翻译"视角形成自身的译学理论意识。西方学者曾借助翻译中国古诗来形成自身的话语论述，生成相应的译论主张，进而对自身的社会历史文化语境作出翻译视角的解读。如美国诗人庞德在英译中国诗歌的过程中形成了"意象主义"诗歌理论，进而引领了美国诗歌的创新与新风尚。换言之，这是将中国古诗作为"他山之石"来思考或解决本土问题。虽然这在客观上促发了中国诗歌的国际传播，但被作为"他山之石"而生成的理论指导被直接拿来观照中国式问题，显然有些不恰当与不合理，对此至少应该心存质疑。因此，作为翻译者或译评人，在重新审视他者的翻译文本以及由此提炼的翻译理论时，可以运用"反向翻译"思维，即通过思考"为何译？如何译？译之效？效之用？"来抵达他者翻译的深层话语语境，进而"取其精华去其糟粕"，在解决本土具体问题时自然生发出自身的译学理论意识。

古诗具有的历史价值与魅力应当在新时代获得跨越时空的话语传播并创造相应的叙事贡献。诗无达诂，译无定法。唯有坚守了"道"层面的宏观要旨，彰显鲜明的民族性，才能在"技"的层面有所建树，体现出真正的世界性。因此，译者与译评人需要充分展现出中国人的诗情文脉和精神气韵，弘扬中华优秀传统诗文，促进中西话语融通，使古诗智慧走向世界。

这有益于人类命运共同体，亦是新时代赋予本土译者与译评人的历史使命与责任担当。

鉴于此，请按照以下要点对 Burton Watson 所译的王安石七言古诗《收盐》进行文本鉴析：

（1）对《收盐》所体现的社会历史文化语境进行思考；

（2）比较原文与译文，思考各自凸显的话语重点。

收盐

州家飞符来比栉，海中收盐今复密。
穷囚破屋正嗟邰，吏兵操舟去复出。
海中诸岛古不毛，岛夷为生今独劳。
不煎海水饿死耳，谁肯坐守无亡逃？
尔来贼盗往往有，劫杀贾客沈其艘。
一民之生重天下，君子忍与争秋毫？

Confiscating Salt

(Salt was a government monopoly and the officials made every effort to prevent people living on the seacoast from boiling water and extracting salt for private profit. The poem attacks the government for depriving the people of a possible livelihood and competing with them for profit. 7-ch. old style.)

From the local office, orders flying thicker than comb's teeth:
along the seacoast, salt confiscation stricter than ever.
Poverty moans and sobs under a broken roof
while boatloads of inspectors patrol back and forth.
Islands of the ocean, from times past lean and barren;
island folk struggling just to keep alive:

boil sea water or starve to death;

who can sit unmoving, not try to escape?

And now they say there are pirates hereabouts

who murder traveling merchants, scuttle their boats —

The life of one subject weighs heavier than the realm!

What true man would vie with others for a hairbreadth's gain?

(Translated by Burton Watson)

四、实践·译笔

半山春晚即事①

王安石

春风取花去,酬我以清阴。

翳翳陂路静②,交交园屋深。

床敷每小息,杖屦或幽寻③。

惟有北山鸟,经过遗好音④。

【注】

① 半山:在江苏江宁,由县东门到钟山,恰好为一半路程,故称作半山。春晚:即晚春,暮春。即事:就眼前景物作诗。

② 翳翳:树阴浓暗的样子。陂路:湖岸,塘堤。

③ 床敷:安置卧具。杖屦:拄杖漫步。幽寻,探寻风景之胜。

④ 北山:钟山。王安石有《思北山》等诗,寄托真心隐逸的心境。遗:赠送,这里引申为留下之意。好音:美妙的叫声。

五、阅读·延展

翻译外国诗是不是"可能"?

翻译外国诗应该不应该有什么一定要遵守的"原则"?

翻译外国诗有什么"好处";换句话说,就是"为什么要翻译外国诗?"

这一串的问题,凡翻译过外国诗的,大概总想起过。对于第一个问题已有许多不同的见解:有人说,外国诗是可以翻译的;有人说不可以;又有人说,外国诗中有可以翻译的,也有绝对不能翻译的,而可以翻译的,也不过是将就的办法,聊胜于无而已。

在这三种说法里,我们赞成的是第三种。我们承认:诗经过翻译,即使译得极谨慎,和原文极吻合,亦只能算是某诗的 Retold(译述),不能视为即是原诗。原诗所备的种种好处,翻译时只能保留一二种,决不能完全保留。所以诗的翻译,又和描摹名画不同。描摹一幅名画,或者竟可以把原画的各种好处,都"具体而微"地表现在摹本里;但是翻译外国诗却不能如此。如果译者勉强要这样做,结果一定是空费气力,反使译本一无足取。翻译"有律"的外国诗,此层尤为显然。所以老实说来,翻译外国诗是不得已的,聊胜于无的办法。

那么,何必翻译外国诗呢?在这里,我们就到了第三个问题:翻译外国诗有什么用处。如果翻译外国诗没有多大的意义,不过是文人游戏而已,本问题就不必多讨论了;如果翻译外国诗不过"报告外国花园里有几种花卉,新开了什么花"而已,本问题也就没有严重注意的价值了;如果翻译外国诗不过因为外国文中既有此种杰作,所以我们不可不有一种译本,那么,本问题也就得否定的答语。我以为翻译外国诗是有一种积极的意义的。

这就是:借此(外国诗的翻译)可以感发本国诗的革新。我们翻开各国文学史来,常常看见译本的传入是本国文学史上一个新运动的导线;翻译诗的传入,至少在诗坛方面,要有这等的影响发生。

据这一点看来,译诗对于本国文坛含有重大的意义;对于将有新兴文艺崛起的民族,含有更重大的意义。这本不独译诗为然,一切文学作品的译本对于新的民族文学的崛起,都是有间接的助力的;俄国、捷克、波兰等国的近代文学史都或多或少地证明了这个例。在我国,也已露了端倪。

(摘自茅盾《译诗的一些意见》)

Within the field of literary translation, more time has been devoted to investigating the problems of translating poetry than any other literary mode. Many of the studies purporting to investigate these problems are either evaluations of different translations of a single work or personal statements by individual translators on how they have set about solving problems. Rarely do studies of poetry and translation try to discuss methodological problems from a nonempirical position, and yet it is precisely that type of study that is most valuable and most needed.

In his book on the various methods employed by English translators of Catullus' *Poem* 64, André Lefevere catalogues seven different strategies:

(1) *Phonemic translation*, which attempts to reproduce the SL sound in the TL while at the same time producing an acceptable paraphrase of the sense. Lefevere comes to the conclusion that although this works moderately well in the translation of onomatopoeia, the overall result is clumsy and often devoid of sense altogether.

(2) *Literal translation*, where the emphasis on word-for-word translation distorts the sense and the syntax of the original.

(3) *Metrical translation*, where the dominant criterion is the reproduction of the SL metre. Lefevere concludes that, like literal translation, this method concentrates on one aspect of the SL text at the expense of the text as a whole.

(4) *Poetry into prose*. Here Lefevere concludes that distortion of the sense, communicative value and syntax of the SL text results from this method, although not to the same extent as with the literal or metrical types of translation.

(5) *Rhymed translation*, where the translator "enters into a double bondage" of metre and rhyme. Lefevere's conclusions here are particularly harsh, since he feels that the end product is merely a "caricature" of Catullus.

(6) *Blank verse translation*. Again the restrictions imposed on the translator by the choice of structure are emphasized, although the greater accuracy and higher degree of literalness obtained are also noted.

(7) *Interpretation*. Under this heading, Lefevere discusses what he calls versions where the substance of the SL text is retained but the form is changed, and *imitations* where the translator produces a poem of his own which has "only title and point of departure, if those, in common with the source text".

What emerges from Lefevere's study is a revindication of the points made by Anne Cluysenaar, for the deficiencies of the methods he examines are due to an overemphasis of one or more elements of the poem at the expense of the whole. In other words, in establishing a set of methodological criteria to follow, the translator has focused on some elements at the expense of others and from this failure to consider the poem as an organic structure comes a translation that is demonstrably unbalanced. However, Lefevere's use of the term *version* is rather misleading, for it would seem to imply a distinction between this and *translation*, taking as the basis for the argument a split between form and substance. Yet, as Popovič points out, "the translator has the right to differ organically, to be independent", provided that independence is pursued for the sake of the original in order to reproduce it as a living work.

(Excerpts from *Translation Studies* by Susan Bassnett)

第七单元

理学至尊·南宋朱熹

一、译事·译研

朱熹（1130—1200），字元晦，号晦庵，世称晦庵先生、朱文公。今江西婺源人，南宋伟大的思想家、哲学家和教育家，理学之集大成者、程朱理学的代表人物，乃孔孟之后中国历史上最伟大的儒学大家。其思想学说被称为"朱子学"，影响深远。朱子理论认为，"理"乃形而上，"气"为形而下，天地万物的形成是"理"赋予其中，加以"禀气"而成"形"。现如今，在面对不断加强社会主义精神文明建设、促进社会健康和谐稳定发展、妥善处理他人与自身、个人与社会之间的关系等问题时，朱熹的思想仍有很多值得借鉴之处，如他提出的"克己""无私""主敬涵养""穷理致知""不以一毫私意自蔽，不以一毫私欲自累"等，对个人修养提高、人格提升、社会赋格有着重要意义。

早在13世纪，朱子学就已流播于朝鲜、日本、越南等邻邦国家，16世纪开始译介入西方，如利玛窦在相关著述中就对朱子学的部分思想持否定和批判的态度。19世纪后，朱子学经历了德译、法译、英译，获得了更为广泛的翻译传播，其学说声望也随之扩大到了全世界，先后影响了西方的怀疑论、偶因论、单子论等（林金水，1997）。

朱子学英译主要始于19世纪初。马礼逊（R. Morrison）是向英语世界传播朱学的第一人（田莎、朱健平，2020）。其在英译《大学》（1812）、编撰《华英字典》（*A Dictionary of Chinese Language*）时融入了朱子注释，引用了朱熹之说释字。在1819年发表的《中国形而上学》（*Chinese Metaphysics*）中，马礼逊更是花长篇幅系统介绍了朱子学，包括理气论中的"太极""理""气"等核心概念。可以说，马礼逊具有首译朱子之功，在随后的1820—1844年间译述朱子学的文章十余篇。汉学家麦都思（Medhurst）于1844年在《中国丛报》（第13卷第10、12期）上翻译发表了《理气》和《太极》，开启了朱子著述之英译。1849年，裨治文也在《中国丛报》上先后英译《朱子生平》（*Memoir of the Philosopher Chu*）和《中国宇宙论》（*Notices of Chinese Cosmogony*），其运用评注等翻译手法改写理气论，将朱熹塑造为一个思想落后的唯物论者（帅司阳，2018）。其后，英国传教士麦丽芝再译朱子理气论（英译《全书》第49卷理气论全篇），造就了朱学首部英文译著。而这部译著也招致传教士湛约翰对其中误译和误释的学术批评，迎来了朱学学术研究及其专业文献翻译的契机。理雅各和卫三畏也分别在英译四书五经（1861—1886）和修订《中国总论》（*The Middle Kingdom*，1883）时系统介绍了朱学，推动了朱学的传播。

到了20世纪，世界大战后弥漫的文化危机意识使得西方学者转向中国传统思想，以期寻求新的精神寄托并进行价值反思，朱学英译也随之进入了"以西释朱"期。最早是由卜道成（J. P. Bruce）在1922年翻译了朱学的哲学内核，以此作为西方哲学参照的价值标准。卜道成在译介朱学思想时认为，"朱熹是中国乃至世界上最伟大的思想家之一……西方哲学和宗教学界可以对照朱熹哲学进行比较哲学和宗教学研究，以进一步丰富西方思想的理论内涵"。随后，美国汉学家卜德（Bodde）在翻译冯友兰的《中国哲学史（上）》时，运用比较哲学的跨文化再诠释，对朱学进行了更为系统的英译与理解。他将朱学和西哲互参互鉴，着力于反思西哲逻辑与脉络。因此卜德指出，"朱熹哲学尽管以伦理为最终旨趣，但他将逻辑与伦理融于一'理'，这一做法十分可贵"（Bodde，1942）。

进入20世纪下半叶，朱学英译从"以西释朱"走向了"以朱释朱"，即前者的比较与比附思维使得朱学真义难以得到彰显。因此，为了还原朱学本来面目，译介的路径也开始变为运用朱子理论内核来解读朱学要义。陈荣捷就是"以朱释朱"的先行者。早在1939年时，他便开始有意识地介绍朱学。1963年，陈荣捷编译的 *A Source Book in Chinese Philosophy*（《中国哲学资料书》）由普林斯顿大学出版社出版，其中第三十四章 *The Great Synthesis of Chu His* 翻译了朱熹的四篇哲学短文（《仁说》《明道论性说》《与湖南诸公论中和第一书》《观心说》），还从《朱子全书》中选译了147条语录。陈氏翻译还注重从纵向角度阐明朱子思想的渊源，如在英译《近思录》（*Reflections on Things at Hand: the Neo-Confucian Anthology Compiled by Chuhsi and LuTsu-Ch'ien*）时，他就从朱熹对周敦颐、张载等所作的批注以及中、朝、日三国儒学家的评注中选译了数百节（陈荣捷，2003），以使读者对朱学有一个纵向的了解。此外，陈氏翻译还最大限度地保持原作风格及语体，显现原作思想，为西方学界研究朱学提供了权威译本，在推动新儒学思想的传播方面作出了巨大的贡献。

朱学不仅属于中国，也属于世界。纵览朱学英译，尽管《近思录》《续近思录》与《家礼》均有英译本问世，但其重要思想著述《朱子全书》仍未译全。因此，在中国文化走出去、中西文化交融互鉴的时代背景下，当代译者应当讲述朱子故事，加强朱子学文献的翻译与出版工作，进一步促进中西文明对话、探求朱学的世界性意义并将其作为构建"人类命运共同体"的丰富思想资源。

二、鉴赏·评析

朱熹以礼持家、知行并用的家训及其思想，不仅为和谐的家庭关系提供了理论依据和行动指南，而且对后世的伦理观念、哲学思想、教育理念等都具有重要的影响，在特定的历史时期着实发挥着道德教化、价值引领的作用。

【原文】

家礼·卷二·冠礼

冠

　　男子年十五至二十，皆可冠。司马公曰："古者二十而冠，所以责成人之礼，盖将责为人子，为人弟，为人臣，为人少者之行于其人，故其礼不可以不重也。近世以来，人情轻薄，过十岁而总角者，少矣。彼责以四者之行，岂知之哉？往往自幼至长，愚騃若一，由不知成人之道故也。今虽未能遽革，且自十五以上俟其能通《孝经》、《论语》，粗知礼义然后冠之，其亦可也。"必父母无期以上丧，始可行之。大功未葬，亦不可行。

　　前期三日，主人告于祠堂。古礼筮日，今不能然，但正月内择一日可也。主人，谓冠者之祖父。自为继高祖之宗子者。若非宗子，则必继高祖之宗子主之。有故则命其次宗子。若其父自主之，告礼见《祠堂》章，祝版前同，但云"某之子某，若某之某亲之子，某年渐长成，将以某月某日，加冠于其首，谨以"，后同。若族人以宗子之命自冠其子，其祝版亦以宗子为主，曰："使介子某。"若宗子已孤而自冠，则亦自为主人，祝版前同，但云"某将以某月某日，加冠于首，谨以"，后同。戒宾。古礼筮宾，今不能然，但择朋友贤而有礼者一人可也。是日，主人深衣，诣其门，所戒者出见，如常仪。啜茶毕，戒者起言曰："某有子某，若某之某亲有子某，将加冠于其首，愿吾子之教之也。"对曰："某不敏，恐不能供其事，以病吾子，敢辞。"戒者曰："愿吾子之终教之也。"对曰："吾子重有命，某敢不从。"地远，则书初请之辞为书，遣子弟致之。所戒者辞，使者固请乃许，而复书曰："吾子有命，某敢不从。"若宗子自冠，则戒辞但曰"某将加冠于首"，后同。

　　……

　　冠者见于尊长。父母堂中南面坐。诸叔父兄在东序，诸叔父南向，诸兄西向。诸妇女在西序，诸叔母姑南向，诸姊嫂东向。冠者北向拜父母，父母为之起。同居有尊长，则父母以冠者诣其室拜之，尊长为之起，还就东西序。每列再拜，应答拜者答拜。若非宗子之子，则先见宗子，及诸尊于父者于堂，乃就私室见于父母及余亲。若宗子自冠，有母则见于母如仪。族人宗之者，皆来见于堂上。宗子西向拜其尊长，每列再拜，受卑幼者拜。

（节选自朱熹：《朱子家礼》）

【译文】

The Capping Ceremony: Capping

(ABSTRACT)

Any young man from fifteen to twenty years of age may be capped, provided that his parents are not in mourning for a period of a year or longer. Three days before the event, the presiding man makes a report at the offering hall, then personally invites the sponsor. The day before, he invites the sponsor again and has the equipment arranged. At dawn on the day of the event, the caps and robes are set out. The participants line up, in order, from the presiding man on down. When the sponsor arrives, the presiding man invites him to enter the hall. The sponsor, with a salute, beckons the initiant to go to the mat, then puts the head-cloth on him. The initiant returns to the side room where he puts on the long garment and shoes before reappearing. The second capping entails a hat, black robe, leather belt, and tie shoes. The third capping entails the scarf-cap, official robes, great belt, boots, and official plaque, or alternatively the ordinary robe and boots. After the pledge, the sponsor gives an adult name to the initiant. The participants leave in order, after which the presiding man presents the initiant in the offering hall and then to the elders. The sponsor is then entertained. Afterward, the initiant goes out to be presented to local elders and his father's friends.

● Any young man from fifteen to twenty years of age may be capped.

The venerable Ssu-ma [Kuang] said, "The ancients performed capping at twenty as a ritual through which a youth was charged with acting as an adult. That is, 'one then expected of the young man the conduct of a son, a younger brother, a subject, and a junior.' Therefore the ceremony had to be treated seriously. In recent times, people are flippant in their attitude toward it. Very few boys are still wearing 'hair horns' beyond ten. What can such boys know about expectations of the four kinds of conduct? All too often they are uniformly foolish from childhood to maturity, for they know nothing of adult ways. Today, although instant change is not feasible, it should be all right to delay capping the young man until he is fifteen or older and can understand the Classic of Filial Piety and the Analects, and has a rough knowledge of ritual and moral principles."

● The ceremony may not be performed if the young man's parents are in mourning for a period of a year or longer.

It also may not be performed if they are in "greater processed cloth" [nine-month] mourning and the burial has not yet taken place

● Three days before the event, the presiding man makes a report at the offering hall.

In the ancient ritual, one chose the day by divination. Today that is not practical, but one may select a day in the first month. The term "'presiding man' refers to the father or grandfather of the initiant when either of them is the descent-line heir of the great-great-grandfather. Otherwise, the descent-line heir of the great-great-grandfather must act as presiding man. If circumstances prevent this, then one of the successive descent-line heirs may act as presiding man.

For the ceremony of the report when the father acts as presiding man himself, see the section on the offering hall [chapter 1, no. 1].

The prayer board begins like the ones described there, then has:

A's son B, or A's such-relative C's son B, who now has grown older and reached maturity, will have a cap placed on his head on such day of such month. Earnestly, ...

When someone caps his own son on orders of the descent-line heir, it should still be the descent-line heir who takes charge of the prayer board, saying that a lesser son, C, has been ordered to carry out the ceremony.

If the descent-line heir's father and grandfather are both dead and he caps himself, then he also acts as presiding man. The prayer board begins the same, but says, "A will, on such day of such month, place a cap on his own head. Earnestly, ..."

● Personally invite the sponsor.

In the ancient ritual, one divined to select the sponsor. Today that is impractical, but one may select a friend who is wise and versed in ritual. On that day the presiding man in the long garment goes in person to the gate of the friend he is inviting, who comes out to meet him, as in ordinary etiquette.

When they finish their tea, the caller rises and says, "A has a son B (or A's such-relative C has a son B) who will have a cap placed on his head. We would like to have you, sir, instruct him."

He answers, "I am not quick and fear that, being inadequate to the task, I will cause you trouble, sir. I presume to decline."

The caller responds, "We still would like you, sir, to instruct him."

He replies, "As you, sir, have repeated your command, I dare not disobey."

If the sponsor lives far away, then write a letter expressing the initial request and send a younger relative to deliver it. When the recipient declines, the messenger insists, at which point he consents. He also writes a reply, saying, "As you, sir, have ordered it, I, X, dare not disobey."

If the descent-line heir is capping himself, then the phrases of the invitation are "A will be placing a cap on his own head ···"

● The initiant is presented to the elders.

His parents sit in the hall, facing south. His younger uncles and elder brothers are on the eastern side, the younger uncles facing south, the elder brothers west. Their wives and daughters are on the western side, the wives of the younger uncles and the aunts facing south, the elder sisters and the wives of elder brothers facing east. The initiant faces north toward his parents and bows to them. They rise for him.

If anyone of a senior generation lives with them, then the parents bring the initiant to the senior person's room to bow to him or her. The senior person rises for him. After he returns, he goes to the east and west sides, bowing twice for each status category. Those who should return the bow do so.

When the initiant is not a son of the descent-line heir, he is presented first to the descent-line heir, then to those who are senior to his father in the hall, then to his parents in a private room, and then to the remaining relatives.

When a descent-line heir caps himself, if his mother is alive he is presented to her, as in the ceremonial described here. Other kinsmen ritually subordinate to him all come to see him be presented in the hall. The descent-line heir bows facing west. Each rank of his seniors bows twice. He also accepts the bows of his juniors.

（Translated by Patricia Buckley Ebrey）

【评析】

根据雅各布森（1971）的分类法，翻译可分为三类：语内翻译（intralingual translation），是指在同一种语言之内以某种语言符号去解释另一种语言符号；语际翻译（interlingual translation），是指在两种语言之间以某种语言符号去解释另一种语言符号；符际翻译（intersemiotic translation），则指以一些非语言符号去解释语言符号，又或相反，以一些语言符号去解释非语言符号。而 Gottlieb（2005）进一步把语内翻译分为四类，即历时性的翻译（diachronic translation）、方言性的翻译（dialectal translation）、语言模式转变的翻译（diamesic translation）和音译（transliteration）。本文节选自《朱子家礼》，根据杨自俭（2005）的观点，"中国清代末年（19世纪中叶近现代汉语分界处）以前的重要文献和书籍"都可界定为"典籍"。而典籍翻译的过程比把一个现代文本翻译成另一个现代文本要复杂，涉及的因素也要多些。典籍翻译过程是"一个二度翻译过程，包括语内翻译和语际翻译两个阶段"（方梦之，2011），这个"翻译过程增加了一个语内翻译阶段，原文为古代或近代汉语，译文为现代英语，中间为现代汉语"（杨自检，2005）。像《朱子家礼》这样的典籍翻译的特点之一，就是它通常要经过语内翻译和语际翻译两个阶段。也就是说，从事语际翻译（如把汉语典籍翻译为现代英语）的人，他通常必须先把用古汉语撰写的典籍"翻译"（"解释"）成现代汉语，然后再根据现代汉语版本翻译成现代英语。在进行语内翻译时，必须考虑包括时间上的差异、社会以及文化习俗的变化等因素。至于在语际翻译之前所做的语内翻译，大致有两种处理办法：一种是把典籍原文变成一个典籍的今译版本；另一种则是译者在头脑中将典籍原文译为今译版本，这个版本只存在于译者的头脑中，并非"看得见摸得着"的"今译"版本。也就是说，把用文言文撰写的典籍翻译成现代汉语的这个语内翻译过程，可以有明显的实际文本，也可以是只存在于译者头脑中的"后源语文本"(post-source-text)，即介于源语与目的语之间的文本。虽然本文译者没有明显采用语内翻译的过程，即没有事先把它翻译成现代汉语版本，然后再把它翻译成英文。但是，在译者的头脑中还是经过了一个语内翻译过程（即把文言文典籍翻译成现代汉语版本）。这是因为，把源语转换成目的语要经过一个"加工"(processing)过程。Bell（1991，2001）对翻译过程进行了深入的阐述，用了好几个图解（有的非常详细、复杂）来说明。他的一个非常简单的翻译过程流程图（详见图7-1），可以帮助我们说明上述的"加工"过程。我们可以借助Bell的翻译过程流程图，对译者做的语内翻译进行分析。

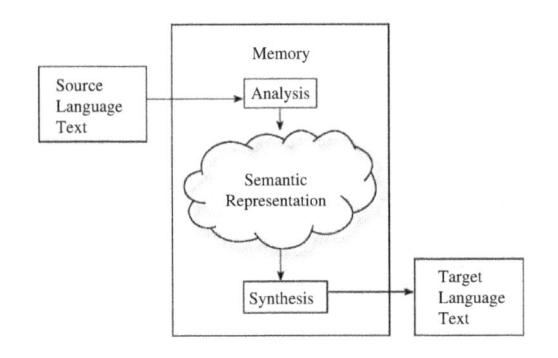

图7-1　Bell的翻译过程流程图

虽然Bell的这个过程流程图比较简单，但它已经清楚勾勒了从源语到目的语的转换过程。该图表明：把源语转换成目的语是在"记忆"（Memory）这个过程中发生的。在进行转换之前，译者必须通过（语言、语境）"分析"（Analysis）来解读、阐释源语所表达和隐含的意义，即理解源语的"语义表征"（Semantic representation）。这里所说的语义表征是比语言表达更为抽象的概念，属于比语言结构更深层的范畴。源语的语义表征一经确定，译者便对语义和信息进行"综合"（Synthesis）处理，然后通过目的语语码来表达这些语义表征和源语所表达和隐含的意义，这样就产生了目的语（译文）（黄国文，2012）。语词有"历时性流变"，即同一语词在一个历史时期中被普遍认可的意义在另一时期会消失或变更。《朱子家礼》成于南宋，译者Ebrey将之翻译为现代英语是在20世纪八九十年代，几百年的岁月变迁使得中文也在不断变化，接下来我们结合原文本和译文分析译者的语内翻译过程。

"人情轻薄"今义为"人与人之间的感情、情谊、互助等关系变得越来越少，缺乏温暖和真诚"，但是译文并没有采取今义。译者根据语境，在头脑中经过了一个语内翻译过程，通过（语言、语境）"分析"（Analysis）来解读、阐释源语所表达和隐含的意义，理解源语的"语义表征"（Semantic representation），即不是人情淡薄，而是人们礼仪观念淡薄，人们对礼仪不再重视，故而译为"people are flippant in their attitude toward it"。

"必父母无期以上丧"中的"无期"今义释为：

（1）无穷尽，无限度；

（2）指无了期；

（3）犹言不知何时，难有机会；

（4）指没有约定日期。

以上四种，皆无"一年"之意，但是根据《墨子·公孟》："伯父、叔父、兄弟，期。"可知，"期"可表为去世的亲属服一年的丧，"期年"也表一整年，与今义相去甚远，所以译者在翻译为"his parents are not in mourning for a period of a year or longer"之前，通过"分析"解读、阐释源语所表达和隐含的意义，理解了源语的"语义表征"。

"戒宾"一词文中指通知各位同僚、朋友，邀请他们届时前来观礼。戒是"告知、通报、邀请"的意思，现代汉语的"戒"在生活中多表"警戒、戒备""留神、当心""戒除"等义，译文采用了古义"邀请"之意，译为"invites"，可见译者在进行语际翻译前进行了语内翻译。

"宿宾"的"宿"文内含义为"恭请"，即前往正宾家，恭请其主持冠礼。现代汉语中几乎不再使用"宿宾"这一表达，"宿"的动词含义也多为"过夜、守夜"，译者将"宿宾"译为"invites the sponsor again"，取古义。

"深衣"在古代指上衣、下裳相连缀的一种服装，为古代诸侯、大夫、士等居家穿的衣服，也是庶人的常礼服。现代一般不再使用"深衣"这一表述，即使使用，也多指深颜色的衣服。译者在语际翻译前进行语内翻译，译为"long garment"。但是我们可以看出，由于"深衣"一词存在文化烙印，译者在语际翻译中也未能完全译出其具体所指，而是采用了一个上义词进行笼统概括。可见在跨文化交际中，如何准确传达原文是译者必须面临的一个挑战。

"病吾子"中的"病"在现代汉语中通常做名词，指生物体发生不健康的现象，如疾病；缺点、不贴切，如语病；损害，祸害；不满、责备，如诟病等。作动词也多为口语，如"病了"。但是古义作动词时可表"担忧、忧虑"，如《论语·卫灵公》："君子病无能焉，不病人之不己知也。"也可表"羞辱、伤害"，如《答韦中立论师道书》："非独见病，亦以病吾子。"本文取"伤害"之意。现代汉语几乎不再使用"吾子"这个称谓,即便使用,也多为"我的儿子"之意。但"吾子"在古时表人的尊称,可译为"您",如柳宗元《柳河东集》"吾子自京师来"以及上文的《答韦中立论师道书》。译者在翻译"病吾子"时,先将古汉语在头脑中翻译为现代汉语,即"给您添麻烦",再进行语际翻译,译为"I will cause you trouble, sir"。

综上所述,典籍翻译通常要经过语内翻译和语际翻译两个阶段,即将典籍译成现代英文时,需要先把用文言文撰写的典籍翻译成现代汉语,然后再根据现代汉语把它翻译成英文。

按照语内翻译、语际翻译和符际翻译的分类,中华典籍的对外传播方式也需要更加多元化,其中符际翻译的作用值得我们探究。蔡志忠的典籍漫画译本俘获了许多国外普通读者。蔡氏用漫画翻译了26部典籍,出版后风靡东南亚和欧美多国,比如在美国,它便吸引了不同年龄和行业的诸多读者。蔡氏译本的符际翻译受到读者喜爱,原因在于它能与解读各阶段的影响要素形成互动,推动读者对译本解读的深化,例如,译本在处理人物勾绘和整体构图等视觉信息成分时,努力寻找中西图像审美的交汇点,强化图像的理据特性,从而吸引读者接收译本信息,增强了读者的感知(黄广哲、朱琳,2018)。除了漫画译本以外,影视作品也可以成为推动典籍对外传播的方式之一。总之,在推动朱子学海外传播的过程中,我们可以充分发挥(语内、语际和符际)翻译的作用。

三、译论·比较

翻译是意义的传译、意义的再生。而时空概念上不断发生的"延异"使翻译的"意义"始终处于一个不断发展的不稳定状态。从本质上说,翻译是一种永无休止的关于理解的对话过程(彭利元、蒋坚松,2005)。典籍翻译可视为对特定时期的文本进行对话理解与构建的行为,这也是对其哲学本质的深入剖析,即通过由翻译主体、翻译客体、翻译环境等要素所形成的对话网络,动态性地分析、解读、重构翻译文本,以此延续文化记忆。

翻译通过对话网络不断地从语内和语际两个方面使原作生命在时间和空间上得以延伸和扩展，这也是典籍翻译的必然过程与方法论。

典籍英译的哲学本质体现为对话，对话的流畅、正确实现是翻译的必要条件，而对话的执行主体是源文本说话人与目的文本潜在听话人。因此，典籍英译的核心就集中于各个翻译主体之间的互动、交流、对话及记忆交往。具体而言，这种对话性哲学本质可体现为两组方法论：

首先，共时对话翻译与历时对话翻译。前者是典籍翻译通过对话理解进行文本构建时受到相关、相近因素的影响，具有相对稳定性特征。后者是典籍文本各要素在历史的发展与演变中不断变化与协调，使之本身能与时代因素发生对话，进而完成文本构建，具有发展动态性。典籍英译以共时对话为依据，发掘"对话"在历时发展中的理解变迁，考察翻译文本的理解差异，进而展现事物的形象演化与记忆流传轨迹。

其次，语内对话翻译与语际对话翻译。典籍翻译过程是一个二度翻译过程，包括语内翻译和语际翻译两个阶段。任何中国典籍，其源语文本是文言文，在其英译之前必然要经过语内同文化语境中文本话语人与潜在听话人的对话博弈，继而以这轮对话为基础搭建语际异文化语境中文本话语人与潜在听话人对话之桥梁。典籍文化的精髓可通过"对话"的形式传译于异文化群体，即首先在语内翻译的基础上历时性地与源文本对话，实现同文化语境的意义阐释，继而通过语际翻译实现不同文化语境的转换和文化记忆的移植，而贯穿其整个翻译过程的始终是"说话人与潜在听话人之间的对话关系"。这一实践过程强调对话主体的平等、互动和共通，体现客观文本的人文精神本质，实现翻译的"和谐共在"，这也体现了典籍英译的目的和宗旨。

鉴于此，请按照以下要点对陈荣捷（Wing-Tsit Chan）所译的朱熹《近思录》选段进行鉴析：

（1）从学术角度了解《近思录》所表达的整体思想概要；

（2）立足于读者（听者）的角度，比较原文与译文，思考其间的语内、语际翻译过程。

诚无为,几善恶。德爱曰仁,宜曰义,理曰礼,通曰智,守曰信。性焉安焉之谓圣,复焉执焉之谓贤。发微不可见,充周不可穷之谓神。《通书》(第三章)

朱子曰:"诚无为",诚,实理也。无为,犹寂然不动也。实理该贯动静,而其本体则无为也。"几善恶",几者,动之征。动则有为而善恶形矣。诚无为,则善而已。动而有为,则有善有恶。

又曰:仁义礼智信者,德之体。曰爱,曰宜,曰理,曰通,曰守者,德之用。

(陈荣捷《近思录详注集评》)

Sincerity engages in no activity, but is the subtle, incipient, activating force giving rise to good and evil.

Sincerity means concrete principle, and engaging in no activity means being absolutely quiet. Concrete principle involves both tranquility and activity, but in its original substance it takes no action. Incipient force means activity at the subtle stage. With activity, good and evil take shape. With sincerity, there is no activity, and there is only goodness. With activity, there will be both good and evil.

The virtue of loving is called humanity, that of doing what is proper is called righteousness, that of putting things in order is called propriety, that of penetration is called wisdom, and that of abiding by one's commitments is called faithfulness. One who is in accord with his nature and acts with ease is a sage. One who returns to his nature and adheres to it is a worthy. And one whose subtle emanation cannot be seen and whose [goodness] is abundant and all-pervasive without limit is a man of the spirit.

Spirit is the character of the sage, mysterious and unfathomable. It does not mean that outside of the sage there is a being called spirit.

(Translated by Wing-Tsit Chan)

四、实践·译笔

儒家讲求"五伦",即君臣有义、父子有亲、夫妇有别、长幼有序、朋友有信。朱熹将儒家仁、义、礼、智、信的思想进行整合发挥,提出了"明伦"这一教育观,体现在《白鹿洞书院揭示》中。

父子有亲,君臣有义,夫妇有别,长幼有序,朋友有信。右五教之目,尧舜使契为司徒,敬敷五教,即此是也。

学者学此而已,而其所以学之之序,亦有五焉,其别如左:博学之,审问之,慎思之,明辨之,笃行之。

右为学之序:学、问、思、辨四者,所以穷理也。

若夫笃行之事,则自修身以至于处事接物,亦各有要,其别如左:言忠信,行笃敬,惩忿窒欲,迁善改过。

右修身之要:正其义不谋其利,明其道不计其功。

右处事之要:己所不欲,勿施于人。行有不得,反求诸己。

右接物之要:其务记览,为词章,以钓声名。

五、阅读·延展

典籍翻译通常要经过语内翻译和语际翻译两个阶段,即将典籍译成现代英文时,需要先把用文言文撰写的典籍翻译成现代汉语,然后再根据现代汉语把它翻译成英文。当然,把用文言文撰写的典籍翻译成现代汉语这个语内翻译过程可以是有明显的实际文本,也可以是只存在于译者头脑中的"后源语文本"(post-source-text)(即介于源语与目的语之间的文本)。有些现当代译者主要是依赖经过了语内翻译的现代汉语译本作为英语译文的源语文本,这就意味着他们根据的"源语"实际上不是严格意义上的源语,而是"后源语文本"。

在这里,有一个问题必须提出来,那就是:"英文(外文)的译者是否有可能不用经过语内翻译过程就直接把用古汉语(文言文)写成的典籍翻译成现代英文（外文）？"也就是说，译者是否不用借助古汉语专家和史学家的专业知识和研究成果就可以直接把典籍翻译成现代英文（外文）。从理论上讲，能够准确解读所要翻译的典籍（如《论语》），并且具有足够的英文（外文）水平来翻译特定的典籍文献的人是有的；但实际上这样的人应该是可遇不可求的，或者说是凤毛麟角的，甚至是没有的。根据 Slingerland（2003）的观点，两千多年来《论语》研究的"注疏"（commentary）传统是一直存在的，没有前人的注疏，研究就无法进行，翻译也是不可能的。他这里所说的注疏与我们所说的语内翻译是相近或相同的，是一致的。因此，他的这一看法与本文所认为典籍翻译通常要经过语内翻译和语际翻译这两个过程的观点是吻合的。

在很大程度上讲，翻译典籍是一件非常具有挑战性的工作，没有足够的相关的古汉语、历史、哲学、文化等专业与百科知识和熟练的外文知识与运用能力以及翻译技能，是无法圆满完成此项工作的。因此，就典籍的翻译而言，我们认为，译者应该能够合理、合适地运用有关专家的研究成果（包括他们对有关典故、事件的考究和解释、注解），然后根据语内翻译过程所产生的现代汉语版本或头脑中的后源语文本进行英文（外文）翻译。

当然，对典籍中的一些词句、段落的考究和解释、注解，有关专家也不一定就有共识，有时甚至是持有对立的观点。例如，《论语·子罕篇第九》的首节（章）是"子罕言利与命与仁"。就这么 8 个字组成的结构，长期以来一直存在多种解释，而这些不同的解释又与儒家思想的解读联系紧密。对于这种长期以来一直在汉语、哲学、历史学界争论的问题，译者是无法将其作为自己的工作或研究重点的，而这点却是翻译研究者必须重视的。对于译者，他们只能根据自己的学识、翻译的目的、读者的对象以及自己的价值取向和个人的因素选择自己认为能够自圆其说或相对合适的观点进行翻译。

（摘自黄国文《典籍翻译：从语内翻译到语际翻译》）

For us, both as linguists and as ordinary word-users, the meaning of any linguistic sign is its translation into some further, alternative sign, especially a sign "in which it is more fully developed", as Peirce, the deepest inquirer into the essence of signs, insistently stated. The term "bachelor" may be converted into a more explicit designation, "unmarried man," whenever higher explicitness is required. We distinguish three ways of interpreting a verbal sign: it may be translated into other signs of the same language, into another language, or into another, nonverbal system of symbols.

These three kinds of translation are to be differently labeled:

1. Intralingual translation or rewording is an interpretation of verbal signs by means of other signs of the same language.

2. Interlingual translation or translation proper is an interpretation of verbal signs by means of some other language.

3. Intersemiotic translation or transmutation is an interpretation of verbal signs by means of signs of nonverbal sign systems.

The intralingual translation of a word uses either another, more or less synonymous, word or resorts to a circumlocution. Yet synonymy, as a rule, is not complete equivalence…

Likewise, on the level of interlingual translation, there is ordinarily no full equivalence between code-units, while messages may serve as adequate interpretations of alien code-units or messages…

Most frequently, however, translation from one language into another substitutes messages in one language not for separate code-units but for entire messages in some other language. Such a translation is a reported speech; the translator recodes and transmits a message received from another source. Thus translation involves two equivalent messages in two different codes.

(Excerpts from *On Linguistic Aspects of Translation* by Roman Jakobson)

第八单元

浩然气节·南宋文天祥

一、译事·译研

文天祥（1236—1283），吉州庐陵人（今江西省吉安市），字宋瑞、履善，号文山，南宋末年政治家和著名诗人，其浩然正气、不甘屈服的人格和气节流传千古。文天祥在抗击元兵的艰苦斗争中创作了大量诗词，其吟咏内容多与时局结合，直抒胸臆，深切感人，气势壮阔，风格阔达，树立了品格高洁的杰出典范。最为大众熟知的是诗体与人格浑然结合的《过零丁洋》。该作既是其人生箴言，也是誓死明志的爱国诗篇，见证并抒发了诗人以死抗争、不求苟活、精忠报国的拳拳丹心和殷殷志向。这种感天悲地的爱国情怀深深融入中华民族的文化记忆之中，世代赓续、传承不息。

曾任法国国立东方语言文化学院图书馆馆长的俄罗斯裔法国汉学家马古礼（Georges Margouliès）对唐宋八大家的散文作品翻译作出了杰出贡献。马古礼对文天祥的诗作予以了极高评价，认为其文风质朴，善于"引经据典""音韵考究"，并"极具感染力的情感抒发"。不过，截至目前，文天祥散文及诗作的海外传播只是片段散译，并不成系统。在中国文化"走出去"的大背景下，文天祥及其诗作具有鲜明的文化代表性，无论是翻译实践抑或翻译研究，都应该推介宣扬文天祥，翻译传播其诗作。

二、鉴赏·评析

景炎元年（1276）三月，文天祥在蒙古祈使团押解下从水路北上大都。到达江苏镇江时，他利用元兵管理的疏漏，在抗元人士帮助下逃脱南下，历尽坎坷辗转至福州，遂以《指南录》为总名，用记叙、诗歌的形式描述了这段经历。

【原文】

脱京口①

二月二十九日夜，予自京口②城中，间道③出江浒登舟，沂金山，走真州④，其艰难万状，各以诗记之。

【注释】

① 脱京口：这是一组诗的题目。包含有《定计难》等十五首带"难"字的诗。
② 京口：今江苏镇江。
③ 间道：偏僻的小路。
④ 走真州：逃往真州。

定计难

予在京城外，日夜谋脱，不得间①者。谢村几去，至平江，欲逃，又不果。至镇江，谋益急，议趋真州，杜架阁浒与帐前将官余元庆实与谋。元庆，真州人也。杜架阁与予云："事集②万万幸，不幸谋泄，皆当死，死有怨乎？"予指心自誓云："死靡悔！③"且办匕首，挟以俱，事不济自杀。杜架阁亦请以死自效，于计遂定。

南北人人苦泣岐，壮心万折誓东归。
若非砑案判生死，夜半何人敢突围。④

【注释】

① 间：机会。

② 事集：事情办成功。

③ 死靡悔：死而不悔。

④ "若非"二句：要不是下定一死的决心，半夜里谁敢突围逃跑呢？斫案，用刀斧砍桌。古人表示决心时的一种动作。《资治通鉴·献帝建安十三年》："因拔刀斫前奏案。"

【译文】

From "The Escape from Jing-kou" (The Account of the Compass)

At night on April 29 we got out of the city of Jing-kou, and taking a shortcut across the floodplain to the river, we embarked by boat. We went upstream past Gold Mountain and hurried toward Zhen-zhou. We ran into hardships and difficulties in every imaginable form. I have given an account of each of these with a poem.

The Difficulty of Deciding on a Plan

Ever since I was taken captive outside the capital, I had plotted to escape but with no success. At Xie Village on the way here, I almost got away. At Ping-jiang I had again wanted to flee my captors, but it hadn't worked out. When we reached Zhen-jiang, making some kind of plan seemed even more urgent. We discussed making a dash to Zhen-zhou. Du Hu, the Archivist, and the Lecturer Yu Yuan-qing plotted with me in earnest. Du said to me, "If this succeeds, we'll be incredibly lucky. If we're not lucky and the plot gets out, we'll all die. Do you resent the prospect of dying?" I put my hand on my heart and swore, "No regrets, even to the death." And I kept a dagger on me to be ready to kill myself if the enterprise did not succeed. Du also asked to die to show his loyalty. The plan was decided.

To go north or south—every man suffers torment at a crossroads,

but bold hearts, whatever the cost, vowed to go southeast.

Had we not then hacked the table[①] and willingly risked our lives,

which man of us that midnight would have dared break free from our guard?

(Translated by Stephen Owen)

【评析】

译者行为批评是由中国学者周领顺教授提出的原创性理论体系,该理论将翻译看作一项社会性活动,并将其置于社会学的视野下进行考察。从翻译的角度看,译者身上只有一种角色,即"译者";而从社会学角度去审视翻译活动的时候,译者的角色并不仅仅是单纯的译者,还有另一个角色——社会人,因为译者是作为具有能动思维和感情的意志体存在于社会中的。当译者具有两种角色时,译者身上就兼具两种属性——语言性和社会性。语言性对应译者的"译者"角色,"反映的是翻译的根本";社会性对应译者的"社会人"角色,"反映社会的需求"。作为中间人的译者,左右两端对应原文和作者与读者和社会。身兼双重身份的译者开展翻译活动时,其行为必然受到两个"角色"的影响。当"译者"角色占据上位时,其语言性得以彰显,译者行为倾向于原文,产生的译文趋向于"求真"——翻译之本;当"社会人"角色占据上位时,其社会性得以彰显,译者行为倾向于读者和社会,产生的译文趋向于"务实"——翻译之用。这也就体现了译者行为批评的核心理论架构——"求真—务实"连续统评价模式。

根据上述模式,现实中的译文可以分为三大类:第一类,译者追求"求

---

① During the Three Kingdoms period, when the Northern warlord Cao Cao invaded the Southern kingdom of Wu, many of the King of Wu's advisers wanted to surrender to him. The king drew his sword and hacked apart the table in front of him, saying that anyone who again suggested surrendering to Cao Cao would end up like the table.

真",弱化"务实",译文靠近原文和作者,如同"异化";第二类,译者追求"务实",弱化"求真",译文靠近读者和社会,如同"归化";第三类,即译者兼顾"求真"与"务实",即所谓的"同化"。三种情况下的译文都有一个"合理度",只不过"合理度"中的"求真度"与"务实度"各有消长。第三种情况应是较理想的翻译,"合理度"达到了最佳状态,但前提是原文和译文所在的社会不存在文化差异等因素的干扰(周领顺,2014)。

我们可以借助译者行为批评理论来分析宇文所安的这篇译文,从中感受译者在"求真度"和"务实度"之间作的取舍。

本文摘自文天祥编著的诗集《指南录》,因在《扬子江》诗中有"臣心一片磁针石,不指南方不肯休"的句子,故作者将其命名为《指南录》。南宋在南方,此处用"南方"指代南宋王朝,用"指南"二字命名意味着作者心指南宋、冒死南归。宇文所安将《指南录》译为"The Account of the Compass",从"求真"的角度来看,译者没有译出"指南"的真正含义。这是因为原文和译文所在的社会存在文化差异,故而"合理度"没有达到最佳状态。译文的人名、地名几乎都采用音译的策略,如:"Jing-kou""Zhen-zhou""Xie Village""Ping-jiang""Zhen-jiang""Du Hu""Yu Yuan-qing"等,译者追求"求真",弱化"务实",尽量保留了异质文化的民族性,用宇文所安(1996)本人的话说就是:"作为译者,我确信这些作品的'中国性'会得以显现,我的任务是发现这个谱系差异的语言风格。"

原文"二月二十九日夜",译者译为"At night on April 29",将中国的农历二月对应西方阳历四月,宇文所安在《中国文学选集》中涉及月份的表达时几乎都是采用这种译法。中国古典诗歌在世界文学史上占有重要的一席之地,凭借的便是"中国性"(Chineseness),即感知与西方诗歌不同的时代、体裁、风格、作家个性的差异,这是中国古诗词的精髓。宇文所安的译诗既追求原诗的"世界性",又保留"中国性",将中国农历译为西方阳历的做法实是把中国地域性改造成为"国际性"的典型案例,因为它们之间存在文化共性。尽管这种美国文化系统内的"国际性"容易产生文化误读,但是，它毕竟进入了国际文化系统的流通，有助于消除 Antoine Berman 所说的"每个文化以本民族为中心"的"特别的自恋情结"（张隆溪，2005）。这便是译者在原文和译文存在社会文化差异等因素的干扰下，其"社会人"角色占据了上位，即社会性予以彰显，更倾向于读者和社会，产生的译文趋向于"务实"，也就是"翻译之用"。

"予指心自誓云：'死靡悔！'且办匕首，挟以俱，事不济自杀。"原文激情慷慨，体现作者视死如归、忠贞于南宋朝廷的情感，译者处理为："I put my hand on my heart"。"合理度"达最佳状态，为第三类译文即"同化"。英语"put（one's）hand on（one's）heart"英文释义为："To swear that something is completely truthful, genuine, or sincere."在西方，尤其是在美国，这是一种礼仪，叫"Pledge of Allegiance"，即"对美国效忠礼"，简称"摸心礼"，表示"祖国在我心中"。美国一般在升国旗时使用此礼，人们面对美国国旗肃立，右手放左胸前。故而此处用英语的审美价值言说原诗，以利于本土读者品鉴，准确地传达了原作者的情感，再现了文天祥爱国凛然的形象。同时"事不济自杀"的"事"译者选用了"enterprise"亦是再现了文天祥等人所谋之事之艰巨且重大。

"南北人人苦泣岐，壮心万折誓东归"一句，身兼双重身份的译者无论是在"求真度"还是"务实度"方面的表现都不尽如人意，这不是因为两种语言所在的社会存在文化差异等干扰因素，而是因为身为译者的宇文所安对这一句所体现的中国古诗词的"中国性"缺乏文化与历史层面的深入了解。"南北"并非南下或北上"to go north or south"，"岐"也非面临十字路口"at a crossroads"，"东归"更不是前往东南方向"go southeast"。此时正是元军入侵、国家被分裂之时，南北人民都为国家的分裂而痛苦流泪，人人都以做元军的俘虏为耻，为国破家亡而痛哭，但他们仍然怀揣着坚定的决心，誓言要东归，即要收复失地，统一国家。"东归"指回故乡。因汉唐皆定都长安，中原、江南人士辞京返乡多言东归。在古代，人们常常把东方看作是吉祥、吉利的象征。因此，东归这个词就有着回归、返回吉祥之地的含义。同时，它还暗示着对家乡、故土的思念和向往。在本诗中，也可理解为作者誓死要回归南宋。因为文化、历史的缺失，译者既无法做到"求真"，也做不到"务实"，可见翻译不可能在真空中产生，也不可能在真空中被接受，它是文化体系中的一个子系统。

"若非砚案判生死，夜半何人敢突围"一句，对于"砚案"这样一个蕴含文化背景的词，宇文所安通过增加脚注的方式具体描述这个词的文化内涵和外延，阐释了这一文化典故。因为目标语文化中不存在这样的文化，故而译文在"合理度"上尚未达到最佳，但是作为译者的宇文所安和作为社会人的宇文所安已经尽力在两种语言间做了很好的平衡，在追求"务实"的时候也兼顾"求真"。

【原文】

高沙道中①

予雇骑夜驱高沙。越四十里，至板桥，迷失道。一夕行田畈中②，不知东西，风露满身，人马饿乏，旦行雾中不相辨。须臾，四山渐明，忽隐隐见北骑③。道有竹林，亟入避。须臾，二十余骑绕林呼噪。虞候张庆右眼内中一箭，项二刀，割其髻，裸于地。帐兵王青缚去。杜架阁与金应，林中被获，出所携黄金赂逻者，得免。予藏处距杜架阁不远，北马入林，过吾旁三四，皆不见。不自意得全。仆夫邹捷，卧丛篠下④，马过，踏其足，流血。总辖吕武、亲随夏仲，散避他所。是役也，予自分必死。当其急时，万窍怒号⑤，杂乱人声。北仓卒不尽得，疑有神明相之。马既去，闻其有焚林之谋，亟趋对山，复寻丛篁以自蔽。既不识路，又乏粮食，人生穷蹙，无以加此。未几，吕武报北骑已还湾头，又知路边鲇鱼坝传闻不尽信。然他无活策，黾勉趋去，倖幸万一。仓皇匍匐不能行。先是自扬州来，有引路三人，牵马三人，至是或执或逃，仅存其二。二人出于无聊，各操梃相随，有无礼之志。逡巡⑥行路，无可奈何。至晚西，忽遇樵者数人，如佛下降。偶得一箩，以绳维之，坐于篓中，雇六夫，更迭负送，驰至高邮城西，天已晓，不得渡，常恐追骑之奄至也。宿陈氏店，以茅覆地，忍饿而卧，黎明过渡，而心始安。痛定思痛，其涕如雨。

【注释】

① 高沙：高邮。

② 一夕：整个夜里。田畈：成片的田。

③ 北骑：元军骑兵。

④ 丛篠：矮小的竹丛。

⑤ 万窍怒号：多种声音同时响起。这里指风声大作。《庄子·齐物论》："夫大块噫气，其名为风。是唯无作，作则万窍怒号。"

⑥ 逡巡：徘徊不进。贾谊《过秦论》："九国之师，逡巡而不敢进。"

【译文】

From "On the Gao-sha Road"

We had hired mounts and were making swift progress toward Gao-sha by night. After having gone more than forty leagues, we came to a plank bridge and lost the road. All evening long we went through the level fields, unable to tell east from west. Our bodies were soaked all over by droplets of mist in the air, and both we and our horses were worn out and hungry. We simply went on through the fog, unable to make anything out.

Then in a moment the hills around us gradually brightened, and all at once I saw the shadowy forms of Northern horsemen. There was a bamboo thicket by the road, and we hurriedly went into it to get away from them. A moment later there were twenty or so horsemen surrounding the thicket and shouting. The Military Inspector Zhang Qing was hit in the left eye by an arrow; he took two blade wounds in the neck; then they cut off his hair and left him naked on the ground. Wang Qing, an officer in the Ministry of War, was tied up and taken off. When

Du Hu and Jin Ying were captured in the thicket, they took out the gold they were carrying, bribed the patrol, and managed to escape. I lay hidden in a spot not far from Du. When the Northern horsemen entered the thicket, they passed right by me three or four times and never saw me. I didn't think I would get out of this alive. Zou Jie, a groom in the Royal Stud, was lying under a clump of small bamboo; a horse had stepped on his foot when passing and he was bleeding. LüWu, of the Office of Military Administration, and his personal attendant Xia Zhong, fled to a different spot. I expected that I was surely going to die in this enterprise.

When things became most desperate, the wind began howling through all the cracks and crevices of the earth, confusing men's voices. The Northerners were in a state of alarm that they hadn't caught everyone and suspected some god must be aiding us. The horses left. Then I heard them making plans to burn the bamboo, and I hurriedly scrambled toward the hill in front of me, looking for another clump of bamboo in which to conceal myself. Not knowing which road to take and on top of that having nothing to eat, no situation in a person's life could be more desperate than this. A little while later when Lv Wu brought me the news that the Northern horsemen had gone back to the Bay, and also let me know that Yu-nian Levee was by the road, I didn't entirely believe what he was telling me. Nevertheless, we had no alternative if we wanted to stay alive, so we did our best to get there as quickly as possible, this being one chance in a million. We were in a panic, scrambling ahead on our hands and knees, unable to walk.

When we had made our way out from Yang-zhou previously, there had been three men leading the way and three men bringing along the horses. Now there were only two left, the others having fled or been captured. When those two came out of their daze, each grasped his cudgel and followed after us, with intent to do us harm. We walked on, not sure what to do, but we had no choice. As it grew later, we suddenly came upon several woodsmen, who seemed to have descended upon us like Buddhas. We happened to find a large basket that a person could sit in, and we fastened it with cords. Then we hired six fellows and took turns being carried; in this way we rapidly came out west of the walls of Gao-you. We couldn't cross the river until dawn had come, and we were in constant fear that at any moment horsemen would appear, chasing us. We stayed over at Chen's inn, lying on its straw-covered floor and enduring our hunger. In the full light of dawn, we crossed the river and our hearts calmed at last. When a hurt is over, a person thinks about it, and then tears fall like rain.

(Translated by Stephen Owen)

【评析】

　　这段文字描写了文天祥在逃跑的途中被元兵追杀,形势紧迫,战事惨烈,命悬一线的情景。逃跑的途中有的同伴被元兵残忍杀死,有的被抓走,有的为躲避元兵与队伍走散。文天祥用了大量的内心活动描写来刻画这险象环生的危恶境地,如"不自意得全""予自分必死""人生穷蹙,无以加此""侥幸万一""无可奈何"以及"常恐追骑之奄至也"。他也多次刻画情况之危急,如"亟""急"等字眼频繁出现,同时用精悍短小的文字,既粗笔提示,又一笔不漏地交代了几名同伴惨烈的死状。短短一段,却让读者生出恍如亲身经历之感。这种叙事中饱含感情的文章需要译者能够准确地抓住原文传递出来的情感,让目的语读者产生与源语读者一样的感受。

　　"风露满身,人马饥乏"一句译者处理为"Our bodies were soaked all over by droplets of mist in the air, and both we and our horses were worn out and hungry"。从"求真"的角度而言,"were soaked"就可以传达出原文的语义,但是作为社会人的宇文所安补上"all over"后语言更加流畅,可读性更强。

　　再现原文的心理描写是翻译的难点之一。本文的心理活动描写诸多,首先是"不自意得全",译者处理为"I didn't think I would get out of this alive",译者充分理解原文的含义,特别是"全"的文化内涵;原文"予自分必死"译为"I expected that I was surely going to die in this enterprise",语气处理得极好,"expected"更是写出了文天祥深知不可为而为之的大义,突出他舍生忘死、随时准备好为国捐躯的高伟形象;"侥幸万一"译者根据英语使用习惯翻译为"one chance in a million",这是译者身份与社会人身份的完美融合,使译文与原文"同化","求真"与"务实"统一;"逡巡行路,无可奈何"译者处理为"We walked on, not sure what to do, but we had no choice"再现了作者一行茫然无措、身处绝处的情景。译者并没有译为"we had no choice but to walk on",而是补充了"not sure what to do"的内容,体现了作者这一路危机四伏、"前有狼后有虎"的进退两难境地;"常恐追骑之奄至也"的译文"we were in constant fear that at any moment horsemen would appear, chasing us"补充了原文没有的"随时"之意,更显作者随时都会有危险。

可以说,译者对心理活动的翻译描写较为妥当,同时也通过扎实的双语功底再现了战事的激烈,直白地让读者明白这是生死存亡之际。文中有两处描写了作者同伴的惨状,分别是"中一箭,项二刀,割其髻,裸于地"和"马过,踏其足,流血",译者分别译为"……was hit in the letf eye by an arrow; he took two blade wounds in the neck; then they cut off his hair and left him naked on the ground"和"a horse had stepped on his foot when passing and he was bleeding"。对于前者,译者借用主被动交替和"leave+宾语+宾补"的手法将作者同伴从殊死搏斗誓不投降到最后任人宰割的凄惨景象呈现出来,令闻者心惊;对于后者,译者借用过去进行时表达现场的血腥,读者仿佛看到了鲜血汩汩流出,同时流逝的还有仆夫邹捷的生命。

以上译文都向目的语读者传达了文天祥一路逃亡之不易。无论目的语读者还是原文读者都会为文天祥的遭遇捏一把汗,这便是译者兼顾"求真"与"务实"所取得的良好效果。

但是译文中也有宇文所安为了"务实"而牺牲"求真"的地方,比如,原文有多处涉及宋朝的官员职称,如"虞候""帐兵""架阁""仆夫"和"总辖"。

对于这种源语中的专有名词，宇文所安在《中国文学选集》中使用的都是近似"归化法"的策略，使译文靠近读者，满足读者的期待视野，积极调动英语读者的文化关联并减轻读者因缺少文化背景带来的阅读负担，从而产生较好的场域效果。另外原文"疑有神明相之"，译者将"神明"处理为"god"，这二者其实并非对等，而译为"god"舍掉了原文的异域性，以"务实"的方式让目标语读者的阅读变得透明，因为这种"透明"式的译文最宜在美国本土化。宇文所安（2003）曾经说，翻译意味着变化，但是不一定意味着异国风味。而"北仓卒不尽得"是指元兵追捕时匆忙仓促，并非是元兵惊恐而未将作者一行全部抓捕回去，故而"The Northerners were in a state of alarm that they hadn't caught everyone"存在语义偏差。这句译文既不是为了"求真"，也不是为了"务实"，而是理解有误。可见在翻译实践中，理解是表达的基础，没有正确的理解就不可能有准确的表达。换句话说，表达建立在理解的基础之上，确切的表达来自透彻的理解。

除了因理解有误而造成译文有误以外，译文中还有几处错误本可以规避掉，比如"虞候张庆右眼内中一箭"被翻译为"The Military Inspector Zhang Qing was hit in the left eye by an arrow"；"右眼"被误译为"左眼"，实在遗憾。另外，"又知路边鲇鱼坝"中的"鲇鱼坝"译者采用音译加直译的方法，但是却将"鲇鱼"音译为"Yu-nian"而不是"Nian-yu"，不知是出于某种考虑还是译者的无心之疏。

三、译论·比较

翻译不仅仅是语言层面的文字转换，也应当包含情感维度的移译与传递。如诗歌、演说等文学作品中富含有情感表达，即使是所谓的一些史学类、科学史类、自然史类文本，也同样夹杂着情感因素。因为文本的编织过程就是作者根据自己的认知对现实客观世界进行加工后的叙事行为，其间或多或少糅纳了作者的认知偏好与情感态度。换言之，文本即叙事，叙事中包含了情感与抒情。相应地，对文本进行翻译的过程也是叙事重构与抒情传递的过程。因此，对某一译本进行翻译批评，可以从翻译抒情的角度审视其效用。首先，可以鉴析原文、译文各自流露出的情感与态度；其次，对比两种情感的契合度，存在哪些共鸣与差异；最后，可以就这些情感异同进行语言学、社会学、跨文化等多视角的分析解读。这不仅可以丰富译本分析的维度，也可以使译本阐释的途径多样化。

鉴于此，请按照上述要点对《过零丁洋》的几个译本进行批评分析与阐释解读。

过零丁洋

辛苦遭逢起一经，干戈寥落四周星。
山河破碎风飘絮，身世浮沉雨打萍。
惶恐滩头说惶恐，零丁洋里叹零丁。
人生自古谁无死，留取丹心照汗青。

A Prisoner's Lamentation—Passing by Lingdingyang

I've taken pains reading classics to be an official,
Four bleak years have been spent in thick battles.
Our land is broken like catkins drifting in the wind,
I roam here and there as duckweed buffeted by the rain.

How panic-stricken I was retreating before the Tartars!
Being a captive, I lamented over my solitary confinement.
Who can avert his death since time immemorial?
Let my heart remain true to shine in the annals.

[Translated by Huang Xinqu（黄新渠）]

第八单元　浩然气节·南宋文天祥

Crossing the Lonely Ocean[①]

Through painstaking mastery of one

Of the Classics, I have risen high;

But four years of raging war have well-nigh

Brought all-round destitution and ruin.

My shattered country does remind

Me of willow-catkins swept by wind;

My life's vicissitudes attain

The aspect of duckweeds beaten by rain.

At th' Frightful Shallows[②] we fought our way,

They'd tell the frightful battle never won,

And on the Lonely Ocean I could but sigh

For being captured, and all alone.

Down through the ages, whoever that lived

Has not in death ended his life?

I wish to leave but a loyal heart

Shining red in History's archive.

[Translated by Wang Zhihuan (王知还)]

[①] The Lonely Ocean is part of South China Sea to the south of what is now the Zhongshan County, Guangdong Province. Song Reizong's Prime Minister Wen Tianxiang (1236–1282), at the end of the dynasty, after being captured by the Yuan Army, was sent under guard aboard a ship to the conquerors' capital Yanjing (now Beijing) in 1278. He was imprisoned for more than three years and executed in 1282, unyielding to the last. Wen is one of the most revered national heroes in Chinese history.

[②] The Frightful Shallows is in Jiangxi Province. It is one of 18 dangerous shallows in the most torrential part of the Gan River. In 1277 Wen was defeated by the Yuan Army there, whence he evacuated to Fujian Province and was later captured.

Sailing on Lonely Ocean

Delving in the Book of Change, I rose through hardship great,
And desperately fought the foe for four long years.
Like willow down the war-town land looks desolate;
I sink or swim as duckweed in the rain appears.

For the perils on Perilous Beach I have sighs;
On Lonely Ocean now I feel dreary and lonely.
Since olden days there's never been a man but dies;
I'd leave a loyalist's name in history only.

[Translated by Xu Yuanchong（许渊冲）]

四、实践·译笔

使举国之少年而亦为老大也，则吾中国为过去之国，其澌亡可翘足而待也。故今日之责任，不在他人，而全在我少年。少年智则国智，少年富则国富，少年强则国强，少年独立则国独立，少年自由则国自由，少年进步则国进步，少年胜于欧洲则国胜于欧洲，少年雄于地球则国雄于地球。红日初升，其道大光。……纵有千古，横有八荒。前途似海，来日方长。

（摘自梁启超《少年中国说》）

五、阅读·延展

翻译家的功绩的伟大绝不下于创作家。他是全人类的最高精神与情绪的交通者。现在的人类被国界与种族界间隔得支离破碎，各国有各国自己的语言。同是两个人，如果是异国的，他们就当面也不能叙谈了。你不知道他的心理，他也不知道你的情绪。误会以生，而战争已起了。唯有文学是满含着人类的最高的精神与情绪的。由文学的交流，也许可以把人类的误会除掉了不少。所以在世界没有共同的语言以前，翻译家的使命是非常重大的。就文学的本身讲,翻译家的责任也是非常重要的。无论在哪一国的文学史上,没有不显出受别国文学的影响的痕迹的。而负这种介绍的责任的,却是翻译家。

俄国文学史中也出了不少的翻译家;他们替俄国文学所尽的责任是很伟大的。最初的俄国文字,就是由马其顿与保加利亚的文字合成的。在1672年的时候,俄皇在某村建筑了一座剧场。在这个剧场上曾开演过好几回由德国翻译来的剧本。到大彼得出而改革俄政的时候,有不少的历史、地理及法律的书籍由外国介绍来。不过,他对于文学却不大注意。所以他的改革,对于俄国文学史没有什么显著的效果可见。然而自他死了不久,文学潮流却由西欧而汹涌的滚滚进来。……近来,俄国的赤色革命成功。他们对于文学更为注意,认定文学对于全人类的联合有非常大的关系。

(摘自郑振铎《俄国文学史中的翻译家》)

The relationship between nations and translation is complex and fraught. The transnational nature of translated texts, which connect two different languages, cultures and often historical periods, challenges deeply held Western concepts of originality and authenticity that underpin the idea of autonomous *sui generis* national cultures…

While it is a widely accepted truth that "the literature of most nations begins with translations", it is no less true that translation has been ignored or suppressed in the literary and cultural histories of modern nations. As Heilbron notes, "Literary history tends to ignore translation since it is commonly conceived as national history". The idea that university departments of language and literature were created in order to document and affirm the "national genius" is supported by their traditional antipathy toward translation—regardless of the cultural significance of those translations— in favor of "original" writing. Indeed, literary historians adopted the model of national historiography, with its preoccupation with origins. What is studied in such historiographies are works that were created in the period under investigation, typically ignoring the "continuous recycling of different texts from the past" that occurs, often with the help of translation. The semiotician Juri Lotman rejects such national histories of literature and culture as marred by a superficial developmentalism that ignores the whole question of a work's actual relevance. Lotman goes on to reference the nineteenth-century Russian writer Nikolai Gogol who, when asked to name the most important writers of his age, replied without hesitation : Walter Scott and Homer. Incidentally, Gogol would have read both of those authors in translation. In fact, the new relevance of Homer to Russian culture of Gogol's time was reflected in the appearance of two much-discussed retranslations of the *Iliad*, by Nikolai Gnedich and Vasilii Zhukovskii. Therefore, a focus on the relevance of literary works as opposed to their origin undermines nationalist historiography, making possible the full integration of translated texts.

(Excerpts from *Nations in Translation* by Brian James Baer)

第九单元

格致泰斗·明代王阳明

一、译事·译研

王阳明（1472—1529），字伯安，名守仁，明代著名哲学家、教育家、政治家和军事家，创"阳明学"，成就冠绝有明一代，与孔子、孟子、朱熹并称为"孔孟朱王"。阳明先生与南昌诸养和之女成婚，后为庐陵县（今江西吉安）知县，有平定江西之功。至今，江西人对阳明先生推崇备至，也有以其命名的道路在南昌、吉安、樟树、赣州皆有，也有以其命名的公园、湖泊、书院、纪念碑。可以说，江西是阳明先生集立德、立功、立言于一身的实践之地，是其心学传承、兴盛之地。王阳明认为"心即理""心外无物""心外无理"，穷极一生探究"心、良知、致良知"，认为这才是认识的主体、对象与根本。因此，无论从本体论还是认识论，"良知"都是贯穿于万物之中的公度性存在与天然法则，即"致知格物"，也产生了所谓的"王门四句教"：无善无恶心之体，有善有恶意之动，知善知恶是良知，为善去恶是格物。可以说，"致良知"是其思想体系的核心，富有创造性转化的内涵与潜力。习近平总书记也充分肯定阳明心学的当代价值，认为王阳明心学是中华传统文化的精华，也是增强中国人文化自信的切入点之一。

随着阳明学的当代价值体现与意义阐释挖掘，其发展传播也构成了一个显性研究分支，如在国内特定地域或领域中阳明后学的分化与发展，在日韩等东亚国家传播的本土化，以及在西方世界的译介传播与思想发微。

1916年，亨克编译本 *The Philosophy of Wang Yang-ming*（《王阳明哲学》）以《传习录》为主体，开了阳明学英译之先河。Jalvies H. Tufts曾为其作序，肯定了亨克对王阳明及其思想在英语世界的首译之功，促进了王学研究的兴起。颜任光也评述了该译本的客观中正以及其中所蕴含的阳明思想：心即理、个人即权威、知行合一与善恶转化。不过，也有学者认为该译本受限于译者的汉学和儒家经典知识水平，有诸多错译及术语滥译现象。如日本知识界领军人物、著名学者姉崎正治（Anesaki Masaharu）就对亨氏译本中的核心理论术语英译表示担忧，对该译本能否恰当地、准确地、系统地呈现王学思想提出质疑，乃至认为"这一骇人的翻译，几乎使王阳明的生命、努力和功绩化为乌有"。可以说，亨氏译文是借助于现成的西方哲学术语和理论来译介王学，一方面能够为西方读者或学者减轻认知负担，使其尽快接纳阳明思想，并迅速提升传播效能；但另一方面也造成了削足适履，存在过度诠释或李代桃僵，使得王学思想被"误读"。

1963年，朱子学权威陈荣捷先生的英译本 *Instructions for Practical Living and other Neo-Confucian Writings*（《传习录》）问世。该译本流畅易懂，颇受好评。陈氏是以一种译研的态度进行译介，他认为《传习录》几乎涵盖了所有传统哲学术语，尤其注重术语的英文表达。另外，该译本的注释详细且严谨，可谓辞必附释、名必加注、追本溯源、考据有加。该译本成为迄今最为广泛接受的《传习录》英文全译之一。诸多学者对陈氏译本赞赏有加，如谢康伦认为译本中的术语翻译较为忠实可靠，运用注译法能够使读者更为全面且准确地理解术语的文化意图与哲学内涵。辛红娟等（2019）认为陈译"以最为简单朴实的语言来表达最为博大精深的阳明思想，让西方读者得以重新认识阳明思想，逐步理解并欣赏西方哲学，为接受并认同中国哲学打下坚实基础"。也有学者对陈氏英译《传习录》标题提出商榷意见，如倪德卫不同意译为 *Instructions for Practical Life* 与 *Instructions for Practical Living*，而是建议译为 *Record of Transmission and Practice*；卜德（Derk Bodde）在英译冯友兰的《中国哲学简史》（*A History of Chinese Philosophy*）时译为 *Record of Instruction*；张君劢在《新儒家思想史》（*The Development of Neo-Confucian Thought*）中译为 *Records of Instructions and Practices* 等。

总体而言，阳明学（以《传习录》为主体）英译与传播受中西哲学思维差异等影响，存在内涵表达不够、思想呈现不足、译研理念欠缺等现实问题与困境。后继翻译与研究应当丰富和完善多语种翻译事业，包括合适的联合翻译主体、创新的传播途径，使其在更忠实可信地传递阳明学思想的前提下更加符合西方世界的思维和认知方式，美美与共，共同推进阳明学在西方世界的翻译传播与研究。

二、鉴赏·评析

【原文】

徐爱录（节选）

爱问："'在亲民'，朱子谓当作'新民'[①]，后章'作新民'之文，似亦有据。先生以为宜从旧本作'亲民'，亦有所据否？"

先生曰："'作新民'之'新'，是自新之民，与'在新民'之'新'不同，此岂足为据？'作'字却与'亲'字相对，然非'新'字义[②]。下面'治国平天下'处，皆于'新'字无发明。如云'君子贤其贤而亲其亲，小人乐其乐而利其利'、'如保赤子'、'民之所好好之，民之所恶恶之，此之谓民之父母'之类，皆是'亲'字意。'亲民'犹孟子'亲亲仁民'[③]之谓，亲之即仁之也。百姓不亲，舜使契为司徒，'敬敷五教'[④]，所以亲之也。《尧典》'克明峻德'，便是'明明德'；'以亲九族'至'平章'、'协和'[⑤]，便是'亲民'，便是'明明德于天下'。又如孔子言'修己以安百姓'[⑥]，'修己'便是'明明德'，'安百姓'便是'亲民'。说'亲民'，便兼教养意；说'新民'，便觉偏了。"

……………

爱问:"'知止而后有定'⑦,朱子以为'事事物物皆有定理',似与先生之说相戾。"

先生曰:"于事事物物上求至善,却是义外⑧也。至善是心之本体⑨,只是明明德到至精至一处便是,然亦未尝离却事物,本注所谓'尽夫天理之极,而无一毫人欲之私'⑩者,得之。"

爱问:"至善只求诸心,恐于天下事理有不能尽。"

先生曰:"心即理也。天下又有心外之事、心外之理乎？"

（选自［明］王阳明撰,黎业明译注:《传习录》）

【注释】

① 所谓"'在亲民',朱子谓当作'新民'",语出朱熹《大学章句》。"在亲民",语见《大学》首章"大学之道,在明明德,在亲民,在止于至善",意为:大学的原则,在于彰显人的完美德性,在于爱护百姓,在于达到至善的境界。

② 然非"新"字义:"新",原作"亲"。

③ "亲亲仁民"意为:君子亲爱自己的亲人,又对百姓仁慈。语出《孟子·尽心上》。

④ "舜使契为司徒,'敬敷五教'"意为:舜于是指派契作司徒之官,敬布五常之教。司徒,古代官名,主管教育、教化。其语出《尚书·舜典》。五教,即《孟子·滕文公上》中所谓的"父子有亲,君臣有义,夫妇有别,长幼有序,朋友有信"。

⑤ 此处引述《尧典》之言,乃本《尚书·尧典》:"克明俊德,以亲九族；九族既睦,平章百姓；百姓昭明,协和万邦,黎民于变时雍。"意为:尧能明其大德,用以亲睦九族；九族得以亲睦之后,则去辨明百官；百官得以辨明之后,又去调和天下万邦,天下民众也因此都变得和睦。

⑥ "修己以安百姓"意为:修养自己来使天下百姓都得到安乐。语见《论语·宪问》:"子路问君子。子曰:'修己以敬。'曰:'如斯而已乎？'曰:'修己以安人。'曰:'如斯而已乎？'曰:'修己以安百姓。修己以安百姓,尧舜其犹病诸！'"

⑦ "知止而后有定"意为:懂得止于至善,而后志有定向。语见朱熹《大

学或问》："能知所止，则方寸之间，事事物物皆有定理矣。"

⑧"义外"意为：义是外在的（而不是发自内心的）。这是告子（告不害，战国时人）的主张。语见《孟子·告子上》："告子曰：'食色，性也。仁，内也，非外也；义，外也，非内也。'"

⑨"本体"，在现代汉语中，一般情况下是指事物的本质；但在古代汉语中，也常常用来指事物的本来状态。在王阳明的《传习录》中，"本体"这个概念很多时候都是指事物的本来状态，而不是指事物的本质。在翻译当中，我们对作为事物的本质的"本体"概念不加翻译。

⑩"尽夫天理之极，而无一毫人欲之私"，语见朱熹《大学章句》，意为：达到天理的极致，而没有一丝一毫的人欲之私心杂念。

【译文】

徐爱问："《大学》'在亲民'一句，朱子说应当作'新民'，后面章节'作新民'的说法，似乎也说明其有所依据。先生您以为应该遵从旧本作'亲民'，也有所依据吗？"

阳明先生说："'作新民'的'新'字，是自新之民的意思，与'在新民'的'新'字不同，这哪里足以为依据呢？'作'字却与'亲'字相对，然而并不是'新'字的含义。下面说的'治国平天下'，都没有对'新'字加以阐发。如说'君子贤其贤而亲其亲，小人乐其乐而利其利'、'如保赤子'、'民之所好好之，民之所恶恶之，此之谓民之父母'之类，都是'亲'字的意思。'亲民'犹如孟子所说的'亲亲而仁民'，'亲之'就是对他们仁爱。正由于百姓不能相亲相爱，于是舜指派契为司徒，'敬敷五教'，目的就是要使百姓相亲相爱。《尧典》所说的'克明峻德'，便是'明明德'；所说的'以亲九族'以至'平章百姓'、'协和万邦'，便是'亲民'，便是'明明德于天下'。又如孔子说'修己以安百姓'，'修己'便是'明明德'，'安百姓'便是'亲民'。说'亲民'，便兼有教养的意思；说'新民'，便觉得有偏差了。"

徐爱问："《大学》'知止而后有定'一句，朱子《大学或问》认为是'事事物物皆有定理'的意思，这似乎与先生您的说法相冲突。"

阳明先生说："从事事物物上寻求至善，这却是像告子那样以义为外在了。至善是心的本来状态，只是明明德达到至精至一的境地便是，然而这也未曾脱离事物，朱子《大学章句》中所说的'尽夫天理之极，而无一毫人欲之私'，这才是得其正解。"

徐爱问："只在心上求至善，恐怕不能穷尽天下事理。"

阳明先生说："心即理。天下哪里又有心外之事、心外之理呢？"

【译文】

I asked : "Chu Hsi said that the phrase 'in loving the people' (*ch'in-min*) in the *Great Learning* should read 'in renovating the people' (*hsin-min*). Since in a later section of the book it says, 'arouse the people to become new,' he seems to have some evidence for his contention. Do you also have evidence for believing that the phrase 'in loving the people' in the old text should be followed?"

The Teacher said, "The word *hsin* in the phrase 'arouse the people to become new (*hsin*)' means the people become new themselves. It is different in meaning from the same word in the phrase 'in renovating the people.' How can it be accepted as evidence? The term 'arouse the people to become' parallels the term 'love' but does not mean the same. The passages that follow in the text on bringing order to the state and peace to the world do not amplify the meaning of renovation. On the contrary, these passages in the text — 'Rulers deemed worthy what they deemed worthy and loved what they loved, while the common people enjoyed what they enjoyed and benefited from their beneficial arrangements', 'Act as if you were watching over an infant', and the ruler 'likes what people like and dislikes what the people dislike. That is what is meant by being a parent of the people' — all express the meaning of love. The meaning of 'loving the people' is the same as in Mencius' saying, 'The superior man is affectionate to his parents and humane to all people.' To love is the same as to be humane.

Because the common people did not love one another, Emperor Shun appointed Hsieh to be minister of education and to institute with great seriousness the five teachings①. This was Emperor Shun's way to love the people. The sentence 'He was able to manifest his lofty character' means the same as 'manifesting the clear character,' and the statements there, 'to love the nine classes of his kindred,' 'to have harmony,' and 'to have unity and accord,' mean the same as 'loving the people' and 'manifesting the clear character to the world.' Also, Confucius said, 'The superior man cultivates himself so as to give the common people security and peace.' Cultivating oneself means manifesting the clear character and giving the common people security and peace means loving the people. Reading the phrase as loving the people expresses both the ideas of educating and feeding the people. Reading it to mean renovating the people, however, seems to be one-sided."

I said, "With reference to the sentence, 'Only after knowing what to abide in can one be calm' in the *Great Learning*, Chu Hsi considered that 'all events and things possess in them a definite principle.' This seems to contradict your theory."

The Teacher said, "To seek the highest good (the abiding point) in individual events and things is to regard righteousness as external②. The highest good is the original substance of the mind. It is no other than manifesting one's clear character to the point of refinement and singleness of mind. And yet it is not separated from events and things. When Chu Hsi said in his commentary that (manifesting the clear character is) 'the realization of the Principle of Nature to

---

① For the father to be righteous, the mother to be affectionate, the older brother to be friendly, the younger brother to be respectful, and the son to be filially pious. See Book of History, "Canon of Shun." Cf. trans by Legge, Shoo King, P. 44.

② Throughout the *Instructions for Practical Living*, Wang attacks again and again the doctrine that righteousness and other moral principles are to be found in external things, a doctrine advocated by Kao Tzu, whom Mencius vigorously denounced.

the fullest extent without an iota of selfish human desire,' he got the point."

I said, "If the highest good is to be sought only in the mind, I am afraid not all principles of things in the world will be covered."

The Teacher said, "The mind is principle. Is there any affair in the world outside of the mind? Is there any principle outside of the mind?"

[Translated and Annotated by Wing-Tsit Chan (陈荣捷)]

I made inquiry regarding "to love the people", which the philosopher Chu said should be translated "to renovate the people," the evidence being that a later chapter uses "to renovate the people." "You feel," 1 said, "that it is correct to follow the original, 'to love the people.' Is there any evidence for your point of view?"

The Teacher said : "The character *hsin* (新) in the later chapter naturally means that the people renovate themselves, a thought which differs from the meaning of this particular passage. Is your evidence for the new edition sufficient? The character 'to make' when used with the character 'to love' does not have the import of renovating. The statement further down, 'govern the state and bring mankind to a state of peace,' does not elucidate the meaning of renovate. For instance, the expressions, 'The princes deem worthy what the people deemed worthy and love what the people loved'; The common people delight in what delighted the princes and benefit by their beneficial arrangements'; or 'Act as if you were watching over an infant'; 'Love what the people love and hate what the people hate,' imply that the superior men are as parents to the people. This gives the meaning of love. The term 'loving the people' (亲民) is the same as Mencius' expression, 'loving one's parents.' Thus loving is an inward and spiritual love of mankind. The people did not love (those above them) and Shun sent Hsieh as minister of instruction reverently to make known the five lessons of duty. This means that he loved them. The canon of Yao which says : 'He was able to make illustrious his lofty virtue,' implies that he made illustrious his own lofty virtue. By loving the nine agnatic relatives up to the point where he made no distinctions between the people and united and harmonized the various states, he illustrated the idea of loving the people and manifested his lofty virtue on all the earth. Again, it is like Confucius' saying, 'To cultivate one's self so as to give peace to the people.' To cultivate one's self is to make illustrious lofty virtue. Giving peace to the people implies loving the people. Loving the people embraces the idea of nourishing and educating. In saying, 'To renew the people,' one becomes conscious of error."

I made inquiry regarding the saying from the Great Learning, "Knowing where to rest, the object of pursuit is determined." "The philosopher Chu," I said, "held that all affairs and all things have definite principles. This appears to be out of harmony with your sayings."

The Teacher said: "To seek the highest virtue in affairs and things is only the objective side of the principles of righteousness. The highest virtues are innate to the mind. They are realized when the manifesting of lofty virtue has reached perfection. Nevertheless, one does not leave the physical realm out of consideration. The original notes say that the individual must exhaust heaven-given principles to the utmost and that no one with any of the prejudices of human passions will attain to the highest virtue."

I made inquiry saying, "Though the highest virtue be sought, within the mind only, that may not enable the individual to investigate thoroughly the laws of the physical realm."

The Teacher said: "The mind itself is the embodiment of natural law. Is there anything in the universe that exists independent of the mind? Is there any law apart from the mind?"

(Translated by Frederick Goodrich Henke)

【评析】

自 20 世纪 90 年代末以来，西方翻译学术界纷纷借鉴布迪厄社会学理论的基本概念与模式，如运用场域（field）、惯习（habitus）、资本（capital）等来分析影响翻译生产、传播和接受、具体策略运用的各种社会制约因素。

布迪厄认为，人类社会是由社会结构和心态结构组成的。生活在社会空间中的行动者是由特定的社会关系网络来确定其社会位置的，即他们凭借各自拥有的特定资本和特定惯习，在一定的社会场域中生活，并在一定的社会制约条件下，不断地同时创造和建构自身以及生活在其中的社会。我们可以把布迪厄的实践概念理解为：行动者在一定的场域中凭借各自拥有的资本，在特定的惯习指导下，为提高自己在场域中的位置以及资本的数量和质量所采取的活动。布迪厄把场域定义为位置之间的客观关系的网络和构型。从布迪厄的社会实践理论体系来解读场域概念，我们可以把它理解为，处在不同位置的行动者在各自惯习的指引下，依靠各自拥有的资本进行斗争的场所。

布迪厄认为惯习贯穿于行动者内外。它既指导着行动者的行为，又展示了他们的风格和气质。惯习不仅记录了行动者的生活经验和受教育经历，而且记录了行动者在不同的环境中实施的创新。惯习具有稳定性和持续性，同时也随时随地受制于社会条件，从而发生变化。此外，惯习既体现了行动者的个性和禀赋，也渗透了他所属社会群体的阶层性质。它既是长期社会结构内在化的结果，以性情倾向的方式系统地表现出来，又在实践中主动外在化，不断再生产新的社会结构。惯习伴随着行动者的生存心态和生活风格，同时也是历史经验和实时创造的统一体，表现为"主动中的被动"和"被动中的主动"，是社会客观条件和行动者主观内在创造力的统一体。惯习源自行动者长期的实践活动，经过一定时期的积累，经验内化为人们的意识，指导和调动着行动者的行为，成为他们社会行为、生存方式、生活模式和行为策略的强有力生成机制。

布迪厄把资本定义为行动者的社会实践工具，他认为资本表现为四种基本形式，即经济资本、文化资本、社会资本和象征资本。

场域、惯习、资本是布迪厄社会学理论应用于翻译研究的三个核心概念，三者之间与社会实践的关系是：【(惯习)(资本)】+ 场域 = 实践（Bourdieu，1984）。也就是说，行动者通过秉持的惯习和享有的资本在场域中参与社会实践。译本作为翻译实践的产物，与译者所处的场域、秉持的惯习和享有的资本密切相关。换言之，场域、惯习、资本导引并制约译者的文本选材与翻译策略（蔡瑞珍，2023）。

1901年，亨克（Frederick Goodrich Henke）作为美国基督教会卫理公会的传教士到江西九江传教，并于1910年在芝加哥大学（University of Chicago）以优等成绩获得哲学博士学位。1911年，亨克应位于上海的皇家亚洲文会北中国支会（the North China Branch of Royal Asiatic Society of Shanghai）的汉学家邀请，对王阳明进行了深入的研究，并成为该会会员。亨克选择翻译王阳明著作，与当时的哲学场域和亨克本人的文化资本紧密相关。20世纪中期之前，西方对中国哲学的译介研究以先秦哲学为主，西方哲学场域整体忽视了宋明哲学的思想价值。而成长于牧师家庭的亨克从小接受基督教思想熏陶，是基督徒与卫理公会牧师，又获得哲学博士学位，是哲学和心理学教授，具备相当的宗教哲学文化资本。

陈荣捷（Wing-Tsit Chan）选择翻译王阳明著作同样与当时的哲学场域和陈荣捷本人的文化资本紧密相关。20世纪五六十年代，美国根据自身发展利益，调整在远东的发展战略，加强对亚洲和中国问题的研究，比如设立福特基金会和亚洲研究协会等资助和研究机构，促进了中国学在美国的迅速发展。陈荣捷翻译《传习录》是在西方阳明学研究逐渐发展的哲学场域中进行的。另外，陈荣捷从小接受儒家经典教育，获得哈佛大学哲学博士学位。他一生致力于中国哲学研究，首次为《大不列颠百科辞典》撰写朱子和王阳明词条，是20世纪80年代发表阳明学著作最多的学者，成为欧美宋明理学研究的权威。可以说，陈荣捷在美国的中国哲学这一子场域中享有较为丰厚的文化资本（蔡瑞珍，2023）。

两位译者不同的资本与惯习必然会在他们的译文中得到体现。将两位译者对关键术语的翻译做一个比较（见表9-1）会发现，受场域、惯习和资本的影响，两人的翻译策略截然不同。总的来说，亨克秉持"以西释中"的翻译理念，采用以目的语为中心的意译归化策略；陈荣捷则沿用"以中释中"的翻译思想，采用以源语为中心的直译异化策略。

表 9-1　陈译本与享译本对关键术语的翻译比较

原文	译文	
	陈荣捷译本	亨克译本
理	principle	principles；natural law
天理	the Principle of Nature	heaven-given principles
天下事理	all principles of things in the world	the laws of the physical realm
新民	in renovating the people	to renovate the people；renew
朱子	Chu Hsi	the philosopher Chu
问	asked	made inquiry
君子贤其贤而亲其亲，小人乐其乐而利其利	Rulers deemed worthy what they deemed worthy and loved what they loved，while the common people enjoyed what they enjoyed and benefited from their beneficial arrangements	The princes deem worthy what the people deemed worthy and love what the people loved'；The common people delight in what delighted the princes and benefit by their beneficial arrangements
百姓不能相亲相爱	the common people did not love one another	The people did not love（those above them）
《尧典》	略	The canon of Yao

首先，在叙述体例上，亨克仅部分保留原文语录体的文体形式，而陈荣捷的英译本几乎完全保留了原文语录体的问答形式。无论问或答，亨克译本很少使用"asked"与"answered"这样直观的问答形式与字眼，绝大部分以"said"为主，间或使用"made inquiry saying"这样的表达法，极少使用"replied"。陈荣捷译本最大程度地保存了原作的思想表达方式，使用"asked"与"said"这种对应形式的频率大大高于亨克。这或许与两位译

者来自不同的哲学场域有关。在中国哲学场域下,圣贤如孔子的对话形式是传授已知知识的场所,所以著作中常见"学生问—老师答"的对话形式;而西方哲人如苏格拉底的对话对已知知识持一种反思态度,把对话当作双方一起探求真知识的过程,体现真正对话的本质。

其次,在哲学术语翻译上,亨克译文倾向于以西方哲学思想诠释中国哲学词汇;而陈荣捷则常用音译加注或提供详细注释,保持哲学词汇翻译的前后一致性。亨克从小接受宗教的洗礼与熏陶,宗教思想已经形塑成稳固的性情倾向,内化为宗教惯习,从而影响着他的翻译策略。亨克在中国传教十余年,其宗教背景与形塑的惯习不可避免地参与到他对阳明学的解读中,故而他以目的语文化为中心,营造西方读者熟悉的文化语境,增加亲近感,引起西方读者的兴趣并从心理上接受阳明学(徐赛颖,2020)。虽然亨克译文使用了厚翻译策略[①],但是他的注释大多仅为一至两行,比较简单,主要为引文出处,未能从中国哲学思想的角度进行详细地阐释与说明。

反观陈荣捷,他生于广东开平,自小接受儒家经典教育,并以《庄子》为题完成了博士论文。在哲学惯习和资本影响下,他采用"以中释中"的策略尽量保持中国哲学本色。例如,对于"天理"的翻译,陈荣捷译为"the Principle of Nature",把"天"解释为"自然";亨克译为"heaven-given principles",把"天"解释为"天堂"。由于彼时中国哲学典籍在西方的哲学场域中处于"边缘中的边缘"(崔玉军,2010),以传教士为主体的中国哲学翻译很大程度上是为了宣扬并传播基督教,亨克也不例外。在哲学场域、传教士的身份所带来的惯习与资本等因素的作用下,他的译文明显带有宗教色彩。同样例子还有"《尧典》",亨克选用"The canon of Yao",其

[①] 根据美国哈佛大学非美文化研究中心的翻译学者夸梅·阿皮亚(Kwame Anthony Appiah)的观点,厚翻译是指"在翻译文本中,添加各种注释、评注和长篇序言,将翻译文本置于丰富的文化与语言环境中,以促使被文字遮蔽的意义与翻译者的意图相融合。只有采用厚翻译的方法,即深厚语境化的方法,在翻译文本中添加注释或术语注解,才能表现出源语言中丰富而深厚的语言和文化语境。"

中"canon"属宗教词汇，有"a Church decree or law（教规，宗教法规）"或"（in the Roman Catholic Church）the part of the Mass containing the words of consecration"之意。

对于关键术语的翻译，陈荣捷很注重前后一致性，如"新民"之"新"处理为"renovate"。但是亨克没有统一，既用"renovate"，也用"renew"。在陈荣捷的译文中，"理"一直译为"principle"；但是亨克的"理"既有"principle"，也有"law"。此外，陈荣捷还严格使用了威妥玛（Thomas Francis Wade）式拼音法（Wade-Giles romanization）对专有术语、人名等进行补充。虽然亨克也使用了威妥玛式音译，但是没有陈荣捷那般严格，如他将"朱子"译为"the philosopher Chu"。威妥玛式音译可以被归为一种陌生化翻译策略，在惯习和资本的影响下，陈荣捷采取此种译介方式目的在于便于西方读者理解，同时保留中国文化的特色。

亨克和陈荣捷的《传习录》英译本促进了英语世界阳明学研究的发端与进展，而两译本的差异则反映了译者背后所持的文化资本及其在场域结构中的位置关系。亨克作为一名传教士，继承了"以西释中"的翻译策略，以西方视角诠释中国哲学概念，以此维护西方哲学宗教场域的逻辑与规则。陈荣捷作为在美国进行中国哲学研究的权威学者，拥有较为丰厚的文化资本，在中国哲学研究子场域中占据一定的位置。他在翻译中沿用"以中释中"的研究路径，用中国哲学思想诠释中国哲学概念，其译本呈现出明显的"学案式"深度翻译特色。

三、译论·比较

翻译主体以及哲学著作的具体翻译经常受到学者们的批评。

乔纳森·里（Jonathan Rée）认为，将法国哲学翻译成英语通常是有问题的，这源于译者假定这两种语言比实际情况更接近。韦努蒂（Venuti）认为，乔伊特（Jowett）19世纪对柏拉图的翻译强调流畅性，这破坏了原始文本特有的"陌生感"。当然，并非所有对哲学文本翻译的批评都是负面的。Rée指出，肯普·史密斯（Kemp Smith）1929年翻译康德的《纯粹理性批判》（*Critique of Pure Reason*），其英译本已被成千上万的学生使用，迄今为止几乎没有发现任何严重的缺陷，许多德国读者在遇到原文问题时反而会参考该译本。对韦努蒂来说，安斯科姆（Anscombe）翻译的《哲学研究》可以说"传达了维特根斯坦的思想，甚至模仿了他的写作风格"。

无论是消极的还是积极的，哲学翻译批评都提供了可用于指导实践和实践理论化的经验参考。事实上，Rée认为任何语言中的严肃哲学"总是听起来已经像是翻译"，因此没有理由担心翻译的哲学听起来像是翻译。哲学有各种各样的体裁——自传、对话、散文、期刊文章、讲稿、信件、冥想、小说、祈祷、散文诗、评论、布道、故事——译者需要灵活应对各种哲学文本类型和风格。

值得注意的是，许多关于不可译性的争论都是围绕哲学术语的翻译展开的，因此斯坦纳坚称"不可译性问题触及了整个哲学事业的核心"，但译哲行为从未停止过。翻译哲学从来都不是直截了当的。哲学的晦涩在于其蕴含的对话和文学性质，以及哲学中的许多术语发展出自己的生命的事实。因此，大多数哲学著作都是由受过适当学术训练的专业哲学家翻译的。例如，维特根斯坦的《哲学研究》在他死后于1953年出版了一个版本，其中包括由著名哲学家、维特根斯坦的学生安斯科姆（Anscombe）翻译的德语文本。

鉴于此，请按照以下要点对Ivanhoe所译的《徐爱录》选段进行鉴析：

（1）将该译本与Wing-Tsit Chan与Henke译本进行对比赏析；

（2）对三个译本中的核心哲学术语作出批评解析。

I asked, "Zhu Xi says thar the phrase 'loving the people' (*qin min* 亲民) in the line from the *Great Learning* that reads '[Making bright one's bright virtue] lies in loving the people' should be changed to 'renovating the people' (*xin min* 新民). Since a later passage in the text says 'Encourage the people to renovate themselves' (*zuo xin min* 作新民), it seems as though there is good evidence for his claim. But you, Master, are of the opinion that it is proper to follow the old version of the text, which has 'loving the people.' Do you, too, have good evidence for your view?"

The Master said, "The word *xin* ['renovate'] in the expression 'Encourage the people to renovate themselves' refers to the people renovating *themselves* [i.e., not *being* renovated]. The word *xin* is not being used in the same way in the expression 'lies in *renovating* the people' (*zai xinmin* 在新民). How can the former [use of *xin*] be regarded as evidence? The word 'encourage' (*zuo*) is parallel to the word 'loving' (*qin*), but they do not mean the same thing. The passages that follow, which talk about 'ordering the state' and 'bringing peace to the world,' do not expand upon the meaning of the word *xin*. When the text says things like, '[Oh! The former kings are not forgotten!] The gentleman regards as worthy what they regarded as worthy and loves what they loved ; the common man enjoys what they enjoyed and benefits from what benefited them,' or '[Watch over the people] as though you were caring for an infant,' or '[The ruler] loved what the people loved and loathed what the people loathed. This is what it means to be mother and father to the people', all of these express the idea of *loving*. The [sense of love] in the expression 'loving the people' (*qin min*) is like Mengzi's teaching that '[the gentleman] *loves* his parents and is benevolent toward people.' To love is to be benevolent toward. It was because "the people are lacking in love" that Emperor Shun employed Xie as minister of education and had him reverently disseminate the Five Teachings. This was how [Shun] loved the people. In the 'Canon of Yao,' the line that reads '[He] was able to make bright his resplendent virtue' describes 'making bright one's bright virtue.' The following lines [in the 'Canon of Yao'], that talk about 'loving the nine classes of his kin', 'pacifying and cultivating [the people of his domain], and 'unifying and harmonizing [the myriad states]' describe 'making bright one's bright virtue throughout the world.' This idea also is seen in Kongzi's teaching that "the gentleman cultivates himself in order to bring peaceful repose to the people.' 'Cultivating himself' describes 'making bright one's bright virtue,' while to bring peaceful repose to the people describes loving the people. Reading [the opening line in the *Great Learning* as] 'loving the people' combines the ideas of educating and nurturing [the people]. Reading it as 'renovating the people' would seem to be one-sided [and incomplete]."

I asked, "Concerning the line 'When one knows where to abide, there is stability,' Zhu Xi thought that 'each thing and every affair has its own fixed principle.' This seems to conflict with your explanation [of the text]."

The Master said, "To seek for the highest good in things and affairs is to treat righteousness as external. The highest good is the original state of the heart-mind; it is simply what results when the effort of making bright one's bright virtue reaches the point of being 'wholly refined and wholly focused.' This being so, it is never separated or found apart from things and affairs. "Zhu Xi got it right when in his commentary on the *Great Learning* he said that '[making bright one's bright virtue] is fully realizing Heavenly principle without the presence of even the slightest human desire.'"

I asked, "If one seeks for the highest good only in the heart-mind, I fear that one will not fully grasp the principles of all the world's affairs."

The Master said, "The heart-mind is principle. Is there any affair outside the heart-mind? Is there any principle outside the heart-mind?"

(Translated by Philip J. Ivanhoe)

四、实践·译笔

1. 学者一念为善之志，如树之种，但勿忘勿助，只管培植将去，自然日夜滋长，生气日完，枝叶日茂。

2. 自朝至暮，自少至老，若要无念，即是已不知，此除是昏睡，除是槁木死灰。

3. 今这里补个"敬"字，那里补个"诚"字，未免画蛇添足。

4. 人心之得其正者，即道心；道心之失其正者，即人心。初非有二心也。程子谓"人心即人欲，道心即天理"。

5. 某今说个知行合一，正是对病的药。又不是某凿空独撰。知行本体，原来如此。

五、阅读·延展

哲学文字有容易译的有不容易译的。哲学可以分为两大部分，一部分差不多完全是理性的，另一部分不完全是理性的。前者靠分析靠批评，后者靠综合靠创作。前者近乎科学，后者近乎宗教。大多数不学哲学的人所注重的是后者，从前的中国人所注重的似乎也是后者。现在学哲学的人有注重前者而不注重后者，也有注重后者而不注重前者，也有二者都注重的。就翻译说，前者是容易翻译的，后者是不容易翻译的。知识论是比较容易翻译的，玄学或形而上学是比较不容易翻译的。中国哲学底纯理成分少，所以也不容易翻译。中国人底"道"字恰巧有希腊文中的 logos，在别的文字如英文似乎就没有相当的字，其他如天，性，命，体，用，诚，仁，义，礼，都是意味深长而意义在别的文字中得不到相当的字眼去表示的。在这种情形下，翻译即令不是不可能的，也是非常之困难的。

即令能译，原动力也许仍得不到。这种困难不必是意义不清楚的困难。有的时候，因为字句底意义底多歧而有意味底丰富，如果翻译出来的字句底意义不是多歧的，而是限于某一方面的意义，原来字句底意味当然会有损失。有的时候，因为字句底意义虽可以翻译，然而翻译底字句没有原来字句底意味。假如我们能够把中国字底意义，先用中文明白地表示出来，能够把它们彼此之间的意念上的关联，精细明白地组织成一意念上的结构，然后在另一文字，例如英文，创造相当的新字以表示此整个的结构，也许我们在意念上把原来的字句完全翻译出来了。在此情形下，原来的字句所表示的意念，就纯思说，或纯理说，已经是翻译成功了，然而就意味说，或就情感说，原来字句所能引起的情感，译文中一点都没有。哲学字句的情感上的寄托有时是原动力，这种情感上的寄托翻译不出来，这种原动力也得不到。即使我们能从译文中懂得原文中的意义，我们也不见得能够受感动。……

哲学文字底另一种困难。以上是就意义虽能由翻译传达而意味不能由翻译传达这一方面着想。这也许还不是普通的情形，也许普通的情形是意念上的意义也难以翻译。哲学有一种情形不是普通所谓科学所常有的。科学不常引用日常生活所引用的字，即不得已而引用，它也用种种方式表示意义底不同。哲学似乎常用日常生活所常引用的字，却不给它们以日常生活中所有的意义，而又引用日常生活中的语言以表示意思，其结果是我们很容易把日常生活中的情感及意义渗入非常的意义。这种情形不但无分于东西而且差不多无分于古今。差不多到最近的多少年内，哲学上的表示方式才有点技术化。在这种情形之下，不但翻译困难而且就是在所谓本国文字也有困难。"性命天道"，一方面有哲学上的意义，一方面又有日常生活中的意义。中国哲学对于中国人本来就有不容易懂的问题（英国哲学对于英国人也有同样的问题）。在本国文有这样的问题，翻译底问题更大。专就意念上的意义说，也许有思想因翻译而清楚的，但是，即令有这样的情形，它也少到可以不必顾虑的程度上去了。

（摘自金岳霖的《论翻译》）

Philosophy is an ancient activity that involves reflecting on how we should live and on the nature of knowledge, and translation has often been the subject of such reflection. As early as the fifth century BCE, for example, Herodotus asked how those with different languages could understand each other. When Wittgenstein became involved in Ogden's English translation of his 1921 *Tractatus Logico-Philosophicus*, he remarked: "It is a difficult business!"; it is the realization of this difficulty that has motivated philosophical involvement with translation. Thus, Crane asserts that we start to philosophize about translation once we see that translating is not a matter of straightforward conversion. And yet, in the context of canonical and/or professional philosophy, relatively little has been written on translation, leading Venuti to refer to translation as philosophy's "dark secret". What attention has been given to translation has largely come from philosophers in the continental tradition, which privileges existential enquiry, most notably Schleiermacher, Nietzsche, Benjamin, Heidegger, Gadamer, Ricoeur and Derrida. However, some philosophers in the analytic tradition, which privileges questions of logic and language, have made important contributions to relevant debates, notably Quine and Davidson. Arrojo suggests that there is increasing interaction between philosophy and translation studies, as evidenced by the growing number of publications and conferences linking the two disciplines. Both disciplines have been influenced by the so-called linguistic turn in the humanities, which may account for growing dialogue. Cassin's *The Dictionary of Untranslatables* (2004, 2014), which examines philosophical terms and their life in translation, is a particularly important development in this direction. Rawling and Wilson provide an overview of canonical philosophers' views on translation.

Translation is important to philosophy for two reasons. First, few philosophers can read all relevant source texts in the original. A contemporary Anglophone undergraduate syllabus, for example, might include works translated from Arabic, French, German, Greek, Latin, Pali and Sanskrit. Second, translation raises issues of conceptual interest to philosophers, because it tells us about language, life and the mind. Nietzsche (1882/2012), for example, examines Roman renderings of Greek texts to show how human affairs inevitably involve a struggle for power, which implies that translation can be read in terms of appropriation, while Derrida argues that with the problem of translation we are dealing with "nothing less than the problem of the very passage into philosophy".

Philosophy is important to translation studies because theorists often use it to support their views. Steiner draws on hermeneutics to develop his translation theory; Tymoczko uses the notion of family resemblance in Wittgenstein to argue that translation is a "cluster concept" that should not be accorded an essentialist definition; the debate on domestication and foreignization introduced by Venuti is rooted in readings of Schleiermacher, and his subsequent support for a hermeneutical model against an instrumental model draws on the hermeneutic tradition in general as well as on Derrida and Peirce. There are risks involved in linking the two fields, however. Pym suspects that "philosophers would not always identify with what has been done in their name" by nonspecialists. If translation studies is to continue to establish itself as a discipline, it must treat its boundaries as fluid and continue to interact with other disciplines, but what is needed is dialogue, not the naive belief that philosophy can solve all the problems of translation.

(Excerpts from *Philosophy* by Philip Wilson)

第十单元

戏剧鼻祖·明代汤显祖

一、译事·译研

汤显祖（1550—1616），字义仍，号海若、若士、清远道人，江西临川人，明代伟大的戏剧家、文学家、思想家，被誉为"中国戏圣"和"东方莎士比亚"，其作品《紫钗记》《牡丹亭》《南柯记》《邯郸记》《紫箫记》构成了一个极具个人色彩与艺术风格的戏剧世界。2015年10月21日，中国国家主席习近平访英期间发表演讲时指出："汤显祖与莎士比亚是同时代的人，他们两人都是1616年逝世的。明年是他们逝世400周年。中英两国可以共同纪念这两位文学巨匠，以此推动两国人民交流、加深相互理解。"此后，中英两国都举办了各种戏剧演出、工作坊、讲座等文化交流活动，在进行一场场"跨越时空与文化的经典邂逅"之时，也借助这一文化纽带加强了异域文明的交流与对话。可以说，中国古典戏剧外译不仅是中国文化对外传播的重要方面，也是中西文明互鉴的特色抓手。因为蕴藏了文化传统的古典戏剧不仅是一种舞台表演，也是一门文学艺术。因此，从翻译对象的文本属性角度而言，古典戏剧兼具典籍与表演的双重功用。

汤显祖系列戏剧中公认知名度与艺术价值最高的当数《牡丹亭》。无论是文字语言、思想内容、情感表现、艺术造诣，《牡丹亭》都达到了古典戏剧创作的巅峰。相应地，其对外译介也颇受关注，得到了异语文化的主动接纳与赞赏,成为中国古典戏剧及其文化走出去的一张靓丽名片。

1939年哈罗德·阿克顿根据《牡丹亭》京剧改写了英译本《春香闹学》(见第七出《闺塾》),乃译介汤剧之开端。1960年杨宪益、戴乃迭夫妇选择能够再现《牡丹亭》主要情节的十一出进行了英译,以一种忠实且不失灵活的译法为英语读者展现了该剧的面貌。1965年美国华裔汉学家翟楚和翟文伯借鉴杨、戴夫妇之译,英译了该剧的三出并收录于其主编的《中国文学瑰宝》。在经历了将近半个世纪的选译、节译之后,1980年白之(Birch)第一次全译《牡丹亭》并由美国印第安纳大学出版社出版。该译本具有一定的文学批评意识,恰当地游走于异化与归化之间,一方面白之注重解读中国文学,保留并再现原文化特色;另一方面也会使用归化语词以靠近读者。之后,国内译者张光前也在1994年全译《牡丹亭》,其间采用了素体诗格式,注重节奏流畅度和音韵协调性。1996年,宇文所安编著《中国文学选集》收录了自己翻译的《牡丹亭》三出以及《作者题词》。

进入21世纪,国内译者汪榕培先生全译《牡丹亭》,译文力主呈现中国文化精华,风格古朴且符合当代英语规范。译者力图"用英语再现原作之美……在中国文化走向世界的过程中贡献一点自己的力量"。该译本也进入《大中华文库》系列丛书。2009年,许渊冲和许明对《牡丹亭》原文部分内容进行了删减和重组,并在"翻译求美"的理念下合译其中的二十二出,实践并再现"音美、意美、形美"。2021年,黄必康《牡丹亭》全译本由商务印书馆发行。该译本忠实于原作品的文学细节和审美意趣,同时更为靠近读者,仿拟莎剧的语言表现与优美韵律。

除去翻译译介,有关《牡丹亭》的文本研究与(汤剧和莎剧)比较研究不断涌现,如汉学家白之发表论文《〈牡丹亭〉或〈还魂记〉》(1974)和《〈冬天的故事〉与〈牡丹亭〉》(1984),史凯蒂(Catherine Swatek)、奚若谷(Stephen H. West)、袁苏菲(Sophie Vilpp)、杜威廉(William Dolby)等学者创作了相关专著和论文。同时,根据《牡丹亭》译本改编的剧目经常在英语国家上演并赢得了诸多赞誉,"这部作品对欧洲、美洲和澳洲的观众具有吸引力",

"观众极其喜爱它"。

中国综合实力的提升离不开翻译传播这一文化软实力的有力补充,而古典戏剧的翻译传播更能凸显中国特色,宣扬中华文化魅力。围绕《牡丹亭》的翻译译介、学术研究、舞台表演、文化交流活动等形成了多层次、立体化的传播效果,如评论所说:《牡丹亭》的舞台演出使杜丽娘已经跨越昆曲的界限,走向了国际大舞台",真正是"以小剧切入,话大国文明"(Swatek, 2002)。

二、鉴赏·评析

【原文】

牡丹亭·第十出　惊梦(选段)

【隔尾】观之不足由他缱[1],便赏遍了十二亭台是枉然。到不如兴尽回家闲过遣。(作到介)(贴)"开我西阁门,展我东阁床。瓶插映山紫,炉添沉水香。"小姐,你歇息片时,俺瞧老夫人去也。(下)(旦叹介)"默地游春转,小试宜春面[2]。"春呵,得和你两留连,春去如何遣?咳,恁般天气,好困人也。春香那里?(作左右瞧介)(又低首沉吟介)天呵,春色恼人,信有之乎!常观诗词乐府,古之女子,因春感情,遇秋成恨,诚不谬矣。吾今年已二八,未逢折桂之夫;忽慕春情,怎得蟾宫之客?昔日韩夫人得遇于郎[3],张生偶逢崔氏[4],曾有《题红记》《崔徽传》[5]二书。此佳人才子,前以密约偷期[6],后皆得成秦晋[7]。(长叹介)吾生于宦族,长在名门。年已及笄[8],不得早成佳配,诚为虚度青春。光阴如过隙耳。(泪介)可惜妾身颜色如花,岂料命如一叶乎!

【山坡羊】没乱里春情难遣[9],蓦地里怀人幽怨。则为俺生小婵娟,拣名门一例、一例里神仙眷。甚良缘,把青春抛的远!俺的睡情谁见?则索因循腼腆。想幽梦谁边,和春光暗流转?迁延,这衷怀那处言!淹煎,泼残生[10],除问天!身子困乏了,且自隐几而眠[11]。(睡介)(梦生介)(生持柳枝上)"莺逢日暖歌声滑,人遇风情笑口开。一径落花随水入,今朝阮肇到天台⑫。"小生顺路儿跟着杜小姐回来,怎生不见?(回看介)呀,小姐,小姐!(旦作惊起介)(相见介)(生)小生那一处不寻访小姐来,却在这里!(旦作斜视不语介)(生)恰好花园内,折取垂柳半枝。姐姐,你既淹通书史,可作诗以赏此柳枝乎?(旦作惊喜,欲言又止介)(背想)这生素昧平生,何因到此?(生笑介)小姐,咱爱杀你哩!

(选自[明]汤显祖著,徐朔方、杨笑梅校注:《牡丹亭》)

【注释】

① 缱:留恋、牵挂。

② 宜春面:指新妆。

③ 韩夫人得遇于郎:唐人传奇故事。唐僖宗时,宫女韩氏以红叶题诗,从御沟中流出,被于祐拾到。于祐也以红叶题诗,投入御沟的上流,寄给韩氏。后来两人结为夫妇。见《青琐高议》前集卷五《流红记》。汤显祖的同时代人王骥德曾以这个故事写成戏曲《题红记》,见王骥德《曲律·杂论》第三十九下。

④ 张生偶逢崔氏:张生和崔莺莺的爱情故事。

⑤《崔徽传》是另外一个故事,见《丽情集》:妓女崔徽和裴敬中相爱,分别之后不再相见。崔徽请画工画了一幅像,托人带给敬中说:"崔徽一旦不及卷中人,徽且为郎死矣!"这里《崔徽传》疑是《莺莺传》或《西厢记》的笔误。

⑥ 偷期:幽会。

⑦ 得成秦晋:得成夫妇。春秋时期,秦、晋两国世代联姻,后世称联姻为秦晋之好。

⑧ 及笄(jī):古代女子十五岁开始以笄(簪)束发,叫及笄,意指女子已成年,到了婚配的年龄。见《礼记·内则》。

⑨ 没乱里:形容心绪很乱。

⑩ 淹煎,泼残生:淹煎,受熬煎,遭磨折;泼残生,苦命儿。泼,表示厌恶,原来是骂人的话。

⑪ 隐几:靠着几案。

⑫阮肇到天台：见到爱人。讲刘晨和阮肇在天台山桃源洞遇见仙女的故事。

【译文】

The Peony Pavilion

Excerpts from "Scene Ten : The Interrupted Dream"

VI

Unwearying joy—how should we break its spell even by visits each in turn to the Twelve Towers of Fairyland? Far better now, as first elation passes, to find back in our chamber some pastime for idle hours.

(They reach the house)

FRAGRANCE :

"Open the west chamber door,

in the east room make the bed,

fill the vase with azalea,

light aloes in the incense burner."

Take your rest now, young mistress, while I go report to Madam.

(She exits)

BRIDAL *(sighing)* :

Back from spring stroll to silent room,

what to do but try on the spring's new adornments?

Ah spring, now that you and I have formed so strong an attachment, what shall I find to fill my days when you are past? Oh this weather, how sleepy it makes one feel. Where has Fragrance got to? (*She looks about her, then lowers her head again, pondering*) Ah Heaven, now I begin to realize how disturbing the spring's splendor can truly be. They were all telling the truth, those poems and ballads I read that spoke of gifts of ancient times "in springtime moved to passion, in autumn to regret." Here am I at the "double eight," my sixteenth year, yet no fine "scholar to break the cassia Bough" has come my way. My young passions stir to the young spring season, but where shall I find an "entrant of the moon's toad palace"? Long ago the Lady Han found a way to a meeting with Yu You, and the scholar Zhang met with Miss Cui by chance. Their loves are told in *Poem on the Red Leaf* and in *Western Chamber*[①], how these "fair maids and gifted youths" after clandestine meetings made marital unions "as between Qin and Jin."[②] (*She gives a long sigh*) Though born and bred of a noted line of holders of office, I have reached the age to "pin up my hair" without plan made for my betrothal to a suitable partner. The green springtime of my own life passes unfulfilled, and swift the time speeds by as dawn and dusk interchange. (*She weeps*) O pity one whose beauty is a bright flower, when life endures no longer than leaf on tree!

VII

From turbulent heart these springtime thoughts of love will not be banished — O with what suddenness comes this secret discontent!

I was a pretty child, and so of equal eminence must the family be truly immortals, no less to receive me in marriage. But for what grand alliance is this springtime of my youth so cast away? What eyes may light upon my sleeping form? My only course this coy delaying but in secret dreams by whose side do I

---

① *Poem on the Red Leaf* (*Tihongji*) is the title of a play by Tang Xianzu's friend, Wang Zhide. The theme is taken from the Tang story of the Lady Han, who wrote a poem on a red leaf, which she set adrift on the water of the palace drain. The leaf was found by Yu You, who returned a message to her by similar means, and eventually met and married her. *Western Chamber* (*Xixiangji*) is Wang Shifu's famous play on the romance, again of Tang times, of the scholar Zhang and Cui Yingying, whom he met by chance on his visit to the temple in which she was lodging. In fact, our text does not name the *Xixiangji* at this point; rather, the *Cui Hui zhuan*, the story of another Miss Cui, but this seems an unnecessary complication.

② Two states of the "Springs and Autumns" period, whose ruling families for generations made marriage alliances.

lie? Shadowed against spring's glory I twist and turn. Lingering where to reveal my true desires! Suffering this wasting, where but to Heaven shall my lament be made!

I feel rather tired, I shall rest against this low table and drowse for a while.

(*She falls asleep and begins to dream of LIU MENGMEI, who enters bearing a branch of willow in his hand*)

LIU MENGMEI:

As song of oriole purls in warmth of sun,

so smiling lips open to greet romance.

Tracing my path by petals borne on stream,

I find the Peach Blossom Source of my desire.[①]

I came along this way with Miss Du—how is it that she is not with me now? (*He looks behind him and sees her*) Ah, Miss Du!

(*She rises, startled from sleep, and greets him. He continues*)

So this is where you were—I was looking for you everywhere. (*She glances shyly at him, but does not speak*) I just chanced to break off this branch from a weeping willow in the garden. You are so deeply versed in works of literature; I should like you to compose a poem to honor it.

(*She starts in surprised delight and opens her lips to speak, but checks herself*)

BRIDAL (*aside*):

I have never seen this young man in my life—what is he doing here?

---

① Allusion to a story of Liu Chen and Ruan Zhao of Han times, who found faery love by following a "peachblossom spring" into the Tiantai ("Terrace of Heaven") Mountains. Even more celebrated is the Peach Blossom Spring of an allegory by Tao Qian describing, at the stream's source, a secluded Shangrila upon which a mortal stumbled.

LIU（*smiling at her*）：

Lady, I am dying of love for you!

（Translated by Cyril Birch）

【评析】

翻译不仅仅是一种语言之间的转换，更是一种跨文化的交际过程。交际双方要想达到预期的交际目的就必须要有共同的背景知识（shared background knowledge）或语用前提（pragmatic presupposition）。有了这一共同知识或语用前提，在交流时就可以省去一些对双方来说不言而喻的东西，从而提高交际的效率。生活在同一社会文化环境中的成员都具有关于这一社会文化的共同知识。因此在交际中，根据语用的经济原则，除非有特殊的目的，他们在运用概念时一般都不会将有关图式中的所有信息全部输出，而往往只是根据交际的需要择重点或典型而用。至于那些对交际双方来说不言自明的内容则往往加以省略。这种被交际双方作为共享的背景知识而加以省略的部分叫作"情境缺省"（situational default）。如果被缺省的部分与语篇内信息有关就叫作"语境缺省"（contextual default），而与语篇外的文化背景有关的就是"文化缺省"（cultural default）。由于文化缺省是一种具有鲜明文化特性的（culture-specific）交际现象，是某一文化内部运作的结果，因此不属于该文化的接受者常常会碰到这种缺省所造成的意义真空（vacuum of sense），无法将语篇内信息与语篇外的知识和经验联系起来，从而难以建立起理解话语所必须的语义连贯（semantic coherence）和情境连贯（situational coherence）。作者在写作时一般都会对自己意向读者（intended reader）的知识结构有一个大致的了解，尤其是对读者的文化经验一般都有比较准确的判断。因此，作者对于一些他认为与读者共有的且无须赘言的文化信息往往会在文中略去。他的意向读者则会在交际（阅读）中根据语篇中某些信号的提示（cue）自觉地填充文化缺省所留下的空位，激活记忆中的有关图式。作者借助文化缺省所要达到的交际意图是通过读者的这种先有知识（prior knowledge）的参与来实现的，文本中受文化缺省影响的语言符号也因此同现实或可能世界连贯起来。我们不得不承认这样一个事实：原文作者在写作时可能不会专门为译文读者的接受能力着想。因此，作为翻译过程主体和中介的译者，必须对文化缺省有高度敏感性和自觉性，有责任对原文重构"文化空缺"，重建语义连贯，使译文对其读者所产生的效果与原文对读者所产生的效果最大限度地趋同（李先进，2013）。译者在补偿文化缺省时可采取多种策略，如：

文外作注，即文内直译，有关文化缺省的说明则放在注释之中；

文内明示，即文内意译，或直译与意译相结合，不借助注释；

归化，即用蕴含目标文化身份的表达方式取代蕴含出发文化身份的表达方式；

删除，即删去含有影响语篇连贯的文化缺省；

硬译，即按字面照译原文，对于影响阅读中连贯重构的文化缺省不作任何交代（王东风，1997）；

直译，原语与译语在表达和语义上接近时，对于原文的文化缺省现象无须任何交代，译出原文内容的同时保留原文形式，既求神似又求形似，达到形式与内容的最佳关联；

意译，即用简洁明了的表达方式释义性解释原文中文化意义浓厚、晦涩难懂的部分，不拘泥于原文细节及形式，译文流畅自然即可。

戏剧承载着丰富的中国文化，如何在不损失原文美学价值的情况下翻译戏剧是译者面临的一个巨大挑战。作为古典戏剧创作巅峰的《牡丹亭》沉淀着独特的中华文化魅力。接下来我们将解读文中的文化缺省及译者的翻译策略。

《游园惊梦》是《牡丹亭》中的一个经典片段，最能体现深闺少女杜丽娘丰富的内心世界，主要内容为：杜丽娘游园惊觉春色之美与春光之可贵，感叹自己的妙龄青春被蹉跎，回屋后，困倦伏案睡去，梦中入情，与书生柳梦梅在花园中相会，而后被母亲"唤醒"。结合整个故事与时代背景，我们知道这反映了青年男女相互爱慕、大胆追求自由爱情、坚决反对封建礼教的精神,故而醒的不仅是梦,更是杜丽娘的自我意识、情感意识和性意识。所以"惊梦"中被缺省的部分既与语篇内信息有关,更与语篇外的文化背景有关。白之采用直译的方式译为"The Interrupted Dream",虽实现了情景连贯,但是目标语读者很难觉察到语篇外的知识。

在这段节选中,白之对【隔尾】与【山坡羊】这种能够体现戏剧文学特征的标志予以省略,但其实这两处携带了重要的信息,不应被省译。读者从这个"隔"字就知道戏唱到这里尚未结束,而【山坡羊】作为曲牌名可以让读者知道接下来便是唱曲。删除后读者无法了解本应知晓的文化信息。这种译法为了使译文语篇处于较好的连贯状态之中,删去了含有文化缺省并可能造成意义真空的内容,因此具有一定的欺骗性。

在处理原文中的舞台指示语如"贴"和"旦"时,白之选择删除的策略。"贴"是指在正旦之外再贴一个次要的旦角。"旦"顾名思义就是旦角,虽然删除后读者也可根据语境理解角色之间的身份,但是从文化的角度而言,这种删除阻碍了彼此间的交流,也剥夺了译语读者领略源语文化魅力的权利。对于角色名,译者采取直译的方式,求其神而舍其形,将"春香"与"杜丽娘"分别译为"FRAGRANCE"和"BRIDAL"。但不知何故,白之没有与前面角色译名保持一致,而是采取音译的方式将"柳梦梅"译为"LIU MENGMEI"。

文中的"映山紫""沉水香""莺"以及"垂柳"等专有名词不仅指事物本身,还富含文化外延。因为寓情于景、寓情于物、托物言志等是中国古代诗歌常见的创作手法,久而久之,一些事物便承载了丰富的文化意蕴,如"杜鹃"有烘托伤春、惜春之情,思乡之情,悲苦、哀怨之情和亡国之情等。"垂柳"有迎接春天的喜悦之情,送别时的不舍与思念之情,对家乡的思念之情,也比喻窈窕多姿的美女以及君子和小人这两种截然相反的形象。在漫长的文化中,中国读者看到这样的信号提示(cue)便会自觉地填充文化缺省所留下的空位,并激活记忆中的有关图式,从而准确理解语境。白之将以上几个专有名词皆做归化处理,分别译为"azalea""aloes""oriole"

和"weeping willow"。这样做的好处是使译文富有诗意和本土美学诗性，但是目标语读者记忆中缺乏这些词所代表的相关图式和相应语义点，无法还原作者的真实意图，从而出现了"意义真空"，读者无法将语篇内信息和语篇外知识与经验相联系，最终产生语义断裂。

"折桂之夫""蟾宫之客"两处带有明显的文化指涉和典故，白之采用直译法分别译为"scholar to break the cassia Bough"和"entrant of the moon's toad palace"，相当佶屈聱口。中文里有"蟾宫折桂"这一成语，意思是攀折月宫桂花。此成语在科举时代比喻应考得中，引申为获得很大的成就或很高的荣誉，多指金榜题名。蟾宫是月宫的意思，因三足蟾蜍是月之精，于是有了蟾宫之说；折桂喻高中进士，因桂树叶碧绿油润，古时科举考试正处在秋季，恰逢桂花开的时候，所以古代把夺冠登科比喻成折桂。"折桂之夫""蟾宫之客"在这里指的是那种出人头地、有能力有地位的好丈夫，与杜丽娘合称"才子佳人"。因为中文读者有了这样的先有知识，作者认为这是作者与读者共有的且无须赘言的文化信息，故而在文中省略了它们代表的真正含义。译者直译后，目标语读者因缺少这部分文化图式，不能读懂它们所蕴含的文化缺省，便会在这两个结点上出现意义真空，无法将这两种表达方式之间以及它们同上下文其他语义单位之间的语义关系连贯起来。

"韩夫人得遇于郎，张生偶逢崔氏，曾有《题红记》《崔徽传》""得成秦晋"以及"阮肇到天台"三处同样存在文化缺省。"韩夫人得遇于郎"取自唐人传奇故事，讲述了宫女韩氏与于祐红叶传情最后结为夫妇的故事；"张生偶逢崔氏"则是家喻户晓的张生和崔莺莺的爱情故事；"得成秦晋"因春秋时代，秦、晋两国世代联姻，故后世称联姻为秦晋之好；"阮肇到天台"化用刘义庆《幽明录》中所载的刘晨和阮肇在天台山桃源洞遇仙之典——刘阮二人后与两位仙女欢会，故此处用阮肇遇仙事，暗示柳梦梅即将遇到杜丽娘，并与之有云雨之欢。译者为了向英语读者补偿原文存在的文化缺省，采用了文外作注的策略。这样做的好处是能较好地体现原作者的艺术动机和原著的美学价值，同时可以利用注释相对不受空间限制的特点，比较详细地介绍有关的源语文化知识，并有利于引进外来语；读者通过注释填补了意义真空点，沟通了上下文，从而建立起语篇连贯。但缺点是读者在正文阅读中会因为出现意义真空而不得不暂时中断去查找注释，于是阅读的连贯性不可避免地会受到一定的影响。值得一提的是，译者在处理"得成秦晋"时，既采用了文外作注，又借助文内明示，译为"made marital unions 'as between Qin and Jin'"。译语读者在不中断正文阅读的情况下依然可以建立连贯，原文含蓄的审美效果不会被削弱，选择阅读注释亦可知晓原文有关文化背景。

中文有大量表示年龄的称谓,本文中的"二八"与"及笄"便是其中之二。译者在翻译"二八"时采用硬译加意译的方式，译为"'double eight', my sixteenth year"，翻译"及笄"时采用直译的方式。前者因为有补充"my sixteenth year"，所以不会对译文读者的语义理解造成障碍。但是在中文里，"及笄"指古时女子满十五岁把头发绾起来，戴上簪子，以示到了可以许配或出嫁的年龄。白之的译文"reached the age to 'pin up my hair'"没有将原文缺省的"女子到了可以许配或出嫁的年龄"文化信息表达出来，故而无法再现原文中杜丽娘感叹自己的妙龄青春被蹉跎的春怨之情。

"拣名门一例、一例里神仙眷"中的"神仙眷"表面指两个人都是神仙并且是夫妻，实则多用于形容世俗中少见的、具有较高才情见识、关系非常默契的正式夫妻或男女。译者采用硬译的方法译为"truly immortals"，对于影响阅读中连贯重构的文化缺省不作任何交代，容易给译语读者造成困惑与文化隔阂。

三、译论·比较

大翻译是一种集体性、协调性的翻译行为，包括了雅各布森提出的三类翻译：语内翻译、语际翻译、符际翻译。大翻译从文本和文化传播的有效性出发，强调各类翻译之间的互动性和建构性，旨在建立一种深层的集体文化记忆，通过模仿、改写、重译、改编等手段，将文学作品经典化、全球化。

换言之，大翻译进一步将翻译置于文化、跨文化、解构等视角下全盘审视，以阐释（interpretation）、翻译（interpreting and translation）、改写（rewriting）、改编（adapting）等操控（manipulating）手法，主张从历史的、文化的、文本与超文本的、民族与跨民族的、跨学科等视角全面解读作品，具有更大的学科包容性，是对翻译学进行的格局提升与立体建构，从而丰富了译学理论研究。

以《山海经》为例，这部先秦古籍在经历了千年"旅行"后，所呈现的形象正是"大翻译"所赋予的。这部经典"应是一个复杂的语内互文改写、语内翻译、语际翻译和符际翻译互为照应的过程，呈现出一种多模态互补的模式"（王敏、罗选民，2017）。从袁珂的"平和"式文本阐释到高行健基于戏剧改编的《山海经传》以及方梓勋（Gilbert C. F. Fong）对其的英译，再到媒体传播改写的各种舞台剧、影视剧、话剧、音乐、杂技、游戏、绘本[①]等，"大翻译"叙事方式将一个文化经典意象塑造得丰满多彩。其间有可能会走样，但却有利于作品发挥现时现用的作用，实现作品或经典的历史性文化传承。

此外，"大翻译"不仅让一个民族的集体文化记忆得以有效地塑造和传承，更有利于这种记忆实现跨民族的文化越界与共享。如"莎士比亚"经过了文本改写、书面到舞台（page to stage）、影视传播改编等多种方式的演绎与阐释后成了英国人民的文化记忆。更重要的是"莎士比亚"跨界来到中国，成了一代甚至几代人共同的文化记忆。正所谓"经过几代人的努力，我们达到了这样一种局面：有了朱生豪等人的好的散文体译本，出了《莎士比亚全集》；上演了若干重要莎剧，开始了用京剧和地方剧形式改编的试验，举行了一次大规模的中国莎士比亚戏剧节"（王佐良，1992）。这些民族的、

[①] 近年依据《山海经》改编的舞台剧有《山海经传》（编剧高行健）、《山海经》（编剧游蕙芬、王文德）、《太阳鸟》（编剧郭馨阳）等；影视剧有《传说》（2010）《山海经之山河图》（2015）《天眼传奇》（2015）、《山海经之赤影传说》（2016）等；话剧有《山海经——老舍之殁》等。此外还有台湾著名摇滚音乐剧《山海经传》（台湾师范大学表演艺术研究所）等；将传统杂技与现代舞相融合讲述的《山海经4.0》（济南市杂技团）和音乐《山海经》（作词徐贤力）、网游《山海游戏》等；以及为适龄儿童改编的《山海经故事》（方锐，2018）等。

跨民族的文化记忆又反推"莎士比亚",使其更具有"经典"意义,而所有这些都是"大翻译"概念提出的有力佐证。"大翻译"有利于整体文化外译,有利于文化走出去,这也正是"大翻译"的核心价值所在。

鉴于此,请按照以下要点对许渊冲所译的《牡丹亭·惊梦》选段进行鉴析:

(1)许渊冲其人其事以及翻译风格;

(2)从"大翻译"的层面分析该译本的舞台拓展潜力;

(3)将该译本与 Birch 译本进行横向对比。

Belle(Singing to the tune of Good Sister):

Be not unsatisfied with what you have not seen.

What even if you've seen twelve bowers scene on scene?

Better to leave when you've enjoyed your fill

Than lingering there still.

Fragrant(Singing on arrival):

"I open the doors east and west,

And smooth the bed for you to rest

I put in vase azelea flowers

And burn incense to perfume the bowers."

My young mistress, will you take a rest while I go in to see if our lady needs me?(Exit.)

Belle: After touring the vernal place,

See if my dress becomes my face.

Oh, spring, you come into my heart.

What could I do to see you part?

What annoying weather! Where is Fragrant Spring?

(Looking left and right and sinking in meditation.)

O Heaven! Now I believe spring is stirring the heart. I have read in long or short poems of ancient days that maidens were moved in spring and grieved in autumn. Now I understand the reason why I'm sixteen years of age, but where is the young man who would win the laureate for me, or fly up to the moon to woo the beauty in the silver palace? Where is the poet to write a love verse on the maple leaf and send it afloat to me? I have read the story of Red Leaf and the Western Bower in which the talent begins by a tryst and ends in a happy wedding with the beauty.

(Shedding tears) How can a young maiden in full bloom pass a floating life like a falling leaf?

(Singing to the tune of Sheep on the Slope):

Oh, how can I get rid of the annoyance of spring?

I hear lovesickness in my heart begin to sing.

Is it a beauty horn in noble house

Must only be in love with a fairy spouse?

Is it a happy pair of heart

Must waste their golden hours far, far apart?

Who knows of whom I'm dreaming and why

Should I pretend to be shy?

Where is my dream gone? To which side?

Has it passed away with spring tide?

Do not delay!

To whom my innermost feeling to say?

Annoyed in life, to whom can I reply?

I can only ask the blue sky.

Tired, I'll lean on the table to take a nap.

(Enter Liu the Dreamer.)

Liu: Orioles warble on fine day;

Men break into broad smile when they are gay.

I follow fallen petals on the stream

As lovers met the fairies in their dream.

I follow the beauty I dream of along the way. How is she lost to my sight? (Looking back)

Ah, my beauty, my beauty!

(Surprised, Belle wakes and meets with Liu.)

I have been looking for you everywhere, and at last find you here. (Belle looking sideways keeps silent.)

Here you are. I happened to see a beautiful willow tree in the garden and I broke off one branch for you. Well known for your verse, will you please write a few lines in its praise?

Belle (Pleased but abashed, about to speak but pausing, sunk in meditation, speaking aside)

I have never seen him before.

How can I know what he is coming for?

Liu (Smiling): I am so deep in love with you, my dear.

[Translated by Xu Yuanchang（许渊冲）]

四、实践·译笔

牡丹亭·题词（节选）

天下女子有情，宁有如杜丽娘者乎！梦其人即病，病即弥连，至手画形容，传于世而后死。死三年矣，复能溟莫中求得其所梦者而生。如丽娘者，乃可谓之有情人耳。情不知所起，一往而深。生者可以死，死可以生。生而不可与死，死而不可复生者，皆非情之至也。梦中之情，何必非真？天下岂少梦中之人耶！必因荐枕而成亲，待挂冠而为密者，皆形骸之论也。

五、阅读·延展

余笃嗜莎剧,尝首尾研通全集至十余遍于原作精神,自觉颇有会心。廿四年春,得前辈同事詹文浒先生之鼓励,始着手为翻译全集之尝试。越年战事发生,历年来辛苦搜集之各种莎集版本,及诸家注释考证批评之书,不下一二百册,悉数毁于炮火,仓卒中惟携出牛津版全集一册,及译稿数本而已。厥后转辗流徙,为生活而奔波,更无暇晷,以续未竟之志。及三十一年春,目睹世变日亟,闭户家居,摈绝外务,始得专心壹志,致力译事。虽贫穷疾病,交相煎迫,而埋头伏案,握管不辍。凡前后历十年而全稿完成(案译者撰此文时,原拟在半年后可以译竟。讵意体力不支,厥功未就,而因病重辍笔),夫以译莎工作之艰巨,十年之功,不可云久;然毕生精力,殆已尽注于兹矣。

余译此书之宗旨,第一在求于最大可能之范围内,保持原作之神韵,必不得已而求其次,亦必以明白晓畅之字句,忠实传达原文之意趣;而于逐字逐句对照式之硬译,则未敢赞同。凡遇原文中与中国语法不合之处,往往再四咀嚼,不惜全部更易原文之结构,务使作者之命意豁然呈露,不为晦涩之字句所掩蔽。每译一段竟,必先自拟为读者,察阅译文中有无暧昧不明之处。又必自拟为舞台上之演员,审辨语调之是否顺口,音节之是否调和,一字一句之未惬,往往苦思累日。然才力所限,未能尽符理想,乡居僻陋,既无参考之书籍,又鲜质疑之师友。谬误之处,自知不免。所望海内学人,惠予纠正,幸甚幸甚!

(摘自朱生豪《〈莎士比亚戏剧全集〉译者自序》)

Theatre translation is distinguished from drama translation principally by its ultimate objective to create a product destined for performance rather than for reading; a performed play-text in translation is intended to be the object of spectatorship and, increasingly, participation. Aaltonen(2000)notes the points of intersection and overlap, as well as the differences, between theatre and drama literary systems. The process of theatre translation, as distinct from the literary translation of dramatic texts, creates a targeted product – the performance text – for active users (theatre practitioners: directors, actors, the creative team) who apply an additional interpretive process to bring a translated play to the stage. Theatre translation thus offers research avenues in a creative process that includes both the generation of a translated text and the methodology of bringing it to performance. The international circulation of performed texts brings into focus a further feature of theatre translation: texts and performances developed with the intention of crossing multiple boundaries, spatially, geographically and linguistically. In such circumstances, the constantly shifting nature of translation emerges more fully into view.

The research potential of the concept of performability has been widely discussed in the wake of a series of interventions by Bassnett (1991, 1998a); a key response is provided by Espasa, who argues for the location of "theatre ideology and power negotiation at the heart of performability", with other factors such as speakability and playability relatively positioned (2000: 58). Translating for performance acknowledges the integral function, as part of the mise-en-scène (Pavis, 2013), of non-verbal elements such as lighting, music and set design and, above all, the tone and physicality of acting and their role in conveying the translated text to the audience. Research focusing on translation for performance is therefore interdisciplinary and has synergies with disciplines such as adaptation studies, film studies and theatre and drama studies.

(Excerpts from *Theatre Translation* by Geraldine Brodie)

第十一单元

科技先锋·明代宋应星

一、译事·译研

宋应星（1587—约1666），字长庚，江西奉新人，明代著名科学家，英国科学技术史学家李约瑟（Joseph Needham）称其为"中国的阿格里科拉""中国的狄德罗"。宋氏博学大才，涉猎广泛，有关于哲学的思考之作，如《论气》《谈天》等；有关于人文的感悟之作，如《野议》《画音规正》等；有关于文学之创作，如《思怜诗》等；有属于自然科技之作，如《观象》《乐律》等。其中《天工开物》是一部集聚生产经验和技术知识的百科全书式杰作，被誉为"中国十七世纪的工艺百科全书"。"天工"取自《尚书·皋陶谟》中的"天工人其代之"，"开物"取自《周易·系辞上》中"开物成务"，二者合力构成宋应星"有益生人"的独特造物思想，也反映了中国的传统造物观。

《天工开物》共十八章，图文并茂，涉农作物栽培、养蚕、纺织、制盐等三十个领域的生产、制造与技术状况。从1637年至2020年，《天工开物》共出现中、日、英、法、西等各类语种版本四十二个，其中汉语版本三十个，外语版本十二个（林宗豪、王宏，2022）。《天工开物》的翻译传播首先进入日本和朝鲜。1771年，日本大阪书商柏原屋佐兵卫刻印了第一个汉文翻刻本，即"菅本"。该版本后来启发明治维新的实业派学者提出富国济民的"开物之学"。1952年，薮内清（Yabuuchi Kiyoshi）将《天工开物》译为现代日文，被列为"东洋文库丛书"。作家与思想家朴趾源在1783年的游记《热河日记》中详载了《天工开物》,开启了该作在朝鲜的译旅。

《天工开物》在欧美的传播主要得益于汉学家、科技史专家的翻译。如汉学家儒莲(Stanislas Julien)曾先后法译《丹青》《五金》《锤锻》等章,并在1869年将所有选译章节汇集为《中华帝国工业之今夕》予以出版。此外,"制盐""制茶"部分在1975年被俄译为单行本《茶盐制作方法》。不过,这些翻译更多是译介形而下的技术与工艺,鲜有挖掘作品中"天人合一"的伦理思想与哲学内涵。

英译《天工开物》较为知名的主要有:

1966年美籍华裔任以都、孙守全夫妇全译本(*T'ien-kung k'ai-wu: Chinese Technology in the Seventeenth Century*),由宾夕法尼亚大学出版社出版。该译本具有深度翻译特征,其策略不仅涉及术语,还涵盖典故。科学史家席文(Nathan Sivin)(1966)认为其英译精准,可称为当时中国古典科技巨著英译本之首位。剑桥大学李约瑟研究所所长何丙郁(Ho Peng-Yoke)(1967)指出,译文的可读性很高,行文地道,灵活运用了重组、译写等翻译策略。"汉学界第一人"杨联陞则认为该译本属于学术翻译,贡献巨大。

1980年化学史家李乔苹全译本(*Tien-kung-kai-Wu: Exploitation of the Work of Nature, Chinese Agriculture and Technology in the XVII Century*),由中华文化学院出版社出版。李乔苹为自然科学领域学者,因此在翻译中更注重对科技术语语义特质的判别与保留。当然,这一翻译观念或许也与译者曾亲历抗日战争、具有强烈的家国情怀相关。他一生始终致力于弘扬中国古代科技成就,形成了最大程度再现原文信息的翻译思想。另外,该译本广泛采用套用、删减、诠释等翻译策略,以求平行移植信息型科技术语。

2011年外语学者王义静、王海燕、刘迎春合译全本,由广东教育出版社发行并入选《大中华文库》,是中国本土译者的第一个全译本。该译本的首要目的在于帮助本土学者重新认识中国古代科技成就,促进科技典籍翻译研究,以此弘扬中华优秀传统文化。因此,译本遵循的翻译原则是:准确规范、术语一致和术语译名的约定俗成，并相应采用意译法、直译法、直译意译兼顾法等，注重句式表达的客观性和谋篇布局的逻辑性（王烟朦等，2019）。

整体而言，《天工开物》的多语种外译对中国传统科技文化的传播产生了不可估量的影响，较好地呈现了中国古代的生态哲学思想和科学成就，讲好了优秀"中国科技故事"，传递了"中国科技智慧"。

二、鉴赏·评析

【原文】

白瓷·附：青瓷（节选）

凡白土曰垩土，为陶家精美器用。中国出惟五六处，北则真定定州[①]、平凉华亭、太原平定、开封禹州，南则泉郡德化（土出永定，窑在德化）、徽郡婺源、祁门（他处白土陶范不粘,或以扫壁为垩）。德化窑惟以烧造瓷仙、精巧人物、玩器，不适实用。真、开等郡瓷窑所出，色或黄滞无宝光。合并数郡不敌江西饶郡产。浙省处州丽水、龙泉两邑，烧造过釉杯碗,青黑如漆，名曰处窑。宋、元时龙泉华琉山（一作"琉华山"）下,有章氏造窑出款贵重，古董行所谓哥窑[②]器者即此。

若夫中华四裔驰名猎取者，皆饶郡浮梁景德镇之产也。此镇从古及今为烧器地，然不产白土。土出婺源、祁门两山：一名高梁山[③]，出粳米土，其性坚硬；一名开化山[④]，出糯米土，其性粢软。两土和合，瓷器方成。其土作成方块，小舟运至镇。造器者将两土等分入白舂一日，然后入缸水澄。其上浮者为细料，倾跌过一缸，其下沉底者为粗料。细料缸中再取上浮者，倾过为最细料，沉底者为中料。既澄之后，以砖砌长方塘，逼靠火窑，以藉火力。倾所澄之泥于中吸干，然后重用清水调和造坯。

....

凡瓷器经画过釉之后，装入匣钵（装时手拿微重，后日烧出即成坳口[⑤]，不复周正）。钵以粗泥造，其中一泥饼托一器，底空处以沙实之。大器一匣装一个，小器十余共一匣钵。钵佳者装烧十余度，劣者一二次即坏。凡匣钵装器入窑，然后举火。其窑上空十二圆眼，名曰天窗。火以十二时辰为足。先发门火十个时，火力从下攻上，然后天窗掷柴烧两时，火力从上透下。器在火中其软如绵絮，以铁叉取一以验火候之足。辨认真足，然后绝薪止火。共计一杯工力，过手七十二方克成器，其中微细节目尚不能尽也。

（选自［明］宋应星：《天工开物》）

【注释】

① 真定定州：真定府定州，明代北直隶境内，今河北省定州市，产白瓷。

② 哥窑：宋代章生一、章生二兄弟在浙江龙泉设的瓷窑，名重一时。

③ 高梁山：高岭，所产瓷土称高岭土，质硬。

④ 开化山：在今安徽祁门，所产瓷土性软而黏。

⑤ 坳口：凹陷的缺口。

【译文】

白陶土叫作垩土，陶坊用它来制造精美的瓷器。我国只有五六个地方出产这种垩土，北方有河北的定县、甘肃的华亭、山西的平定及河南的禹县，南方有福建的德化（土出福建永定，窑却在福建德化）、江西的婺源和安徽的祁门（其他地方出的白土，拿来造瓷坯不够黏，但可以用来粉刷墙壁）。德化窑是专烧瓷仙、精巧人物和玩器的，但不实用。河北定县和河南禹县的窑所烧制出的瓷器，有的颜色发黄，暗淡而没有光泽。上述所有地方的产品都没有江西景德镇所出产的瓷器好。浙江处州府的丽水和龙泉两县烧制出来的上釉杯碗，墨蓝的颜色如同青漆，这叫处窑瓷器。宋、元时期龙泉郡的华琉山山脚下有章氏兄弟建的窑，出品极为名贵，这就是古董行所说的哥窑瓷器。

至于我国四方闻名、人人争购的瓷器，则都是江西饶郡浮梁县景德镇的产品。自古以来，景德镇都是烧制瓷器的名都，但当地却不产白土。白土出自婺源和祁门两地的山上：其中的一座山名叫高梁山，出粳米土，土质坚硬；另一座山名叫开化山，出糯米土，土质黏软。只有两种白土混合，才能做成瓷器。将这两种白土分别做成方块，用小船运到景德镇。造瓷器的人取等量的两种瓷土放入臼内，舂一天，然后放入缸内用水澄清。缸里面浮上来的是细料，把它倒入另一口缸中，下沉在底下的则是粗料。细料缸中再倒出上浮的部分便是最细料，沉底的是中料。澄过后，分别倒入窑边用砖砌成的长方形塘内，塘靠近火窑，借窑的热力吸干水分，然后重新加清水调和造瓷坯。

…………

瓷器坯子经过画彩和上釉之后，装入匣钵（装时如果用力稍重，烧出的瓷器就会凹陷变形，再也周正不了了）。匣钵是用粗泥造成的，其中每一个泥饼托住一个瓷坯，底下空的部分用沙子填实。大件的瓷坯一个匣钵只能装一个，小件的瓷坯一个匣钵可以装十几个。好的匣钵可以装烧十几次，差的匣钵用一两次就坏了。把装满瓷坯的匣钵放入窑后，就开始点火烧窑。窑顶有十二个圆孔，叫作天窗。烧二十四个小时火候就足了。先从窑门发火烧二十个小时，火力从下向上攻，然后从天窗丢进柴火入窑烧四个小时，火力从上往下透。瓷器在高温烈火中软得像棉絮一样，用铁叉取出一个样品用以检验火候是否已经足够。火候已足就应该停止烧窑了。如此造一个瓷杯所费的工夫，合计要经过七十二道工序才能完成，其中许多细节还没有计算在内呢。

【译文】

WHITE PORCELAIN (SUPPLEMENT : BLUE PORCELAIN)

The raw material used by porcelain makers for their finest wares is a white soil known as white clay, which is produced at only half a dozen places in China. They are: in north China, Ting-chou in Chen-ting prefecture [in Ho-pei], Hua-t'ing district in P'ing-lang prefecture [in Kansu], P'ing-ting in T'ai-yuan prefecture [in Shansi], and Yü-chou in K'ai-feng prefecture [in Ho-nan];

in south China, Te-hua in Ch'üan-chou [in Fukien] (the clay is actually obtained from Yung-ting district, but the kilns are in Te-hua), and Wu-yuan and Ch'i-men in Anhui (white clay produced in other places than these does not stick together when molded into pottery ware, and so is often used as plaster for walls). The Te-hua kilns specialize in making porcelain buddhas and delicate figurines, things that are of no great practical value. The products of Chen-ting and K'ai-feng kilns, on the other hand, have an earthy color and lack lustre. The porcelain of all these places together cannot compare with that produced in the Yao prefecture of Kiangsi province. In the districts of Lung-ch'üan and Li-shui in Ch'u-chou prefecture, Chekiang province, however, there is manufactured a kind of glazed bowls and cups that are blue-black like lacquer and are called "Ch'u-kilns ware." At the foot of Hua-liu Mountain in Lung-ch'üan district there were, during [late] Sung and Yüan dynasties, kilns operated by two Chang brothers, whose wares were highly prized. These are the pieces called in curio shops the "Brothers-kiln ware."

But the porcelain which has enjoyed far-flung fame, and which all China's neighboring countries are eagerly seeking, is that produced from the kilns of Ching-te-chen in Fu-liang district of Yao prefecture. From ancient times to the present day this place has been a center of porcelain manufactures. White clay, however, is not locally available, but must be obtained from two [nearby] mountains in Wu-yuan and Ch'i-men. One [mountain] is called Kao-liang Mountain, where "nonglutinous rice" clay [China-clay] of a hard character, is found; the other is called K'ai-hua Mountain, and here "glutinous rice" clay [China-stone] is found, which is soft and pliable in quality. Porcelain wares can be fashioned only out of a mixture of these two clays.

These run-of-mine clays are molded into square blocks, and transported to Ching-te-chen on small boats. The porcelain makers then put an equal amount of each kind in a bowl, and pound the mixture for an entire day, after which [the powdered clay] is placed in a large water jar to be classified [by means of decantation]. The fine particles suspended in the upper part of the water column are poured into a second jar, whereas the coarse particles settle on the bottom of the first jar. The particles in the second jar are further classified to result in a suspension of superfine material, which is poured into a third jar. The particles that sink to the bottom [of the second jar] are called medium-sized material. After decantation, the fine-sized clay pulp is poured into an oblong ditch built of bricks beside the kilns, so that the clay pulp can be dried with the help of the [waste] heat. The dried clay is again mixed with clear water to form a paste, which is used for making the body of porcelain ware.

...

After being decorated and glazed, the porcelain wares are packed into box frames or saggers (a slight heavy-handedness in packing them will result in warped shapes after firing). The saggers are made of coarse clay; each packed [piece of] porcelain ware is supported by a clay disk; and the empty space at the bottom of each sagger is filled with sand. One sagger will have room for one large porcelain article, or about one dozen small pieces. Good saggers can be used repeatedly for more than ten firings, but poorly made ones will disintegrate after one or two. After the kiln is completely loaded with packed saggers, a fire is kindled. Toward the top of the kiln there are twelve round holes, called skylights. The firing should continue for twenty-four hours, of which the first twenty hours consist of firing from the kiln door, allowing the heat to rise from the bottom upward; then lighted wood is thrown in through the skylights and burns for four more hours, allowing the heat to travel from the top downward. While they are in the burning kiln the porcelain pieces are soft like cotton wool. To test the extent of firing, one article is taken out of the kiln with a pair of iron tongs, and the fire is stopped when the specimen is determined to be sufficiently heated. In sum, without counting the minute details, a portion of clay must pass through seventy-two different processes before it is finally made into a cup.

（Translabed and Annotated by E-Tu Zen Sun and Shiou-Chuan Sun）

【评析】

这篇科技译文不同于其他文体，现主要从词汇、语法和句型三方面进行文本分析。

首先是词汇层面，科技文的词汇大致来说具有以下几个特点：

（1）科技英语一般将常用词汇当作专业术语，但是汉语讲究正名，且赋义于形，使某一专业的术语尽量带上该专业的色彩。本文中，原文"白陶土"顾名思义是做陶器所用的土，即使是非专业人士也知这是陶瓷行业的术语，具有专业色彩，但是英语"white soil"为常用词汇。同理还可见："臼（bowl）""舂（pound）""瓷坯（paste）""画彩（decorate）""上釉（glaze）"等。

（2）科技英语中同一词往往具有多个专业含义，但是汉语讲究专词专用。例如中文的"锻造"通常是工业用语（修饰手法除外），但是英文"mold"不仅可用于工业，同时也是农业科学的术语，表"霉菌"；"pulp"不仅用于工、农业表示"浆状物"，还表医学中的"牙髓"；"article"既是文中所指的"某件"，同时也是法律术语"条款"，还表"冠词"之意。

（3）术语统一问题。译者通过悉心的词义辨析获得该词词义以后，即应严格遵循某专业技术领域的用语习惯，给概念以约定俗成的译名。某一词语一经译出，即应保持一贯性（Consistency），不应在不同的上下文中随意改变引起概念上的混乱。但是本文"瓷坯"这一术语存在多个译文，如"paste/ pottery ware/ porcelain ware/ porcelain article"；"瓷器"也有多个译文，如"porcelain/ porcelain ware/ porcelain pieces"等。

（4）科技英语词汇构成法有多种，包括缩略词、合成词、混成词、词缀法、剪截法、逆序法、造词法、词性转换法以及借用外来语等构词法构成通用或专用词语。合成法（Compounding），即将两个或两个以上的旧词组合成一个新词。科技英语中的合成词有合写式（无连字符）与分写式（有连字符）如：本文"skylight"由"sky"+"light"合成（无连字符）；"China-clay"、"China-stone"分别由"China"+"clay"和"China"+"stone"合成（有连字符）。混成法（Blending），即将两个词在拼写上或读音上比较适合的部分，以"前一词去尾、后一词去首"加以叠合混成，混成后新词兼具两个旧词之形义，如本文的"specimen"。词缀法（Affixation），即利用词缀（前缀或后缀）作为词素构成新词。英语中许多词缀的构词能力很强，因此词缀法就成为科技英语构词的重要手段。本文"nonglutinous"由前缀"non（非）"加在词根（word base）"glutinous（黏性的）"之后构成相反的语义。"disintegrate"由表示"相反、分开、去掉、不"等意义的前缀"dis"与词根"integrate"共同构成，表示分解、分裂或瓦解为原始或更小的部分，即与词根"integrate"（整合）词义相反。剪词法是指从一个词的某个部分或几个部分中剪切出来，形成一个新词，通常是为了缩短词语，使其更加简洁或易于使用，如本文中"curio shop"的"curio"由"curiosity"剪切而来。

其次，对科技英语语法的讨论主要集中在词法和谓语形态两方面。

词法，即用词倾向方面的特点，这里着重介绍名词化与名词连用。科技英语在词法方面的显著特点就是名词化（Nominalization）。名词化倾向主要指广泛使用能表示动作或状态的抽象名词（如本文的"decantation""suspension"）或起名词功用的非限定动词（如本文的"firing"）。科技英语的名词化倾向是与科技文体的基本要求密切相关的。科技文章的任务是叙述事实和论证推断，因而要求言简意明，其基本问题之一是语言结构的简化。与名词化密切相关的是名词连用。"名词连用"是指名词中心词前可有许多不变形态的名词，它们是中心词的前置形容词，被称为"扩展的名词前置修饰语"（Expanded Noun Premodifiers）。名词连用可以有效简化语言结构，本文涉及较多"名词连用"，如"pottery ware""curio shops""Brothers-kiln ware""clay pulp"以及"kiln door"等。科技英语词法上的另一个特点是倾向于多用表示行动的动词代替表示存在的动词 be。

由于科技英语在大多数情况下都是描述行为、过程、现象及发展等，因此多用表示行动的动词，文章具有较鲜明的动态感，比较生动；表示存在的动词给人以静态感，比较凝滞。本文大量使用表示行动的动词，十分符合科技英文这一特点，如："use""produce""obtain""mold""manufacture""pour""mix""throw""stop"等，不一而足。

关于谓语形态，科技英语倾向于多用动词现在时表述"无时间性"（Timeless）的"一般叙述"（General Statement），即通常发生或并无时限的自然现象、过程等，目的在于给人精确无误的"无时间性"（Timelessness）以排除任何与时间牵连的误解，使行文更生动。除"宋、元时龙泉华琉山（一作'琉华山'）下，有章氏造窑，出款贵重"（有明确时间标志——宋、元时）、"大器一匣装一个，小器十余共一匣钵。钵佳者装烧十余度，劣者一二次即坏"这两处外，全文皆为一般现在时，符合科技英语的行文特点。

此外，科技英语倾向于多用被动语态。这是因为科技英语叙述的往往是客观的事物、现象或过程，而主体往往是从事某项工作（试验、研究、分析、观测等）的人或装置。这时使用被动语态不仅比较客观，而且可以使读者的注意力集中在被叙述的事物、现实或过程，即客体上。本篇译文使用的被动句高达36处，动词形态趋势非常明显。最后，为避免表露个人感情，避免论证上的主观随意性，科技英语总是力求少用或不用描述性形容词以及具有抒情作用的副词、感叹词及疑问词。科技英语力求平易（Plainness）和精确（Preciseness），因此尽力避免使用各种旨在加强语言感染力和宣传效果的修辞格，忌用夸张、借喻、讥讽、反诘、双关及押韵等修辞手段，以免行文浮华、内容虚饰。

最后是句型层面。科技英语虽然不像公文文体那样程式化，但由于它在语法结构方面有较强的倾向性，因此许多固定句式出现的频率很高。熟练掌握这些句式的翻译规律，既能保证译文的准确性和可读性，又能提高翻译效率。如上文提到的科技英语倾向于多用被动语态，从而派生出一系列以被动式为基本谓语形式的常用句型，如：It is believed that（人们认为／

据信），It is suggested that（有人建议），It has been proved that（已经证明）等。熟悉这类句式的形态及各种译法，有助于提高翻译质量和速度。又如：科技英语注重逻辑性，因此分词连接成分（Participle Connectors）的使用率很高，如 supposing that（假定、假设），assuming that（假设、假定），provided that（倘若、只要），seeing that（由于、鉴于）等。熟悉这类常用结构的翻译无疑是十分必要的。掌握尽可能多的科技英语常用结构，也是科技翻译的基本功之一（刘宓庆，2019）。

在科技英语中，状语性分词词组用得十分普遍，原因可能是这种词组相当于副词从句（Participles as Adverb Clause Equivalent），使用词组以代从句，有助于行文的简洁化。这种组合，一般都存在某种逻辑意念上的内在联系，不是随意的连缀。这种内在联系是：前句表示某种前提条件或事实，后句表示某种结果或后续情况。组合后的句子以紧凑的结构表达了前后两句之间存在的逻辑关系。这是所有的状语性分词词组所具有的语法理据与特点，也是这种状语结构的一大优点。本篇译文当中的典型例句便是"allowing the heat to rise from the bottom upward"和"allowing the heat to travel from the top downward"。

科技英语非常注重文章的逻辑性与准确性，这就要求译者"既见树木，也见森林"，既关注文章的衔接（cohesion），也要关注文章的连贯（coherence）。我们认为，在衔接方面，本篇译文有几处需要关注，如"In the districts of Lung-ch'üan and Li-shui in Ch'u-chou prefecture, Chekiang province, however, there is manufactured a kind of glazed bowls and cups that are blue-black like lacquer and are called 'Ch'u-kilns ware'", "White clay, however, is not locally available, but must be obtained from two [near-by] mountains in Wu-yuan and Ch'i-men"。前者后半句存在句式杂糅之嫌，后者"however"与"but"使用是否得当有待商榷。另外，译文个别地方存在漏译现象，如"装时手拿微重，后日烧出即成坳口，不复周正"，其中"不复周正"是为了强调手拿轻放的重要性，否则后果就是"再也周正不了了"，这也可体现科技文的

210

严谨。译文"a slight heavy-handedness in packing them will result in warped shapes after firing",丢失了"不复周正"之意。

关于连贯方面,原文第一段在比较全国各地瓷器时指出"合并数郡不敌江西饶郡产",而后在第二段第一句再次点出"若夫中华四裔驰名猎取者,皆饶郡浮梁景德镇之产也"。译者翻译时并未对这两句进行逻辑整合,使得译文啰嗦重复,同时逻辑混乱,不易于读者理解。若是省略译文"The porcelain of all these places together cannot compare with that produced in the Yao prefecture of Kiangs province",使第一段后半段以并列的方式比较景德镇以外的中国各地瓷器,第二段句首再以"The porcelain that outshines all the ones produced in these places and has enjoyed far-flung fame and is early sought by people from home and abroad is produced in the Ching-te-chen in Fu-liang district of Yao prefecture"承上启下,或许会使译文更有逻辑、更加紧凑,且更加符合英语读者的习惯。

整体而言,本篇译文较符合科技英语的文体特点。译者除了正确理解了原文的意义外,也跨越了文化障碍,将原文中半隐半现、若隐若现的文化现象进行了文化信息解码,从而准确地传达了原文。比如"德化窑惟以烧造瓷仙、精巧人物、玩器,不适实用"句,译者并没有望文生义将"瓷仙"译为"porcelain fairies"或"porcelain immortals",而是对这个词进行文化解读,根据词的文化内涵选择适当的译文。"瓷仙"指瓷器的人物造像,以福建省德化县所制白瓷为最精,旧时多塑仙佛,因此统称"瓷仙",故而译者选用"porcelain buddhas"颇为贴切。

严谨的科技英语表达严谨的科学事实或预测,因此在翻译中不容有任何差错。科技翻译工作者必须培养和发扬严谨的翻译作风,切不可由于翻译上的疏误,给科研或生产带来损失。

三、译论·比较

探究科技翻译,不得不审视"科技"这一概念或定义。在现代性横扫全球的当下，科技也成为各个国家发展与进步的重要衡量指标。然而，随着"李约瑟难题"的提出，中国是否有科学悄然成为一个"值得深思的问题"。但是，何为"科学"，或者说已经深入人心的"科学"概念是在谁的主导之下形成的呢？进一步而言，"科学"是否不应当成为一个确定的约束性概念，而应当成为一种包容的求知精神或求真态度？奈达曾认为翻译不仅仅是一门科学（science），还是一门艺术（art）。将翻译视为科学，正是取"科学"严谨、务实、求真的态度与精神。

张光直先生曾明言："西方的社会科学所演绎出来的许多原则、法则、法理，是根据从苏美尔文明以来的西方文明的历史经验中综合归纳出来的。就像我们从中国古代五千年或更长的历史中，也可以综合归纳出许多社会科学的法则一样。问题在于'欧风东渐'——西方社会科学输入中国以来，有许多西方的法则便直接地套到中国的史实上去"（张光直，1990）。这套观念的套搬体现在方方面面，翻译实践也不例外。甚至"science—科学"这一对译本身就是假定式的对等，被急切性解读为中西共有。当然，在西周确定"science—科学"的对译之前，"science"曾与中国文化中的"格物、格致、穷理"等词有过对译之缘，如傅兰雅主编的《格致汇编》，其初始英译名便是 *The Chinese Scientific Magazine*。然而，"就中国传统文化本身而言，'格致'不是科学，而它终于演变为'科学'，是在开放的条件下不断接受外来文化冲击的结果"（樊洪业，1988）。

因此，科技翻译不应盲从外来的理论、策略与方法，而应因地制宜，基于本土的实践与现实生发属于本土的地方性知识，发挥并彰显本土特色与优势。

鉴于此，请按照以下要点对《白瓷》的另一译本进行鉴析：

（1）从"知识翻译"的层面评析该译本对于本土性知识的彰显；

（2）将该译本与 E-Tu Zen Sun 和 Shiou-Chuan Sun 的译本进行横向对比。

White Porcelain

White soil known as white clay is the raw material used by porcelain makers for their finest wares. There are five or six areas producing white clay. In the north, there are Dingzhou of the Zhending Prefecture, Huating County of the Pingliang Prefecture in Gansu Province, Pinging County of Taiyuan in Shanxi Province, and Yu County of the Kaifeng Prefecture in Henan Province. In the south, there are Dehua County (the producing area is Yongding County, but the kiln is in Dehua) of Quanzhou in Fujian Province, Wuyuan County of the Huizhou Prefecture and Qimen County. (White clay in other places is not sticky enough to make pottery, but it can he used to paint walls.) The Dehua kilns only make porcelain fairies, delicate figures and toys, which are not practical. Some porcelain made in Zhending and Kaifeng Prefecture is a little yellow and dull. The above-mentioned porcelain can not match the porcelain made in the Raozhou Prefecture of Jiangxi Province. Lishui and Longquan County of Chuzhou Prefecture in Zhejiang Province make glazed cups and bowls, which are named the Chu kiln and black as black lacquer. During the Song and Yuan dynasties, at the foot of Liuhua Mountain in Longquan there was Zhangshi kiln, which turned out precious porcelain. This is the Brother kiln mentioned in antique business.

Jingdezhen porcelain produced in Liang County of Raozhou Prefecture is the most famous and popular throughout the country. Jingdezhen is the place producing porcelain from ancient times, but white clay doesn't exist in Jingdezhen, it comes from Wuyuan and Qi-men. One is called Gaoliang Mountain, which yields hard rice clay ; the other is called Kaihua Mountain, which yields soft glutinous rice clay. By mixing these two kinds of clay together, porcelain can be made. Clay is made into blocks and shipped to Jingdezhen by boat. Porcelain makers mix the same amount of the two kinds of clay, pound them in a mortar for a day and settle them with water in a vat. The small quantity of powder floating on the surface is fine material and should be poured into another vat. The one settling at the bottom is rough material. The fine material in the latter vat should be taken out and poured into another vat. The material floating on the surface of the small quantity powder vat, it is the best, and the material at the bottom is the next. After settling, dry by fire in the kiln and mix them with water again to make unburnt bricks.

（Excerpts from *Library of Chinese Classics*：*Tian Gong Kai Wu*）

四、实践·译笔

1. 凡煤炭取空而后，以土填实其井。经二三十年后，其下煤复生长，取之不尽。

2. 草木之实，其中韫藏膏液，而不能自流。假媒水火，凭借木石，而后倾注而出焉。此人巧聪明，不知于何禀度也。

3. 凡苗自函活以至颖栗，早者食水三斗，晚者食水五斗，失水即枯（将刈之时少水一升，谷数虽存，米粒缩小，入碾、臼中亦多断碎），此七灾也。汲灌之智，人巧已无余矣。

五、阅读·延展

在我国翻译史上，明末清初是翻译西方自然科学的时期。这时期的翻译力量，一是来中国传教的西方耶稣会教士，二是从事科学研究或对科学感兴趣的中国士大夫，二者结合，开展了翻译活动。从明万历到清康熙这段时间内，前来传教的耶稣会教士，知名的有七十人以上，一般都有译著，共成书三百余种，其中有关自然科学的占一百二十种左右，属于利玛窦、汤若望、罗雅谷、南怀仁等四人的译著，就达七十五种。明末参与耶稣会教士的科学翻译活动的中国士大夫中，比较著名的有徐光启、李之藻、李天经、王澂诸人，而徐光启乃是佼佼者。

……徐光启就非常重视《几何原本》的翻译,认为"此书为用至广,在此时尤所急须"。然而利玛窦只口译了欧几里得原作的拉丁文译文部分,至于克拉维斯的注解以及他所收集的欧几里得《原本》研究者的论述,几乎全都删去了。徐光启的笔录却花了不少心力。译本中的许多名词,如点、线、直线、曲线、平行线、角、直角、锐角、钝角、三角形、四边形等等,都是由他首次定下来的,不但在我国沿用至今,而且影响到日本、朝鲜等国。译稿经过反复订正,一校二校,乃至三校,遗存的《三校〈几何原本〉》尚有那一年徐光启点窜的手笔。其后,徐光启在编译的《大测》二卷里把平面三角和球面三角介绍进来了;而《割圜八线表》则是三角函数表。在测量方面,徐光启又与利玛窦合译了《测量法义》一卷。中国人有经纬度的精确观念,当始于此。徐光启在翻译过程中善于吸收西洋科学中对中国科学可以互相启发、互相补苴的地方加以发挥。例如他译了《测量法义》之后,接着写出《测量同义》和《勾股义》两书。在《测量同义》中,他比较了中西的测量方法,认为我国古代的方法与西洋的方法基本相同,理论根据实际上也是一致的,他运用《几何原本》中的定理来解释了这种一致性。《勾股义》则是仿照《几何原本》的方法,并运用其逻辑推理思想,企图给我国古代的勾股术加以严格的论述。

徐光启热衷于农业的科学研究和试验,《农政全书》的编著是他一生中最大的贡献。他在1612年与熊三拔(Sabatino de Ursis,1575—1620,意大利人,1606年来华)合作,译出《泰西水法》六卷。他翻译时,是在中国原有水利灌溉方法和工具的基础上,选择其中对当时具有实用价值,或确实属于先进方法者,经过制器和试验,才编译入书的。译成之后,他又在天津开辟水田,试用新的水法,获利甚丰。他在《自笑扎》中说:"如今岁偶尔讲求数种用水之法,试一为之,颇觉于民为便",就是指的此事。

……徐光启主持修改历法时,对西历的翻译并不盲目地生搬硬套。他认为制定历法的任务是正确反映日月五星的运转规律,使之与天行符合。当时西历的精密程度是超过《大统历》的,对《大统历》"每遇一差,必寻其所以差之故",对西历"每用一法,必论其所以不差之故"。因此译书时非常重视测验,"昼测日,夜测星",他不顾高龄,亲自观测,以致失足受伤。《崇祯历书》中的"节次六目"和"基本五目",是他根据"熔彼方之材质,入《大统》之型模"这一原则所事先确定的编译范围和内容。所谓"熔",并不是生搬硬套,而是通过"会通",以求"超胜"。徐光启修改历法,在"洋为中用"方面为我们树立了光辉的榜样。

(摘自马祖毅《徐光启与科学翻译》)

Addressing research questions and issues relevant to scientific translation requires reflection on two key concepts, science and translation. The concept of translation is critically examined in a variety of ways by translation scholars who seek greater understanding of the place of translation in the world. The concept of science, no less complex, receives abundant critical examination in a different body of scholarship. The overlapping fields of science studies, science and technology studies (STS), and science, technology and society (also STS) are concerned with greater understanding of the place of science in the world. Both science studies and translation studies are inherently interdisciplinary and employ a wide range of theoretical and empirical approaches to address historical, philosophical, social, cultural and political questions. Our understanding of the place of scientific translation in the world may therefore benefit greatly from scholarship at the confluence of these two disciplines.

… It could be argued that scholarship on scientific translation is following a similar trajectory, though with an interlude of some decades. The majority of publications that focused on scientific translation prior to the 2000s aimed to serve as guides to translators or translation students. Early contributions reflected an underlying conception of science as knowledge and of scientific discourse as communication of invariant referential meaning. Manuals produced during the 1960s, 1970s and 1980s were designed and used as practical guides to scientific and/or technical translation. Many fulfilled their didactic function through a strong normative emphasis on techniques for achieving terminological accuracy and precision of expression. A small number of contributions focused on the translator's development of conceptual scientific knowledge and understanding (Hann, 1992, 2004). Since the turn of the century, guides to scientific translation have reflected a growing understanding of the social and cultural importance of scientific translation as part of scientific practice, and increasingly offer a much more contextualized view of scientific communication, providing insights into the activities of professional scientific and technical communication and/or focusing on specific scientific genres.

Aligned with universalist and positivist views of science, many of the earlier contributions on scientific translation that involved textual analysis were limited by an understanding of scientific texts as serving primarily informative or referential functions, a view that is reflected in Ortega y Gassett's (1937/2000: 50) assertion that scientific translation is easier than translation of literary texts, due to a perceived universality of the language of science and/or of scientific thought. This perspective overlooks the significant expressive and operative functions of scientific discourse, as the means by which authors construct meanings, make claims, challenge others, enrol allies and preempt contestation, seek to build consensus within a scientific community, exclude or include non-members of that and other communities and establish and drive research agendas. Failure to acknowledge these social and rhetorical functions of scientific discourse can lead to a focus on precision of terminology and accuracy of description, and moreover a consideration of both as somehow culturally invariant. This conceptualization of science, in turn, may be responsible for the relative lack of attention to scientific translators' social and textual practices, compared to the breadth and depth of research on their counterparts in literary domains.

The typical backgrounds of translation researchers, for example in literary and linguistic studies, may also mean that they are less prepared to engage with scientific disciplines, ideas and discursive practices.

(Excerpts from *Scientific Translation* by Maeve Olohan)

主要参考文献

[1]Anesaki, M.Reviewed Work（s）: The Philosophy of Wang Yang-ming by Frederick Goodrich Henke[J]. *The American Journal of Theology*, 1918（04）: 599.

[2]Bassnett, S.*Translation Studies*[M].London : Methuen & Co.Ltd, 1980.

[3]Bell, R.T. *Translation and Translating : Theory and Practice* [M]. London : Longman/Beijing : Foreign Language Teaching and Research Press, 1991/2001.

[4]Bhabha, H.K.The *Location of Culture*[M]. London and New York : Routledge, 1994.

[5]Bodde, D.（trans）The Philosophy of Chu His by Fung Yu-Lan [J]. *Harvard Journal of Asiatic Studies*, 1942（1）: 1-51.

[6]Bourdieu, P.*Distinction : A Social Critique of the Judgement of Taste*[M].Cambridge : Harvard University Press, 1984.

[7]Bruce, J.The Theistic Import of the Sung Philosophy [J]. *Journal of the North China Branch of the Royal Asiatic Society*, 1918（49）: 111-127.

[8]Henke, S.M.The Philosophy of Wang Yang-ming（Review）[J]. *Journal of Asian Studies*, 1965（4）: 688.

[9]Gottlieb, H.Multidimensional Translation : Semantics Turned Semiotics

[A]. *EU-High-Level Scientific Conference Series*[C].MuTra, 2005.

[10]Ho Peng-Yoke. T'ien-kung K'ai-wu : Chinese Technology in the Seventeenth Century [J].*Harvard Journal of Asiatic Studies*, 1967（27）: 295-299.

[11]Jakobson, R.On Linguistic Aspects of Translation[A].*Word and Language（SelectedWriting*2）[C].The Hague : Mouton, 1971 : 260-266.

[12]Owen S.*An anthology of Chinese literature : beginnings to* 1911[M].New York : Norton, 1996.

[13]Schirokauer, C.M.Instructions for Practical Living and Other Neo-Confucian Writings by Wang Yangming. Wingtsit Chan（Review）[J].*The Journal of Asian Studies*, 1964（1）: 151-152.

[14]Sivin N.T'ien-kung K'ai-wu : Chinese Technology in the Seventeenth Century[J].*Science, New Series*, 1966, 153（3737）: 730-731.

[15]Swatek, C.Boundary Crossings : Peter Sellars' Production of Peony Pavilion[J].*Asian Theatre Journal*, 2002（1）: 147-158.

[16]Venuti, L.*The Translator's Invisibility : A History of Translation*[M].Shanghai : Shanghai Foreign Language Education Press, 2004.

[17]Wang Yang-ming.*Instructions for Practical Living and other Neo-Confucian Writings*[M].Wing-tsit Chan, trans.New York : Columbia University Press, 1963.

[18]Wang, Yang-ming.*The Philosophy of Wang Yang-ming*[M].Frederick Goodrich Henke, trans.Chicago : Open Court, 1916.

[19]Watson, B. *The Columbia Book of Chinese Poetry : From Early Timesto the Thirteenth Century*[M].New York : Columbia University Press, 1984.

[20]Yen, Kia-Lok.The Philoso phy of Wang Yang-ming by WangYang-ming and Frederick Goodrich Henke（Review）[J].*International Journal of*

Ethics，1917（2）：241-244.

[21] 蔡瑞珍. 布迪厄社会学视域下《传习录》两译本对比研究 [J]. 外国语言文学，2023，40（03）：87-97+136.

[22] 陈福康. 中国译学史 [M]. 上海：上海外语教育出版社，2015.

[23] 陈荣捷. 西方对朱熹的研究 [C]// 韩钟文主编. 儒学与西方哲学. 北京：中华书局，2003.

[24] 陈荣捷. 新儒学的术语解释与翻译 [J]. 张加才，席文，编译. 深圳大学学报（人文社会科学版），2013（06）：52-56.

[25] 陈湘琳. 欧阳修的文学世界与生命情境 [D]. 复旦大学，2010.

[26] 崔玉军. 美国的中国哲学研究 [M]. 北京：社会科学文献出版社，2010.

[27] 樊洪业. 从"格致"到"科学"[J]. 自然辩证法通讯，1988（03）：39-50+80.

[28] 方梦之. 中国译学大词典 [D]. 上海：上海外语教育出版社，2011.

[29] 冯友兰. 中国哲学简史 [M]. 赵复三，译. 北京：生活·读书·新知三联书店，2014.

[30] 傅修延. 生态江西读本 [M]. 南昌：二十一世纪出版社，2019.

[31] 葛兆光. 中国思想史·导论 [M]. 上海：复旦大学出版社，2013.

[32] 宫留记. 布迪厄的社会实践理论 [J]. 理论探讨，2008（06）：57-60.

[33] 胡开宝，谢丽欣. 基于语料库的译者风格研究：内涵与路径 [J]. 中国翻译，2017，38（02）：12-18+128.

[34] 黄广哲，朱琳. 以蔡志忠典籍漫画《孔子说》在美国的译介谈符际翻译 [J]. 上海翻译，2018（01）：84-89+95.

[35] 黄国文. 典籍翻译：从语内翻译到语际翻译——以《论语》英译为例 [J]. 中国外语，2012，9（06）：64-71.

[36] 蒋林. 后殖民视域：文化翻译与译者的定位 [J]. 南京社会科学，2008（06）：146-151.

[37] 李德俊. 基于语料库的西方描述性翻译研究：回顾与展望 [J]. 中国翻译, 2019, 40（06）: 30-41+190.

[38] 李先进. 关联理论视角下的文化缺省及翻译策略 [J]. 外国语文, 2013, 29（03）: 112-116.

[39] 梁启超. 中国文学讲义 [M]. 长沙：湖南人民出版社, 2010.

[40] 林金水. 福建对外文化交流史 [M]. 福州：福建教育出版社, 1997.

[41] 林宗豪, 王宏.《天工开物》三英译本作者"误见"之译者行为批评研究 [J]. 上海翻译, 2022（06）: 73-79.

[42] 刘军平. 西方翻译理论通史 [M]. 武汉：武汉大学出版社, 2009.

[43] 刘孔喜, 许明武. 亨克及王阳明心学著作在英语世界的首译 [J]. 国际汉学, 2019（03）: 45-53+204.

[44] 刘宓庆. 翻译美学导论 [M]. 北京：中国对外翻译出版公司, 2005.

[45] 刘宓庆. 文体与翻译 [M]. 北京：中译出版社, 2019.

[46] 鲁迅. "题未定"草 [C]// 鲁迅全集（第六卷）. 北京：人民文学出版社, 2005.

[47] 鲁迅. 我怎么做起小说来 [C]// 鲁迅全集（第四卷）. 北京：人民文学出版社, 2005.

[48] 罗新璋. 翻译论集 [M]. 北京：商务印书馆, 1984.

[49] 罗选民. 从"硬译"到"易解"：鲁迅的翻译与中国现代性 [J]. 中国翻译, 2016（05）: 32-37.

[50] 罗选民. 大翻译与文化记忆：国家形象的建构与传播 [J]. 中国外语, 2019, 16（05）: 95-102.

[51] 马祖毅. 伟大的佛经翻译家玄奘 [J]. 中国翻译, 1980（02）: 18-19.

[52] 马祖毅. 中国翻译简史："五四"以前部分 [M]. 北京：中国对外出版公司, 1998.

[53] 冒国安. 实用英汉对比教程 [M]. 重庆：重庆大学出版社, 2004.

[54] 彭利元, 蒋坚松. 语境·对话·翻译——巴赫金语境对话理论对翻

译的启示[J].外语与外语教学,2005(09):47-51.

[55] 钱锡生,季进.探寻中国文学的"迷楼"——宇文所安教授访谈录[J].文艺研究,2010(09):63-70.

[56] 全灵.从"硬译"说起[C]//鲁迅研究文丛第一辑.长沙:湖南人民出版社,1980.

[57] 帅司阳.重塑朱熹——"译名之争"语境下裨治文对《御纂朱子全书》的节译[J].翻译界,2018(01):25-40+142.

[58] 谭载喜.西方翻译简史[M].北京:商务印书馆,1991.

[59] 田莎,朱健平.朱学英语译介二百年[J].外语教学与研究,2020,52(02):296-308+321.

[60] 汪次昕.英译中文诗词曲索引——五代至清末[Z].台北:汉学研究中心,2000.

[61] 王东风.文化缺省与翻译中的连贯重构[J].外国语(上海外国语大学学报),1997(06):56-61.

[62] 王建国.汉英对比视角下的翻译实践分析[M].北京:中译出版社,2023.

[63] 王敏,罗选民.文化预设与中国神话的多模态互文重构——以《山海经》英译为例[J].中国外语,2017(03):92-100.

[64] 王倩.中国文化外译传播中的译者身份建构[J].社会科学战线,2018(9):266-270.

[65] 王烟朦,王海燕,王义静.《大中华文库》(汉英对照)之《天工开物》英译者访谈录[J].外国语文研究,2019,5(01):1-8.

[66] 王佐良.翻译:思考与试笔[M].北京:外语教学与研究出版社,1989.

[67] 王佐良.《论诗的翻译》[M].南昌:江西教育出版社,1992.

[68] 吴梅影.欧阳修[M].北京:中华书局,2019.

[69] 萧公权.萧公权文集:迹园文录[M].北京:中国人民大学出版社,

2014.

[70] 辛红娟,费周瑛.陈荣捷《传习录》英译的转喻视角研究[J].国际汉学,2019（02）:160-168+126+206-207.

[71] 徐赛颖."厚重翻译"观照下的亨克英译《传习录》探析[J].浙江大学学报（人文社会科学版）,2020,50（03）:231-240.

[72] 许多,许钧.中国典籍对外传播中的"译出行为"及批评探索——兼评《杨宪益翻译研究》[J].中国翻译,2019,40（05）:130-137.

[73] 严晓江.古诗英译推动中华文化国际传播[N].中国社会科学报,2023-01-17（008）.

[74] 杨宪益.杨宪益自传[M].薛鸿时,译.北京:人民日报出版社,2010.

[75] 杨自俭.对比语篇学与汉语典籍英译[J].外语与外语教学,2005（07）:60-62.

[76] 宇文所安.把过去国有化:全球主义、国家和传统文化的命运[C]//他山的石头记——宇文所安自选集.南京:江苏人民出版社,2003.

[77] 张光直.从商周青铜器谈文明与国家的起源[C]//中国青铜时代（二集）.北京:三联书店,1990.

[78] 张隆溪.中西文化研究十论[M].上海:复旦大学出版社,2005.

[79] 周领顺.译者行为批评:理论框架[M].北京:商务印书馆,2014.

[80] 周晓梅.译者的声音与文化身份认同——路易·艾黎与宇文所安的杜诗英译对比[J].外语与外语教学,2019（06）:80-89+147-148.

[81] 邹振环.20世纪中国翻译史学史与近代史学新领域的拓展[J].河北学刊,2019,39（02）:63-72.

[82] 左晓婷.《浣溪沙》研究[D].河北师范大学,2012.

参考答案（实践·译笔）

第二单元

1. 归去来兮，田园将芜胡不归？既自以心为形役，奚惆怅而独悲？

汪榕培：

Homeward ho! Why not return now that my fields will go into weeds?

Since I took up a position against my will, there is no need for me to lament by myself.

林语堂：

Ah, homeward bound I go! Why not go home, seeing that my field and garden with weeds are overgrown?

Myself have made my soul serf to my body: why have vain regrets and mourn alone?

罗经国：

Going home! The land will soon lie in the waste. Why shouldn't I go home?

Since I willingly let my mind be enslaved by my worldly desires, why should I feel remorseful and sad?

2. 云无心以出岫，鸟倦飞而知还。

汪荣培：

The careless clouds float from behind the hills；

The weary birds know that they should return.

林语堂：

There the clouds idle away from their mountain recesses without any intent or purpose, and birds, when tired of their wandering flights, will think of home.

罗经国：

Clouds drift out aimlessly from behind the mountains.

Birds will return to their nest when tired.

3. 羁鸟恋旧林，池鱼思故渊。

汪榕培：

Birds in the cage would long for wooded hills；

Fish in the pond would yearn for flowing rills.

William Wacker：

The tame bird longs for his old forest——

The fish in the house-pond thinks of his ancient pool.

4. 方宅十余亩，草屋八九间。

汪榕培：

My farm contains a dozen mu of ground, my cottage has eight or nine rooms around.

William Wacker：

My land and house — a little more than ten acres,

In the thatched cottage only eight or nine rooms.

5. 开荒南野际，守拙归园田。

汪榕培：

So I reclaim the land in southern fields, to suit my bent for reaping farmland yields.

William Wacker:

I too will break the soil at the edge of the southern moor,

I will guard simplicity and return to my field and garden.

第三单元

Ah! A beautiful scenic spot is rarely seen, and a sumptuous banquet like this one is even less likely to be held again. The grand gathering at the Orchid Pavilion is an event in history and the famous Jinggu Garden is now in ruins. I have the good fortune to attend this feast and I would like to leave this farewell message at the time of parting. I count on all the gentlemen here to ascend the tower and contribute their writings. I humbly compose this short piece in all sincerity. Since every one of us is required to write a poem, the following is what I write;

The lofty King Teng's Tower overlooks the River.

The jade pendants tinkle, and the carriage bells jingle.

The banquet's over. the guests are leaving, and the singing and the dancing have stopped.

In the morn the rosy clouds from the southern shore flit across the painted pillars.

In the eve the rain in the western mountains is drawn in by the red curtains.

The lazy clouds are reflected in the water and the days pass in leisure.

Things change and stars move; how many years have passed since the building of the Tower?

Where is its builder, King Teng?

Only the River outside the railing flows to the cast all by itself.

第四单元

Breaking Through the Ranks (Po zhen-zi)

That time of year when swallows are set to go,
 and in high rooms last night, west wind.
I sought a small party in
 this mortal world,
we held our golden cups beside
 clumps of chrysanthemums.
The songs lasted long, and faces
 powdered white flushed red.

Then sinking sunlight again
 pierced the curtains,
light chill progressively touched the beech.
 So much in the heart I could not say—
on slips of fine paper
 I wrote into melody
these feelings, in thousands, one after another.

(Translated by Stephen Owen)

第五单元

For autumn is the minister of punishments, the dark Yin among the four seasons. It is also the symbol of arms, metal among the five elements. Hence it is said to be the breath of justice between Heaven and Earth, and its eternal purpose is stern execution. By Heaven's design for all things, spring gives birth, autumn ripens. That is why in music the note Shang reigns over the scale of the west, and Yi-tse is the pitch-tube of the seventh month. Shang means grief, the grief of things which grow old. Yi means "destruction"; things which have passed their prime deserve to be killed.

(ANNOTATION: Autumn is the season in which the ch'i (breath) which energizes heaven and earth is on the wane, having passed from its Yang or active to its Yin or passive phase. Its place among the four seasons corresponds with that of the board of punishments among the five departments of state, of metal among the five elements, of justice among the five cardinal virtues, of Shang among the notes of the pentatonic scale, of the west among the four cardinal points. The seventh month, which is the first month of autumn, corresponds with Yi-tse among the twelve tubes which determine musical pitch.)

(Translated and annotated by A.C. Graham)

第六单元

Impromptu: Late Spring at Pan-shan

(Pan-shan or "Halfway-to-the-Mountain" was the place where the poet lived in retirement, so called because it was halfway between Nanking and Mt. Chung. 5-ch. regulated verse.)

Late spring has snatched away the blossoms,
left me this cool shade instead,
the sloping road quiet under its covering of shadows,
the garden cottage deep in intertwining green.
Bench and mat whenever I want a little rest,
walking stick and shoes for visiting secluded spots —
otherwise I've only the north mountain birds
that pass this way, leaving their lovely notes behind.

第七单元

According to Zhu Xi, the real purpose of education is to enable the student to understand moral principles so he can cultivate himself and extend them in dealing with others. To this end, he composed the chieh-shih, literally "posted notice", and had it posted on the lintel. The chieh-shih is usually called "Articles for Learning", but it must be understood that they do not mean compulsory rules but moral precepts. The text of the chieh-shih is as follows :

Between father and son, there should be affection.

Between ruler and minister, there should be righteousness.

Between husband and wife, there should be attention to their separate functions.

Between old and young, there should be a proper order.

And between friends, there should be faithfulness.

The above are the items of the Five Teachings.

Study it extensively, inquire into it accurately, think over it carefully, sift it clearly, and practice it earnestly.

The above is the order of study.

Let one's words be sincere and truthful, and one's deeds be earnest and reverential. Restrain one's wrath and repress one's desires.

Move toward the good and correct one's mistakes.

The above are essentials for self-cultivation.

Rectify moral principle and do not seek profit. Illuminate the Way and do not calculate on results.

The above are essentials for handling affairs.

Do not do to others what you do not want them to do to you. If you do not succeed in your conduct, turn inward and seek for its cause there.

The above are essentials for dealing with others.

第八单元

If all Chinese youth become a decadent generation, then China would be doomed to be left behind, whose demise could be imminent. Therefore, the responsibility of our times should be shouldered by youth rather than anyone else. A country could be smart and rich once the youth are smart and rich. A country could be strong and independent once the youth are strong and independent. A country's freedom could be achieved once the youth have free will. A country could press ahead once the youth are making progress. Also, a country could outperform Europe and stand firmly and proudly among the nations in the world once the youth are capable to outshine others. A rising sun illuminates the bright path ahead ... China enjoys a long history and a vast territory whose huge potential will be further unleashed in the near future.

——Liang Qichao

Should the nation's youth be rendered decrepit, then our China would regress to its miserable past, so much so that its demise could be expected soon. Today's responsibilities, therefore, rest on the shoulders of no one but the youth. If our youth are intelligent, then our country is intelligent; our youth wealthy, then our country wealthy; our youth strong, then our country strong; our youth independent, then our country independent; our youth liberal, then our country liberal ; our youth progressive, then our country progressive ; our youth outperform the European counterparts, then our country outperforms the European counterparts ; our youth tower over the global rivals, then our country towers over the global rivals. A brilliant red sun is rising up, casting its glorious rays on the road ...With an enduring history in vertical dimension of time and an expansive territory in horizontal dimension of space, China has a bright future, as vast as the ocean, stretching endlessly ahead.

——By Liang Qichao

If Chinese young people become prematurely senile, China will remain as backward as it likes in the old days and its downfall can be expected soon. Therefore, today's responsibility of revitalizing the Chinese nation falls on no others but Chinese young people. If Chinese young people are wise and intelligent, the nation is full of talents ; if Chinese young people are affluent, the nation is wealthy ; if Chinese young people are vigorous, the nation is prosperous ; if Chinese young people are independent, the nation emerges as a sovereign power ; if Chinese young people are self-determining, the nation is self-reliant ; if Chinese young people make progress, the nation will take bigger steps forward ; if Chinese young people outperform their counterparts in the European countries, the nation will end up surpassing those countries ; if Chinese young people come out on top among their world's peers, the nation will take the lead in the world. The red sun is rising over the eastern horizon, shining in all its splendor... China enjoys a long history tracing back thousands of years and vast territory stretching far and wide in all directions. The future of Chinese young people is as boundless as the vast sea and their long life journey is just ahead.

——by Liang Qichao

第九单元

1. 陈译：If only he neither forces it to grow nor neglects it, but keeps on cultivating and nourishing it.

亨译：The seed of the tree should neither be helped nor forgotten but banked up.

2. 陈译：He can't do so unless he is sound asleep or dead like dry wood or dead ashes.

亨译：It be that he is sound asleep or dead, or that he is a worthless fellow.

3. 陈译：To add the word seriousness here and the word sincerity there is as superfluous as to draw a snake and add feet.

亨译：To say at this time that reverence needs to be added here and sincerity there, makes an exaggeration inevitable.

4. 陈译：When the human mind is rectified it is called the moral mind and when the moral mind loses its correctness, it is called the human mind. There were not two minds to start with. When Master Ch'eng I said that the human mind is due to selfish desires while the moral mind is due to the Principle of Nature.

亨译：When a selfish mind is rectified it is an upright mind; and when an upright mind loses its rightness it becomes a selfish mind. Originally there were not two minds. The philosopher Ch'eng said, "A selfish mind is due to selfish desire; an upright mind is natural law (is true to nature)."

5. 陈译：My present advocacy of the unity of knowledge and action is precisely the medicine for that disease. The doctrine is not my baseless imagination, for it is the original substance of knowledge and action that they are one.

亨译：By saying that knowledge and practice are a unit, I am herewith offering a remedy for the disease. I am not dealing in abstractions, nor imposing my own ideas, for the nature of knowledge and practice is originally as I describe it.

第十单元

Has the world ever seen a woman's love to rival that of Bridal Du?

Dreaming of a lover she fell sick; once sick she became ever worse; and finally, after painting her own portrait as a legacy to the world, she died. Dead for three years, still she was able to live again when in the dark underworld her quest for the object of her dream was fulfilled. To be as Bridal Du is truly to have known love.

Love is of source unknown, yet it grows ever deeper. The living may die of it, by its power the dead live again. Love is not love at its fullest if one who lives is unwilling to die for it, or if it cannot restore to life one who has so died. And must the love that comes in dream necessarily be unreal? For there is no lack of dream lovers in this world. Only for those whose love must be fulfilled on the pillow and for whom affection deepens only after retirement from office, is it entirely a corporeal matter…

第十一单元

1. 任译：After a coal mine has been depleted, the shafts are then filled with earth, and more coal will appear there again after twenty or thirty years—it is inexhaustible.

李译：When the coal is exhausted, the shaft is filled up with earth. After twenty or thirty years, the coal forms again, and repetition of the process makes the source inexhaustive.

王译：After the coal has been exhausted, fill the coal mine with earth. People once thought it would grow out coal again after twenty or thirty years.

2. 任译：Stored in the seeds of grasses and trees there is oil which, however,

does not flow by itself, but needs the aid of the forces of water and fire and the pressure of wooden and stone [utensils] before it comes pouring out in liquid form.[Obtaining the hidden oil]is an ingenuity of man that is impossible to measure.

李译: The seeds or nuts of plants contain oil or fat, which is unable to flow out by itself. When they are subjected to water and fire, they pour out under the action of wood and stone machines. It is not clear how the mankind managed to invent such things.

王译: The seeds of grasses and trees are rich in oil, which can't flow out by itself. When people do something to the seeds of grasses and trees with the help of the forces of water and fire and the pressure of wooden and stone utensils, the oil will come out. We don't know how the skills and the wisdom of the ancient people are handed down from one generation to another.

3. 任译: A seventh disaster is the lack of water and drying up of plants, for between the formation of the tassels and the maturing of the grains the water needed [per plant] is three pecks for the early variety and five pecks for the late variety (if the plants are short of one pint of water just before harvest, the grains will still be there, but their size will be small, and are easily broken when husked). Human ingenuity has, however, developed the arts of irrigation and watering to the utmost.

李译: With respect to the water required, from the time of transplanting the seedlings in the fields, to their ripening, three tou (斗) are needed for the later varieties. If there is any deficiency in the water supply, the rice plant will wilt and die. (If water is lacking by one sheng (升), at the time of harvest, even though the rice grains may not be reduced in number, they will become less plump and more rice will be broken in milling). This is the seventh form of crop disaster. It is important that the farmers use all their ingenuity and skill in irrigating the fields.

王译: From growing blades to earring up and bearing fruit, the seedlings require irrigation, without which the rice withers. The early season rice needs three dou of water and late season rice five dou (toward harvesting, a shortage of one sheng of water will cause the shrinkage of the grains of rice and though the number of the rice grains remains the same, and when being ground, the grains will be smashed). This is the seventh disaster. This means that irrigation is imperative and the farmers are well skilled therein.